Putting the Charter to Work:
Designing a Constitutional Labour Code

The entrenchment of a Charter of Rights and Freedoms in the Canadian constitution raises a host of fundamental issues, both theoretical and practical. As the American experience makes abundantly clear, expanding the focus of judicial review means that the symbiosis between law and politics will become more intertwined than ever before. *Putting the Charter to Work* investigates the extent to which judicial review offers a means by which social justice in our community can be enhanced.

Rather than considering the relationship between the three branches of government in the abstract, David Beatty focuses on legal practice as it functions in labour law and shows how the Charter could be used both to reform labour law and to protect against attempts to reverse gains made in labour legislation in the past. Beatty's critical analysis rests on two principles: that the Charter provides equal liberty for all workers to participate in determining the conditions that govern their working life; and that fundamental rights should be limited only by laws employing the least repressive alternative. These principles are applied to the constitutional validity of rules: prohibiting discrimination, requiring payment of minimum wages, excluding groups from collective bargaining laws, mandating retirement at a specified age, and requiring membership in trade unions. Beatty argues that the current model of collective bargaining cannot be constitutionally sustained and that voluntary and/or plural representation of employee interests is more compatible with the Charter.

In the final sections Beatty shows that the process of judicial review can be instrumental in extending meaningful institutions of industrial democracy through all sectors of our economy and argues that interest group advocacy can be an effective means by which the least advantaged in our community can have more influence in determining the law which governs their working lives.

David M. Beatty is a member of the Faculty of Law and the Centre for Industrial Relations at the University of Toronto.

Putting the Charter to Work

Designing a Constitutional Labour Code

DAVID M. BEATTY

McGill-Queen's University Press
Kingston and Montreal

© McGill-Queen's University Press 1987
ISBN 0-7735-0600-4 (cloth)
ISBN 0-7735-0601-2 (paper)

Legal deposit second quarter 1987
Bibliothèque nationale du Québec

Printed in Canada

(∞) Printed on acid-free paper

This book has been published with the help of a grant
from the Social Science Federation of Canada, using
funds provided by the Social Sciences and Humanities
Research Council of Canada.

Canadian Cataloguing in Publication Data

Beatty, David M.
 Putting the Charter to work : designing a
 constitutional labour code
 Includes index.
 ISBN 0-7735-0600-4 (bound) ISBN 0-7735-0601-2 (pbk.)
 1. Labor laws and legislation – Canada. 2. Judicial
 review – Canada. 3. Civil rights – Canada.
 I. Title.
 KE3109.B42 1987   344.71'01   C87-093458-9

To Helen and Bob
who pointed this path out to me
and to Timothy, Colin, and Adam
who followed with me to where it has led

Contents

Preface

With the entrenchment of a Charter of Rights and Freedoms in our
constitutional order of government, a new process of validation has
been added to our system of creating law. In addition to complying
with a set of formal, procedural requirements, our laws must now respect
a set of substantive criteria – our fundamental rights and freedoms
– in order to qualify as valid assertions of legal authority by the state.

My impression is that most Canadians do not as yet realize the full
significance of this event. Although a few decisions concerning laws
controlling doing business on Sundays, the right to practise abortions,
and the legality of mandatory retirement have caught the public's
attention, by and large the Charter seems to have had little direct impact
on the everyday lives of most Canadians. But, as the American experience
has made abundantly clear, expanding the focus of judicial review beyond
that conventionally tolerated in the Anglo-Canadian traditions of law
inevitably carries with it a transformation in the relationship between
the legislative, executive, and judicial branches of government. Whatever
else it may come to mean, entrenching a set of fundamental rights
and freedoms in our constitution means the symbiotics between law
and politics will become more intimate and intertwined than ever before.

Such an important innovation in our system of government will raise
a host of fundamental issues, both theoretical and practical, which
lawyers, political scientists, and philosophers will grapple with for years.
A theory and principles within which a court may overrule a decision
by any one of the three branches of government will have to be worked
out. Procedures through which, and the institutions to which, individuals
will be appointed to resolve such fundamental questions about the nature
of our social order will have to be designed. The qualifications required
to participate in this novel addition to our structures of state will have
to be decided. Now that an entrenched bill of rights is an integral

part of our system of government, these matters and more will have to be confronted and settled. The decisions we make on each of them will vitally affect the nature and character of the role that judicial review will play in our system of government and ultimately in the democratic quality of our country.

As important as each of these issues is, my ambition here is to concern myself, in a very partial and preliminary way, only with the circumstances in which a member of the judiciary can invalidate the decision of some other governmental actor. I will not address any of the other difficult questions that arise when such a charter of rights is grafted onto a democratic system of government. Nor will I attempt to respond to those who question the legitimacy of the entire enterprise. I have started from the premise that our Charter of Rights and judicial review are accepted constitutional facts.

Although most Canadians may not be sensitive to the magnitude of the institutional questions concerning the constitutional character of the Canadian state, there is no doubt many others are alert to the theoretical issues which are at stake. Indeed, for many of those on the political left it is now conventional wisdom that we should be wary of the enhanced position given to the courts to define when it is legitimate to use the coercive authority of the state. Prominent members of the New Democratic Party, the Canadian Labour Congress, and the Civil Liberties Association have all voiced concern regarding the role an unelected, professional class should have in reviewing – they would say frustrating – the will of the people. As they see it, judicial review could prejudice even further the opportunities and entitlements of those who are already among the least advantaged in society.

An important purpose of this inquiry is to question whether this widely held view is well grounded. It is intended as a beginning in exploring whether the process of judicial review can help those who traditionally have not been very powerful in our system of government increase their influence over the laws which organize and regulate their lives. I want to consider the extent to which judicial review offers a means by which social justice in our community can be enhanced.

In pursuing this objective I have narrowed my focus in one additional way. Rather than considering the relationship between the three branches of government in the abstract, I have limited my inquiry to the legal practice we have constructed to regulate the places where we work. Analysing a discrete body of legal rules, like our labour laws, for their constitutional integrity will allow us to keep our theoretical deliberations within manageable bounds. It will identify specific individuals and groups in our society who can legitimately claim to have been disadvantaged by the rules we have included in our labour code and who can, therefore, put the nature and character of judicial review to a litmus test. Working the beginnings of a theory of judicial review through our labour laws will also have the practical advantage of being able to show, quite dramatically, the resultant impact interest-group advocacy can have on the everyday working lives of Canadians. It should provide a set of discrete and easily described examples to explain to ordinary Canadians what this alteration in our constitutional order of government is all about and why it will be so important in their lives.

Many friends have helped me work this project through to its completion. George Adams, Bernie Adell, Harry Arthurs, Rick Brown, Innis Christie, Harry Glasbeek, Marc Gold, Karl Klare, and Brian Langille all read an earlier draft of the manuscript in its entirety and made positive suggestions as to how it could be improved. Ninette Kelley, Alfred Pankert, Carol Rogerson, Clyde Summers, Michael Trebilcock, and Ernie Weinrib read parts of it and made similar contributions. While I am satisfied the quality of the published version has been strengthened considerably by their insights and inquiries, I have no illusions that I have satisfied any of them or that I have fully met the force of their reservations and comments. Peter Downard, Howard Law, Patrick Macklem, Roman Stoykewych, and Elizabeth Yip each provided invaluable research assistance for different parts of the manuscript. Their efforts were tireless, their suggestions always helpful. Verna Percival, Diana Koczka, and Mary Ellen Yeomans looked after all the secretarial and administrative details that are associated with the production of a final manuscript in as patient and supportive a manner as anyone could ever expect to enjoy. Philip Cercone at McGill-Queen's University Press was simultaneously encouraging and tolerant in the editorial changes he initiated and allowed until and even while the manuscript was going to press. Diane Mew made my turgid style and convoluted sentence structure as readable and digestible as it can be.

The book was written in part while I was on sabbatical leave as a visiting associate at the International Institute for Labour Studies at the International Labour Organization in Geneva and in part while I was at my own university in Toronto. Both these institutions provided as congenial and supportive environments as one could wish to have to complete a project of this kind. As well, the financial assistance of the Connaught Program in Legal Theory and Public Policy; the Social Science and Humanities Research Council, which provided funds for a leave fellowship which allowed me to travel to Europe; and the Social Science Federation of Canada, which assisted in the defrayal of the expenses associated with the publication of the book, are gratefully acknowledged. Anyone who has undertaken a project of this kind knows how large my debt is to all of these people for their contributions and support. To them, to Tim Johnson and Rob Prichard, two friends who supported my efforts in their special ways, and to Ninette Kelley whose idealism and integrity have been a source of great strength, I will always be grateful.

Putting the Charter to Work

Introduction:
Law, Politics, and the
Least Advantaged

The practical purpose of this study is to explore, in a preliminary way, the impact of the Charter of Rights and Freedoms on the laws that govern people's relations at the places they are employed to work.[1] My objective is to develop and apply a principled method of analysis which will assist citizens and courts to formulate and then test the laws that regulate people's behaviour at work against the new constitutional constraints embodied in the Charter.

The method of analysis I develop is rooted in principles formulated to recognize the equal right of every person to choose and pursue his or her own goals and purposes in life. I refer to these principles collectively as providing some measure of equality of self-definition and self-government, or equality in liberty and autonomy for short. Although the method of analysis will be relevant to a wider range of problems, my intention is not to write a comprehensive treatise on every constitutional question that may arise with respect to our labour relations laws.[2] Rather I have selected a group of issues that arise at different stages of the employment relationship – hiring, performance, termination. This will allow us not only to consider particular features of the major components of our labour code[3] against the general requirements of the Charter but also to provide a method of addressing a range of general issues concerning our labour relations laws beyond those specifically addressed in the text.

Although the substantive focus will be on the major principles of our labour code, my primary objective relates to the more basic question of the role the courts are now being asked to play in our liberal democratic system of government. Labour law simply poses a convenient collection of related issues through which we may begin to explore the relationship of our third arm of government with the legislative and the executive branches. It provides an opportunity to examine the extent to which the process of judicial review will further the capacity of the less powerful in our society to respond to their relative lack of influence in the formulation of the legal rules which most directly control their lives. The analysis will allow us to begin[4] the task – which is at the heart of all constitutional law – of interpreting and better understanding the political theory and ethical principles that underlie our new constitutional order.[5]

The particular focus of the inquiry is prompted in part by the circumstances in which many of our relatively less advantaged workers at present find themselves. Labour is under siege. Or at least labour thinks it is, and many would not disagree. Just as the Charter is coming into force, public and political opinion seems cool, if not hostile, to the continuation of a legal and social environment which appears far too accommodating to the wishes and whims of workers. Though he expressed these views over twenty-five years ago, Friedrich Hayek seems to have captured the mood of many in our own community when he wrote:

Public policy concerning labour unions has, in little more than a century, moved from one extreme to the other. From a state in which little the unions could do was legal if they were not prohibited altogether, we have now reached a state where they have become uniquely privileged institutions to which the general rules of law do not apply. They have become the only important instance in which governments signally fail in their prime function – the prevention of coercion and violence.[6]

In our recent past, calls for wage and price freezes, economic free zones, restrictions on the right to strike, and repeal of various pieces of labour legislation have tended to dominate public debate. Proposals such as those aimed at reducing minimum employment standards, inhibiting certain groups from engaging in collective bargaining, re-stricting unemployment compensation, and fettering the powers of human rights commissions are other noteworthy broadsides in what, to some workers, seems like a sustained attack on the legal environment which regulates their relations at work. We have moved from a period of relative quiet in employment regulation to an era in which legislative initiatives to take away or diminish the protection that the law affords to workers are being put forward and/or enacted with increased regularity.[7] Proposals for free-market zones of labour are a logical corollary for those who believe the law has been too solicitous of the interests of workers and wage-earners at the expense of those who employ them and/or consume the output they produce.

So the political and economic circumstances in which working people, and especially those who are most hard-pressed, now find themselves, provide an excellent opportunity for a case study of what impact our Charter of Rights and Freedoms can be expected to have on people's everyday lives. Through the example of our most disadvantaged workers we can begin to make out what kind of a declaration of human rights our Canadian construct will turn out to be.

Covenants of human rights and freedoms are intended to protect the members of a society who are least adequately represented in, and most vulnerable to abuses by, the political and legislative processes.[8] In the United States various groups of individuals, including blacks,[9] women,[10] and those who are caught up in the criminal justice process,[11] as well as the poor,[12] have been able to utilize the process of judicial review to have a more direct input into the formulation of some of the most basic rules affecting their lives. These instances provide dramatic evidence of how significant this new process of constitutional validation can be.

Can those Canadian workers, who are among the least advantaged by, and most poorly represented within, the processes of politics, harbour a similar expectation? Can they succeed in securing a measure of concern and respect by litigation, which so far they have been unable to obtain in legislation? Will it be possible for them, through the more principled process of decision-making that a written constitution entails, to participate more meaningfully in the policy-making process than they have in our democratically elected legislatures, where inequalities in resources are allowed a much greater influence?[13] The current political and economic circumstances of the most poorly treated workers in our community provide a real opportunity to evaluate whether judicial review and interest-group advocacy will enhance their influence in the policy-making processes. It will allow us to hold up the possibilities for judicial review against Mill's hypothesis that "in the absence of its natural defenders, the interest of the excluded is always in danger of being overlooked; and when looked at, is seen with very different eyes from those of the person it directly concerns."[14]

After working our way through this analysis my conclusion will be that disadvantaged and relatively powerless workers should be able to put the Charter to work in the cause of enhancing the social justice of the legal environment in which they are employed. On the analysis I propose, this new, second stage through which social policy must be validated offers a unique opportunity for what I will call a conversation of justification, in which workers who have not been particularly well treated by some agent or arm of government will be able to insist that the rest of the community show them that degree of concern and respect they claim for themselves. If the courts interpret the Charter according to principles which lie at the root of liberal theories of justice, the most enduring and uncontroversial components of our labour code will be confirmed, while many of the most indefensible invasions of personal rights and freedoms can be repaired.

Indeed, in the final parts of this study, I endeavour to show how, armed with the Charter, judicial review can be utilized as a process of government through which workers can insist that the places in which they work be democratized and regulated by legal rules and procedures which parallel those we use to regulate the other environments of our community in which we live. By examining the constitutional validity of the principle of employee representation in our system of collective bargaining, we will be able to sense just how far the interests of the least advantaged workers can be promoted by our third branch of government. For those whose interest is limited to the validity of the principle of exclusive representation – which is without question one of the most central principles of our system of collective labour relations – it is possible to proceed directly to this discussion in Part Four.[15]

To carry out this project the analysis is divided into four separate parts. In Part One I begin the substance of the inquiry by reviewing the importance of work for our capacity for personal autonomy. My purpose here is simply to recount the ways in which work has become so integral to the human experience. I then trace a chronology of the laws we have used to regulate our relationships at work. If the current political debate is about whether we have gone too far in striking a balance between the interests of consumers (buyers) and producers (sellers) in the performance of work, it is important to know the direction in which we are moving. Until we understand where we are going and how our present laws came about, we cannot know if we have passed or have yet to arrive at the destination to which, consciously or not, we seem to be headed.

Most of this part will focus on the ways in which our labour code has developed. As we follow the evolution of the legal rules which we and our ancestors have crafted to govern the employment relationship, at least three broad characteristics stand out. Perhaps the most prominent, yet often most forgotten, feature of labour law over the course of the last five hundred years, is the degree to which every society has subjected this activity to detailed social regulation. A free, private market for labour is, as we shall see, a matter of myth.

Secondly, when it is interpreted as part of a continuing story, as a kind of chain novel,[16] the labour relations rules that have been formulated can be seen to manifest an increasingly sensitive (but by no means constant) concern for the most vital interests people have in their work. Over time, the focus of labour law has gradually expanded, both in terms of the persons that are caught within its field of vision and in the interests it is intended to protect. As members of the working class have been able to participate more effectively in the legislative and executive branches of government, the law has, haltingly and sporadically, come to recognize principles and rules to reconcile relations at work which promote the autonomy of those they govern. A larger percentage of the labour force now enjoys the benefits of a wider range of common and legislated law which endeavours to respect their interests as industrial citizens[17] than at any time in the past.

Thirdly, tracing the evolution of the major principles used in various labour laws in the past makes it plain that there are real limits on the extent to which the political processes and the legislative institutions of government can act as forums for relief for the weakest in our midst. The current anxiety which many sectors of our labour force feel about their identities and the survival of their organizations is not unique. History teaches us that those who have dominated the processes of government have been inclined to act in their own self-interest. The history of the law governing work relationships is one of interest-group politics which is consistent with conventional political theory espoused by the left as well as the right.[18] As even the cursory chronology I will trace clearly shows, the extent to which workers' interests have been recognized and protected in our legal codes correlates closely to their opportunity to participate in the processes and institutions of government. As Mill's hypothesis reminds us, it is no accident that when working people have been excluded from the processes of politics and law their interests have, by and large, been sacrificed by and for the benefit of those who governed them.

Thus, even though the balance which has been effected by our law has gradually shifted to accommodate more of the vital interests each of us has in our work, frequently it has not been drafted comprehensively or applied consistently. There are still a large number of workers, especially those employed in the agricultural, service, and unorganized and secondary sectors[19] in our own community who are legally or practically denied the protection of some of the most basic parts of our labour code. For these individuals, the increasing sensitivity of our labour code to the most important purposes work serves in our lives has not been nearly so meaningful. For them, much of our labour law does not live up to the political ideals to which the Charter now commits us. For them, rather than going too far, our legislators still have not gone far enough.

Within this historical context, then, we should be able to see how the circumstances of workers who are relatively less advantaged in our own community are quite similar to those which constrained much larger percentages of workers in the past. The pragmatic and often unprincipled method of our legislative and executive branches of government has frequently meant that the vital concerns of those workers did not always receive the concern and respect they deserved.

Of the different lessons this chronology teaches, this last one is perhaps the most important. Much of the remainder of this study is devoted to exploring whether and to what extent we can respond to the limits and inequalities, which are inflicted by the legislative and executive institutions of government, through the process of judicial review. Though there are strong parallels between the circumstances of those who are most prejudiced by our current labour legislation and those who have laboured in the past, in this one respect the situation of our own workforce is unique. On earlier occasions when working people sought to effect any change beneficial to their interests, they were more or less committed to struggling within the forums of politics and policy where, because of their relative lack of material and natural resources, they could only participate at a serious disadvantage.[20] There was little that the courts, committed to the logic of the common law, could or would do.

Today, however, with the entrenchment of the Charter, a second forum of relief – that of judicial review – is available. Unless a legislature expressly declares the Charter will not apply to some part of our labour laws,[21] anyone who feels aggrieved by the enactment of any particular rule or policy can initiate a constitutional conversation before our courts to determine whether the challenged part of our labour code meets the standards of the Charter. The adjudication of such claims simply cannot be avoided. Challenges to some of the most basic aspects of our system of work relations have now been initiated and will eventually find their way to the Supreme Court.[22] Inevitably, that court will have to rule on whether the balance that is affected by our labour laws is consistent with the criteria of social relations that the Charter now requires our legislatures to meet. In particular, they will have to decide whether laws that establish or authorize minimum wages, mandatory retirement, affirmative action, or compulsory membership in trade unions, or the provisions of those laws that deny certain individuals the benefit and protection of their terms, are consistent with the requirements of the Charter.

In developing answers to these questions, the court will be required to think through an overriding theory of what the Charter itself represents and what purpose it serves in our system of politics and government. The second part of this monograph is devoted to exploring how the Supreme Court ought to proceed in discharging this novel feature of constitutional jurisprudence. My purpose here is to distil those principles of judicial review which are most consistent with the explicit text of the Charter and to our legal practice as a whole. My objective is to derive principles of interpretation which will provide as close a fit, and as strong a justification for our legal practice as possible. In this way, when they are invoked to evaluate some aspect of our laws of employment, we can be confident about the conclusions they yield.

In the text I will suggest at least two principles which may be employed by a court whenever it holds some rule in our labour code up to the Charter. One principle relates to the ends our legislators are entitled to pursue; the other to the means by which they may endeavour to accomplish those goals. The first will validate legislative initiatives designed to promote the rights and freedoms of those in our community whose choices for their lives are already the most constrained. The second will ensure that our lawmakers pursue those policies in a way that is as respectful of the rights and freedoms of others in the community as possible. Together the two principles will encourage our governors to respect some degree of equality in the liberty of every worker to control and participate in the formulation of the rules which govern the productive side of his or her life.

Authority for the recognition of these principles is grounded primarily in the text and judicial interpretations of the Charter itself. Further support lies in the accommodation of both of these principles by most, if not all, of the contemporary constitutional theories which accept the coherence and integrity of judicial review. As importantly, the two principles provide a powerful justification for the most enduring and fundamental laws governing the work relationship.

Part Three is devoted to holding up various parts of our labour code to these principles of judicial review. First, I apply the two principles to those parts of our legal system of work relations, such as our anti-discrimination and minimum wage laws, in which we have most confidence. Then I examine how the principles respond to the plight of some of the most vulnerable and least well represented groups of workers in our community to see what the Charter can do for them. If, properly interpreted, the Charter cannot assist groups such as domestics and agricultural workers, or if it cannot put an end to invidious discrimination between workers on the basis of their personal characteristics such as their age or their sex, it is unlikely it will be of much assistance to anyone. If the constitutional conversations end in these ways, judicial review will not have enhanced the democratic character of our processes of government.

In each of these cases the analysis will remain the same. Each of the rules and parts of the labour code I review is tested for the integrity of its purpose and the reasonableness of its method. The principles

I have proposed yield conclusions which accord, I believe, with our most basic and felt intuitions of justice. Even though the principles of interpretation are quite cautious and conservative, both as a positive and normative description of judicial review, these initial examples will demonstrate that our Charter is capable of redressing serious injustices which afflict our existing legal regime. They will show how the Charter can be used to reinforce the representation of persons whose personal and material circumstances have traditionally inhibited their effective participation in the debates and dialogues which take place within the executive and legislative processes of government. Just as the American Bill of Rights has offered protection to blacks, women, the poor, and those caught up in their criminal justice system, so with our Charter, it turns out, can our courts redress inequities created and tolerated by the legislative and executive processes against those workers who are least able to represent themselves effectively in those branches of government. Indeed, not only can the Charter and the process of judicial review be used to fend off challenges to much of the legislation which protects employees' most basic interests, but it can also be employed to encourage our legislators to enact new rules which will further the evolutionary process our law has been following for the past six hundred years.

With the legislative past as prologue and with the integrity of our principles of constitutional review confirmed by the conclusions they yield to the claims of those workers most deserving of protection, I move on, in the fourth part, to assess the full force of the Charter as an instrument of social justice. Here I construct a full constitutional conversation and consider whether the Charter can support a claim brought by those who have been called the unskilled, unlucky, and unorganized, to require our legislators to substantially reform the processes of collective decision-making, that is, our collective bargaining laws. At the end of a rather extended dialogue my answer is that it can, and it is on the basis of that conclusion that the full significance of the Charter, as an instrument of social justice, can be appreciated. By structuring a conversation according to the same principles of judicial review, those working people who today are least able to participate in the processes of decision-making that characterize the collective bargaining processes will be able to insist on alternate models of industrial government. They can claim, on behalf of all working people, entitlement to an employment standard of good government, of a fair process of decision-making, which our model of collective bargaining has not and cannot satisfy. With the Charter in their hands, working people, whose interests traditionally have received the least attention from the legislative and executive process of government, will be able to demand that their governors continue the logic that is manifested in the evolution of the law that has regulated the workplace over the preceding hundreds of years. Part Four is intended to illustrate how dramatic and important the victories of interest-group advocacy can ultimately be.

Before we begin to explore the role that the Charter can play in promoting justice between people in the places we work, I should acknowledge at the outset that the principled argument that drives the analysis (our constitutional commitment to some equality in personal self-government) is not likely to be initially appealing to either of the interests that have conventionally dominated the formulation of our labour laws. As a matter of substantive law, all of the changes effected by the Charter that we will consider require our legislators to protect and enhance the worker's interests more equally and more consistently than they have in the past. For that reason both consumers and employers of labour might be expected to resist the interpretation of the Charter I have proposed and the conclusions to which it leads. Equally, the major interest groups promoting the interests of workers are likely, initially at least, to be similarly sceptical. Trusting to the processes of law and the institution of the court will not, given the treatment workers and unions have received from the judiciary in the past, be something that will come easily or naturally to the working class and its representatives.[23]

With respect to the opposition of the employers and consumers there is little I can add to the analysis itself. I am content to let the coherence of the argument and the conclusions to which it leads speak for themselves. With respect to the scepticism of workers and their organized representatives I would add, by way of encouragement to overcome a long-standing antipathy to judicial law-making, that there are good reasons to be optimistic. When judges review the constitutional validity of the legal rules we have adopted to regulate the employment relationship, they will insist that the interests of the least advantaged workers be shown the respect which is now their constitutional due.

In the first place, in theory and especially in the present political climate, the process of judicial review should be more hospitable than the legislative and executive processes of government to the interests of workers who are least advantaged, simply because of the nature of the interpretative process through which courts develop the law. As a matter of institutional design, groups which historically have been poorly represented in the political process should have a comparative advantage in the forum where the force of one's principle, and not the power of one's resources, determines the quality of participation in the processes of law-making and the integrity of the law itself.

Adjudication, not political organization, may be the most effective process by which the least powerful and most poorly organized groups in our society can ensure their interests are properly considered in the process of policy formulation. Where historically working people have had to devote enormous amounts of time and energy to petition for the protection of law which others already enjoyed, the Charter of Rights and Freedoms offers a forum of principle[24] in which their relative lack of resources should not count as heavily against them.

The historical record described in Part One offers another reason to hope that the courts will provide relief to workers when legislatures do not show them the concern and respect to which they are now entitled. While many of the rulings courts have handed down in the past have been hostile to the interests of workers as a group, their judgments have never been entirely one-sided. There have also been important instances in which courts have developed common law principles which have protected and benefited the interests of the working class.[25]

Finally, optimism for judicial review can also be justified in the recognition that in all the rulings the courts author which will promote the interests of the working class, the method and criteria of their constitutional adjudication will conform closely to the traditional roles they have performed in the past. On the theory of the Charter I will work with, our courts would endeavour to effect a balance between the competing interests in the workplace and a set of values which is similar to those they have conventionally turned to when they developed and applied the common law.[26]

To ensure our labour code is consonant with the conceptions of social justice our Charter now guarantees, courts will be required neither to adopt activist postures against the legislative and executive branches of government nor to develop radical theories of law. On the interpretation I propose they will be asked only to measure the validity of policy initiatives against a written text which flows from and expresses a commitment to equality between Canadians in their opportunities for personal self-government. It is this value which the courts, in their development of the law of private relations, have always been vigilant in protecting, even if on occasion they mistakenly[27] made it serve what they saw as a deeper ethic of free and unrestricted trade.[28] By petitioning the courts to exercise their traditional functions against values they have historically honoured the most, workers who generally have not participated effectively in the development of social policy in the legislative and executive branches of government can be optimistic that they will be able to represent their interests more vigorously and secure results more sympathetic to their needs.

PART ONE

The Legal Regulation of the Employment Relationship

Security is indivisible.
Albert Einstein

ONE

A Purposive Interpretation of Work

To assess the rationality and integrity – that is, the constitutionality[1] – of any legal regime, liberals, logicians, and lawyers all recognize the necessity of having a clear understanding of the purposes of the activity or behaviour being regulated or the good being distributed.[2] Any evaluation of a legal system, such as our labour relations laws, presupposes a set of objectives which that law is expected to facilitate. Commonly, there are a variety of purposes, often in competition with one another, which the law is required to reconcile. In the case of working, one can identify two broad constituencies whose ambitions are partly congruent and partly antagonistic: those of the worker – the producer of the goods and services – and those of the consumer – the user of that which is produced. All the purposes and objectives in a work relationship can be subsumed under the act of producing: the doing of a task and the product, the output that is the consequence of that behaviour. As conventional economic analysis recognizes, even the employer's interests are connected to, and ultimately parasitic on, the competing objectives of the producer and consumer.[3] Thus, while it has distributional objectives all its own, the employer's role can be understood to be broadly allied with the workers to whom his capital is made available and against the consumer to whom employer and employees will sell the product of their joint endeavour.[4] By contrast, in his act of hiring – that is, purchasing – the services of those he employs, the capitalist acts in the interest of the consumer by endeavouring to secure those services and the products that are manufactured at the lowest possible cost. While obviously possessing a separate and independent interest of his own, the capitalist's position in the labour exchange can be seen as being analogous to that of a broker who trades upon the conflicting interests of the producers and consumers in a way that best advances his own separate interest in the transaction.

Within this framework of analysis we can easily identify a list of more specific goals served when people work. Doing so will underscore why this activity is so central to each of us personally and to the communities within which we live. Our interest as consumers in the products of others' labour follows directly from the realization that the output – the goods and services generated by work – provides the resources available for us to use in whatever plans we have for our lives. Each of our projects is fundamentally affected by the fact that large numbers of persons have chosen, for their own reasons, to produce autos rather than art, steel instead of steroids, hamburgers rather than tofu dogs. Extrapolated to the society at large, the products of our collective labour define the physical environment within which and the material resources with which each of our personal sagas must unfold.[5]

Moreover, it is not just the physical character of the community that is affected by our efforts at work. What we do at work and who does it will have an impact on the social character of our society. A nation whose members are all productively employed will manifest an industriousness and a tranquillity, a cohesiveness and seriousness of purpose, that will not likely be found in a community that tolerates widespread idleness and unemployment. The material and psychological deprivations that can accompany enforced idleness have long been recognized as leading to family breakdown, vandalism, violence, and other forms of social disturbance which can ultimately undermine the social fabric of the community.[6]

Similarly, a society that distributed all of its remunerative work only to its male population would present a radically different legal structure of social relations to one that provided for a more egalitarian treatment of both sexes. Taken together, both the material and the sociological dimensions of our labours are vital to the very definition of society itself. Karl Renner, the Austrian legal scholar, captured its essence when he described work as doing for a social organization what the digestive tract does for the animal organism.[7] It is in no small part because work serves these vital public functions that, as we shall see, it has always been the subject of detailed social regulation.[8]

But however essential our working activities are to the definition of the society in which they are performed, for most of us it is the producer's, not the consumer's, objectives that makes labouring so vital to our lives. Popes,[9] philosophers,[10] psychologists,[11] and popularizers[12] all agree that it is the personal purposes of the individual who is working which underlie most of the claims made about the fundamental significance of this activity and the legal principles which organize it. From each of their different perspectives work is seen as the most basic activity by which we define and maintain ourselves, and its enormous importance lies in how it serves the physiological, psychological, and sociological imperatives of our existence.

The biological need is obviously the most basic function satisfied by work. For most people, I suspect, working is, sadly, little more than getting a pay cheque. For too many, the objective of survival, of consumption, is the most compelling inducement to engage in paid-for-productive activity. In the psychologist's terms, it is the most basic of the motivational needs.[13] It is the reason why, even in the most dull and dirty and dangerous environments, people will seek out and ultimately devote themselves to this activity eight hours a day, five days a week, fifty weeks a year for approximately half of their natural lives. Except for those of independent means, it is only by working that we are able to maintain ourselves in a style of physical well-being (of nourishment, attire, and shelter) compatible with the society in which we live.

But even in the least attractive surroundings, work is usually not just getting a pay cheque. Even when it is performed at minimum, poverty-level wages, work can, if done in safe surroundings, ensure a sense of health and well-being unavailable to those who, while sheltered and clothed and fed by various public assistance programs (welfare, unemployment benefits, and so on), are deprived of the opportunity to work. Physiologically it is work, the exertion of effort, the creation and expenditure of energy, and not simply the income we receive from the sale of our labour, which most effectively ensures our physical well-being.

Yet if we are to explain the unique significance that is attributed to labour activity in human affairs, and to understand how work defines and distinguishes humans from all other species, we must look beyond the biological purposes pursued by people when they work. The explanation lies, of course, in the conceptual and psychological side of our humanity. Work is as basic to our spiritual health as it is to our physical well-being. It is the primary means by which the vast majority of persons can secure for themselves the dignity that is part of being human. Studs Terkel, in an essay introducing his anthology of autobiographical sketches of American workers, made the point this way:

During my three years of prospecting, I may have, on more occasions than I had imagined, struck gold. I was constantly astonished by the extraordinary dreams of ordinary people. No matter how bewildering the times, no matter how dissembling the official language, those we call ordinary are aware of a sense of personal worth – or more often a lack of it – in the work they do. Tom Patrick, the Brooklyn fireman whose reflections end the book, similarly brings this to a close: "Last month there was a second alarm, I was off duty. I ran over there. I'm a bystander. I see these firemen on the roof, with the smoke pouring out around them, and the flames, and they go in. It fascinated me. Jesus Christ, that's what I do? I was fascinated by the people's faces. You could see the pride that they were seeing. The fucking world's so fucked up, the country's fucked up. But the firemen, you actually see them produce. You see them put out a fire. You see them come out with babies in their hands. You see them give mouth-to-mouth when a guy's dying. You can't get around that shit. That's real. To me, that's what I want to be. I worked in a bank. You know, it's just paper. It's not real. Nine to five and it's shit. You're lookin' at numbers. But I can look back and say, 'I helped put out a fire. I helped save somebody.' It shows something I did on this earth."[14]

If for no other reason than the time we commit to it, the work we do has a crucial impact on our self-respect. The opportunity to master a task, develop an expertise, or do a job well can provide a sense of achievement, of personal development, and of independence which is fundamental to our self-esteem. By discharging a responsibility, making a contribution, work allows us to secure the recognition, appreciation, and admiration of others in our community.[15]

Just how fundamental work is to a person's sense of his self-worth is revealed in the circumstances of those who are out of work, or are employed in jobs too small for their spirits, or who, like women, seek emancipation and freedom from a status of dependency. In the general malaise, the lifelessness and disillusionment of those who perform the most marginal, least meaningful, and the dirtiest work in our community, we see how powerful an effect work has on a person's identity.[16] Euphemistic job titles, invoked to soften the violence done to the spirit of workers doing menial jobs, as well as quality of work-life programs which purport to enhance the opportunity of workers to control their own environment, underscore the causal link between anomie and inhuman work. Not to have a job can be just as destructive. Being unemployed is to be a person who has nothing to offer which is valued by others in the community. It was Camus who, in describing the depth of the connection between work and a person's identity, observed that without work all life goes rotten, but when work is soulless, life stifles and dies.

In the recent experience of women and the feminist movement we have perhaps the most dramatic evidence that work (or again the lack of it) permeates and indelibly influences our personal identities. The point is most tellingly made when, in response to the question, "Who are you?" women can now reply, "I am a hod carrier or a heart surgeon," and not "housewife," as most of their mothers were obliged to say.

In the emancipation of women one is able to see perhaps more clearly than anywhere else how a large group in our community, which had traditionally been confined by notions of custom and status to narrow, one-dimensional identities, sought independence through the workplace. The enormous increase in their participation in the labour market can be explained, at least in part, by their recognition that employment can provide a vastly wider set of opportunities for self-expression and definition than exists in the home. Feminism is in part the opportunity to master a project, learn a skill, make a contribution, and secure self-esteem in more than one socially determined way. For many women, the connection between work and identity is so strong that equality between the sexes translates first and foremost into equality of opportunity in the workplace. Work is recognized as providing the primary opportunity for self-realization; for a woman to be what she determines for herself she is capable of becoming.

In our own society, then, work is an activity which is fundamental to the very experience of being a human.[17] People must work if they are to maintain the physical and mental condition essential for continued existence in our communities. These last three words are important and warrant extending our interpretation of work, to make two additional observations. So far I have only described the purposes work serves that are private or internal to the individual. I have said nothing about the impact the social dimension of work has on the worker's purposes and plans. And that is a serious omission. After all, work is ultimately a public, not a private, activity. Work is by definition different from leisure precisely because what is produced is valued by another person.[18] Indeed, given the vast quantity of time most people devote to it, it seems certain there is no other activity that so effectively coordinates our personal ambitions as consumers and producers with those being pursued by the other members of our society. Work is unquestionably the most important means by which each person is integrated into the larger social purposes of the community of which he or she is a member.

Moreover, the social dimension of work, for the producer at least, goes well beyond the exchange relationship that is effected most commonly through an employer. In addition, in most work settings, individuals labour in teams or groups, on assembly lines or in departments of fellow workers which provide a sense of belonging and of being involved in a smaller and more intimate segment of society. It is in the workplace that many of an individual's closest friendships are formed and in turn where many of his or her other social activities come to be chosen.[19] Indeed, when generalized across the community, it is these social relationships that ultimately form the basis of sociologists' ideas of status and class. In our own society it has traditionally been the case that the father's working activities would largely determine where a family lived, where the children went to school, and what social activities it pursued; these together defined the class to which the family belonged. Today economists' measures confirm the causal link that holds between a parent's (and traditionally this has meant the father's) occupation and the lifestyle and life chances of every other member of the family.[20]

Labour Relations Laws: Pre-Industrial Society

Given the significance of work for the human condition, it would be difficult to exaggerate the importance of the legal code which is designed to regulate it. Every labour code will strike some balance between the various objectives which are pursued in the workplace. Depending on the legal rules that make up the code, the balance will shift in favour of one purpose or interest or another. In this and the next two sections I want to inquire into the extent to which our own legal institutions, processes, and rules have facilitated or impeded the realization of the personal objectives most of us pursue when we go off to work. By focusing on the particular balance our labour code strikes between the competing interests which are at play when people work, we will be able to highlight its most distinctive features and the most basic moral values that underlie it.

To facilitate this analysis I propose to compare our own labour code with those that have preceded it. By tracing a chronology of the major rules of work relations we can explore how the recognition and protection of the interests of people in the workplace have evolved over time. Although all labour codes can be understood as serving the various personal and social objectives that individuals and communities have in work, it is clear, from even the most cursory examination of labour law, that there are drastic differences in how these two basic interests have been weighed and reconciled.

Compared to earlier codes, the most distinctive ethical feature of our own labour law lies in the quality rather than the quantity of its legal rules. Our labour code is unique not so much in the volume and detail of its rules as in the extent of the protection it offers to the interests workers have in their employment. In advancing this view I recognize that not everyone would agree. For many, one of the most striking features of our labour code is the sheer volume of the rules and regulations courts, legislators, and their subordinate agents have generated to govern relations in the workplace. In their view, vast numbers of rules have been promulgated by legislators, the executive, and the courts to govern the most detailed phases of the employment relationship. Employment standards, establishing minimum terms for all the major conditions of employment (wages, hours of work, leisure time, and so on); human rights codes, proscribing most forms of arbitrary and discriminatory treatment of workers; health and safety legislation, providing varying degrees of protection from potentially hostile physical environments; collective bargaining legislation, establishing collective processes of decision-making within an enterprise – all these represent an awesome, and for some suffocating, assertion of public control. And, beyond those legislative initiatives, critics point to the common law rules developed by courts to deal with wrongful dismissals, restrictive covenants, and the like, as well as other statutory enactments providing for unemployment insurance, workers' compensation, public pension and old age security plans stipulating a person's entitlements during periods when he or she is separated from his/her job. In this view, the legal practice in which we have enveloped the employment relationship involves an unwarranted and unprecedented limitation on personal choice.

For the moment I want to leave aside the question of whether the extensive detail and scope of the legal rules we have adopted to regulate relations in the workplace can be adequately justified. That will be the focus of our attention in parts Three and Four. In the meantime, one can dismiss quite summarily any claim that the density of our legal practice is, at least in our own tradition, in any way unusual or unique. As any history of work relations will show, every community, acting in its own self-interest, has subjected this activity to extensive social regulation. Given its importance to the vitality of the individual and the community alike, work has always been one of the most intensely regulated of human activities. Whenever a society, or more accurately its rule-makers, has perceived that the individual or the social order was threatened by the patterns and processes of work, it has consistently acted to preserve what it thought was in its most vital interest.

What is most distinctive about our own labour code is its qualitative rather than its quantitative dimension. In this, the critics of our current legal practice are correct. When one compares our existing code with the versions that preceded it, it is readily apparent that our system of employment relations is unique in the extent to which it recognizes and endeavours to protect the producer's interest in her or his work. In our system of employment we have identified a wide range of rules providing for minimum wages, maximum hours, health and safety, equal opportunities, collective decision-making, and so on, in which society's interest in a person's work is made to respect the objectives of the workers. Although it is true that earlier societies have organized their labour relationships so as to give some recognition and protection to the purpose pursued by the producer in the performance of her or his work, none has done so to the extent and degree that we have. If one casts one's eye over the distance which labour law has travelled over time, our own legal regime falls naturally at the end of an evolving continuum which evinces an increasing concern and respect for the personal importance workers attach to their jobs.

This distinctiveness is highlighted most vividly when our labour code is compared to how these same interests were reconciled in the legal practice of enslavement. Slavery was, of course, simply a different legal device through which certain forms of work could be accomplished. Like employment, slavery was a legal institution which governed a relationship for the provision of services. As such, it entailed a code of rules stipulating the terms on which the relationship would be established, terminated, and services would be rendered. It was tolerated by a wide variety of pre-industrial societies from the classical Greek to our own feudal and mercantile ancestors. It was used often, though not exclusively, to govern the performance of the most menial, mundane, and mechanical work in those communities.[1]

What was remarkable about this method of organizing production, of course, was that all the personal characteristics we now recognize in the performance of work were completely denied. Slavery was so exceptional (and to us such an anathema) precisely because it was intended to benefit the society – or, more properly, the rule-makers within those societies – which employed it without regard to the interests of those who laboured under it. Slavery was a legal code which allowed those who consumed the worker/slave's services and output to control every aspect of that person's life, whether productive or otherwise, entirely according to their own interests. Although the personal dignity and the associational relationships of the slave which were fixed by this social arrangement of production were not always entirely negative,[2] nevertheless the life of the slave was entirely beyond his or her control. The slave could only expect his or her purposes to be recognized when they were congruent with and furthered the interests of the slave-holder and the larger social structure of the community.

Slavery is, undeniably, exceptional in terms of the balance it strikes between the interests of workers and those who employ or consume their services. It is the clearest case of what is involved in one person treating another wholly as a means. It stands at one end of the spectrum of the legal institutions available to a society to regulate its labour relationships, where the personal meaning that has come to dominate our own understanding of work is completely denied. Indeed, it is precisely because the ethical principle underlying slavery is so repugnant to the values of human dignity, self-esteem, and self-determination that for quite some time[3] this method of organizing production has not been permitted, even when two people create such a relationship by a "voluntary and private" agreement. The personal meaning of work for the slave is so nihilistic, the identity it fixes so negative and destructive of all we think essential to a human life, that everywhere it is now accepted as being an illegitimate system of organized labour relationships.

Slavery could not survive in our own legal culture because it was predicated on a status that was antithetical to the condition of freedom on which the coherence of contract and our law of employment ultimately depend. Slavery denies even the very limited and formal definition of liberty and consent on which the integrity of employment by contract is grounded. Legal scholars long ago recognized that slavery by contract or consent was a logical impossibility.[4] Blackstone put the matter shortly in doctrinal terms. According to his now standard analysis, contract implies in law an exchange, a quid pro quo. In the jargon of legal doctrine, contracts require "consideration." But it is just this requirement that could not be satisfied in a "contract of enslavement." Precisely because all the property of the slave would devolve to the slave-owner at the instant the "contract" was formed, consideration would be a logical impossibility. "Contracts of enslavement" denied the legal personhood essential to the giving and receiving which is at the heart of an "exchange" relationship. By definition, the slave could receive nothing in law and the slave-owner, with an absolute right to the latter's life and liberty, could give nothing in return. Contracts of enslavement could have no validity in a society where the idea of contractual obligation was justified on the deep normative goals of individual liberty and self-determination. Again, early on, legal scholars were alive to this deep contradiction. Blackstone put the point rhetorically when he asked, "Of what validity ... can a sale be, which destroys the very principles on which all sales are founded?"[5]

Although slavery is the most extreme example of a legal regime which fails to show any concern and respect for the interests individuals pursue in their work, it is by no means unique in this respect. In fact, if not in design, the same ethical orientation seems to underlie the most important laws which organized the work relationship in the feudal and mercantile societies which preceded our own. Although there is a tendency to be overly romantic about our pastoral past, the reality was that the laws invoked by our ancestors in the centuries preceding the Industrial Revolution did not offer much protection to the personal ambitions individuals had in their work.

It is true, however, that even though the underlying tendency of the Elizabethan Code was the opposite to our own, its laws and institutions of work organization did modestly acknowledge the basic needs of the worker, and in so doing could be said to have made some advancement over those regimes which practised slavery. Workers did receive some marginally greater recognition of their interests in these later models of labour relations than was accommodated in a legal state of enslavement, and to that extent their circumstances offer some evidence for the broad evolutionary process I have noted above. Even though most of the labour legislation of these pre-industrial societies was hostile to, and indeed punitive of, the worker's interest, there was still, in the words of one commentator, "the shadowy image of a benevolent corporate state."[6] Central to the legal regulation of the work relationships in this period was a principle of formal equality before the law and, within the (admittedly strict) bounds of birthright, a liberty of the person to pursue his or her self-interest which differentiated it from an institution such as slavery.

For almost two hundred years prior to the Industrial Revolution, the labour code of our ancestors was organized around two basic enactments: the Statute of Artificers and Apprentices (1563) and the Poor Laws (1601). Together these legal artifacts guaranteed workers the right to live.[7] Even if the life it accommodated was modest and rudimentary, the labour code which was built on these two statutes did give some social recognition to the inviolability and integrity of the producer's physical person. It was a central principle of the Statute of Artificers and, indeed, of legislation going back to the middle of the fourteenth century (the Statute of Labourers), that wages were fixed, either by statute, or by a system of compulsory arbitration presided over by local magistrates, according to scales that were tied closely to the price of basic provisions such as bread. Thus, while a person worked, he was generally ensured either by direct or delegated legislative authority that he would be paid a wage that would guarantee his physical survival. Moreover, by working for a year, an individual was guaranteed that he would have a "settlement" in the parish in which he worked, which entitled him to "outdoor relief" when he was not gainfully employed. In the hierarchy of personal motivations we noted in the last section, the Elizabethan Code of Labour guaranteed the minimum physiological needs of the worker. At the very least, for those who had worked a year, it ensured the means of survival.

In addition to these statutes, the common law, the "unwritten law" which the courts developed in this period, also showed some sensitivity to the natural fact that most people had to work for a living. For example, very early on courts formulated a rule that, in the absence of an explicit provision to the contrary, every hiring was assumed to last for a year. In this respect the common law recognized an obligation on the employer to sustain the worker as much as "when there was work to be done as when there was not."[8] Unless the master had reasonable cause to dismiss a worker, it was assumed a hiring would last that long. The labour relationship was understood to be a personal one in which the employer and ultimately the consumer of the product were made to bear the "overhead costs" of maintaining the physical well-being of the worker.[9]

Another principle of the labour code promulgated by the courts which, in result if not design, offered some protection to workers was the doctrine which invalidated restraints on free trade. By this principle the courts were able, especially in the employment context, to limit the ability of some members of society from curtailing the opportunity of others to pursue livelihoods of the latters' own choosing. Indeed, some courts even held to this rule when the person sought to be constrained in the pursuit of a particular vocation had previously agreed (by way of a restrictive covenant in his contract of employment) to such a limitation on his freedom to work. It is true that this principle was largely justified on the abhorrence the common law was said to have for idleness and the attendant social costs implicit in such a state of affairs. Nevertheless, these covenants were also seen to offend against the commitment of the common law to the liberty and freedom of the individual to work at any lawful trade.[10] Regardless of the motives for initiating these common law rules, they facilitated, if only marginally, the ability of individuals to choose for themselves what services they would contribute to the communities in which they lived. This part of the pre-industrial labour code also offered some limited protection for the purposes people had in their work. As well, the courts were able to promote the liberty of the individual to work at the vocation of his choice by ruling that the seven-year apprenticeship requirement in the Statute of Artificers would be restricted to those trades in existence at the time of its enactment.[11] That piece of judicial law-making can also be understood as an attempt by the third branch of government to enhance the capacity of each individual to define what work he would do and what role he would play in the community.

Finally, and seemingly paradoxically, the Statute of Artificers itself can be interpreted as a rule of the labour code of this period which, again in its impact if not its design, was sensitive to the distinctively human purposes we now recognize people have in their work. In effect, through its apprenticeship requirements this statute codified and

extended the guild system as the governing principle for the organization of work in the crafts and trades it regulated. By recognizing the
craftsmen's exclusive right to practise in and set the terms of these
trades, and by limiting access to its membership, more than any other
component of the labour code of that day, it had the effect of creating
a legal environment most congenial for a select group of people to
satisfy the full range of objectives in their work. Maximizing the control
artisans had over the manner in which their skills and expertise were
applied created the greatest opportunity possible for these workers to
realize a sense of achievement, dignity, and self-respect.[12] Of course,
the defect in this particular statute, and the explanation for the courts'
refusal to extend its terms to newly emerging skills and crafts, lay in
the means by which the enactment accomplished its objectives. Quite
simply (and in a pattern which, as we shall see, continues to infect
some of our own legislative regulation of work relations), the opportunity
of those craftsmen and tradesmen to realize all the goals people pursue
in their jobs was achieved only by denying everyone else an equal
opportunity in their work.[13]

It would be misleading to romanticize the extent to which the labour
laws in the medieval and mercantile periods protected the workers' private
and personal interests in their work. The fact is, the laws regulating
labour relationships before the Industrial Revolution had an overwhelmingly social rather than personal bias in the interests they protected.
Certainly the laws of this period are decidedly closer to the institution
of slavery than they are to our own system of work relations. Duties
not rights, status not freedom, were the principles of justice which
distinguished the pre-industrial labour codes.[14]

It is generally recognized that in this period there were three
fundamental principles around which the labour code was organized.
Each of them had the effect of promoting the consumers' and employers',
rather than the workers', interests in production. The first of these rules
was that every able-bodied adult person without means of support (e.g.,
ownership of land or mastery of a craft) was compelled to work on
pain of imprisonment and corporal punishment. This obligation was
first imposed immediately following the Great Plague of the mid-
fourteenth century.[15] It was, like slavery, a type of enforced labour.
As such, it would be expected to enhance the public's well-being in
the usual ways. A duty to work, by eliminating or at least reducing
the incidence of idleness and begging, would be expected to facilitate
the creation of a well-ordered community.[16] By such a rule everyone
would be integrated into the society in a positive, contributing, and
reciprocal way. It was expected that by requiring every able-bodied
person to be productively employed, a social environment would develop

which would be more conducive for everyone else in the society being able to realize her or his own projects and plans. As well, subsequently, in a community whose laws were committed (by the Poor laws) to a right to live, the duty to work would, by limiting the financial implications of that right, also accrue to the fiscal well-being of the community. If a society's philosophical and/or religious values called on it to respect the right of each of its members to remain alive, attaching a duty to work was not only morally justifiable but made economic good sense.

The second fundamental idea around which labour law was organized during this time was that the most basic terms and conditions on which work was rendered – wages and hours – would be publicly fixed by statute or, alternatively, by a process analogous to our own system of compulsory (interest) arbitration. Again this feature of labour regulation dates back to the Statute of Labourers (1349) and was expressly enacted to respond to the prejudice consumers (employers) would otherwise have suffered in their purchase (and/or employment) of labour as a result of the acute labour shortage which followed the plague. By fixing maximum wages and minimum hours of work, these statutory enactments were intended to deny workers the opportunity of profiting from a natural catastrophe. When this wage-fixing feature is set alongside the duty to work, as it was in both the Statute of Labourers and the Statute of Artificers, it is difficult to quarrel with the conventional wisdom that most of the laws regulating labour relationships in the pre-industrial period were designed to secure for the community, or at least for its governors, a cheap and docile labour force. It was, in the words of one commentator, "class legislation" which was aimed at "industrial slavery."[17]

Indeed, even the apprenticeship requirements of the Statute of Artificers, the third great pillar of the pre-industrial labour code, were generally justified by their positive contribution to the public, not the private, purposes of work. While conceding that these provisions had the potential of adversely affecting the well-being of the community,[18] advocates of the system of seven-year apprenticeships argued that the public interest would be promoted because those provisions would minimize, if not eliminate, unskilfulness in the practice of the trade. Insisting on a certain level of qualifications of the workforce was expected to enhance directly the quality of the goods and services produced. In addition, it was said, "apprenticeships [were] useful to the commonwealth by employing ... youth and learning them to be early industrious."[19] This observation underscores how long the connection between the legal institutions governing work and the social order and cultural environment which affects everyone's opportunity to realize their own personal goals has been recognized. Such a justification for the apprenticeship rules is an early version of the now standard "externality" or "public goods" argument, which says that unless the training and acculturalization of youth is made mandatory for everyone, unless people are prohibited from entering a vocation "without having undergone the same discipline," no one will be inclined to choose seven years of servitude. If such a state of affairs were allowed to prevail, both the quality of goods and services and the environments within which they are produced were expected to suffer accordingly.

Viewed in their entirety, it seems clear that the labour codes of pre-industrial England did show a greater degree of respect for the personal objectives of the worker than rules which sanctioned enslavement. Nevertheless, on balance they were drawn very heavily in favour of the interests of the consumers and users of labour. While the codes did not allow society to acquire labour power for nothing, they did allow its consummation at a price less than what it would have had to pay if the forces of supply and demand and individual autonomy had been given full play. Indeed, in addition to the three basic principles which distinguished the feudal and mercantile labour codes, there was a variety of related rules and regulations pertaining to the work relationship which tended toward the same imbalance. Settlement laws restricting a worker's freedom of mobility,[20] the conspiracy laws inhibiting his freedom of association,[21] and criminal sanctions restraining his freedom to quit his employment,[22] further tilted the balance in favour of the purchasers' and employers' objectives in how work was performed. In short, even though more respect was gradually shown for the interests of the worker, all the labour codes of pre-industrial England were much more confining and coercive than our own.

Although it is not my purpose to provide an elaborate explanation of how this particular balance between the competing purposes came to be drawn, the historical record makes it plain that each culture and each generation acts according to its own social circumstances and system of moral values. Any society's labour code will be strongly influenced and ultimately constrained by the social, political, philosophical, technological, and economic environments in which it must arrange its affairs. Pre-industrial England is no exception in this respect and in its circumstances virtually all of these forces tended to elevate the purchaser's expectations for its labour relationships over those pursued by the persons doing the work.

For our purposes one of the most striking features of this social landscape was the political disability of those whose lives were governed by these regulations. The fact that workers were, by and large, excluded from the very processes in which such rules and regulations were formulated offers an obvious explanation of why the laws of this period gave so little credence to their interests. In English feudal and mercantile societies it was those who used and employed the services of labour, and not the workers themselves, who had access to and were represented in the institutions of state authority. Consistent with Mill's hypothesis, the gross imbalance in the protection which the labour code provided to the competing interests in the workplace seems directly related to the general disability under which workers laboured in presenting their cases to the legislative and executive branches of government.

There were, of course, other powerful forces at play in pre-industrial English society which supported and legitimated what appear today as arbitrary and arrogant acts of self-interest. The smaller population base, made so scarce by events like the plague, provided strong moral and economic incentives for the governing classes to act as they did. As already noted, the Statute of Labourers was introduced in the wake of the Black Death essentially to protect the consumers' collective interest against the dramatic increase in prices which would otherwise have followed naturally from and compounded this human tragedy.

Moreover, the conventional moral and legal wisdom of the day embraced ideas that there was a just or fair price for each resource or artifact; that there was some objective measurement available to ensure an equivalency in exchange. Notions like those lent an aura of legitimacy to legislation which otherwise seems so blatantly partial to the interests of those who enacted it. The belief that there existed some predetermined, fair value to be paid in exchange for a worker's services provided justification for such legislation. It was looked upon as an effort to prevent objective standards and principles of distributive justice from being eroded by the morally arbitrary and deleterious forces of nature. Without legislation freezing wages at rates fixed according to the moral standards of the day, workmen would have been able to "exploit" the misfortune and necessitous circumstances of employers and consumers and obtain wages which, in this environment at least, would have been regarded as excessive and unjust.

Indeed even if, initially, the labouring classes had not been entirely persuaded by the logic of a theory of just wages, in time the Protestant religious orthodoxy, to which much of the working classes were drawn, would eventually have inclined many of them to accept this legal code.[23] The dignity of hard work, the fantasy of future kingdoms, the subordination of economic materialism to spiritual salvation all in turn facilitated, if not justified, the balance being struck as it was.

THREE

Labour Relations Laws: Industrial Society

When one turns to the labour code of industrialized England, it is clear that virtually all of the social phenomena present in pre-industrial England underwent radical change.[1] In the first place, the demographic circumstances of the two societies were exactly the opposite. By comparison with its mercantile and feudal ancestors, the population base of industrial England expanded dramatically. What had been a scarcity of labour became a surplus through both natural increase and the influx of Irish immigration.[2] The excess supply of labour created circumstances whereby the social interest in employing and consuming the services and products of workers on the most favourable terms (that is, at the lowest possible price/wage) could be accomplished without imposing statutory freezes or ceilings on wages as had been done in the past. Natural market forces would do the job just as well. It seems more than a coincidence that the massive shift away from a "public" (statutory) to a "private"(contractual) code of work regulation coincided with the radical demographic transformation in early industrial English society.[3]

In fact, this shift in social policies, which seems to have been of far greater magnitude than the deregulation movement we are experiencing today, provides another example of how vulnerable the forum of politics is to the influence of wealth, hypocrisy, and self-interest. Allowing market forces to run free when it suited their consumptive interests contrasts sharply with the earlier reaction of the rule-makers of pre-industrial society when natural phenomena appeared to threaten their way of life. Unlike their feudal and mercantile ancestors, industrial communities no longer thought individuals were being unscrupulous and overreaching when they profited from the weakness of others and took advantage of the natural environments around them whenever and however they could.

Although the comparatively broad population base of early industrial English society provided fertile ground for the dramatic change in the form (but not, as we shall see, in the balance) of the laws regulating the work relationship, it does not provide the rationale for the legislative activity which ensued. To explain this fundamental shift we must look to the dominant political and philosophical circumstances which accompanied the birth and development of industrial communities. It is there, in the theories and structures of government, that we find the generally accepted explanations for the great transformation which occurred in the legal institutions within which most of the members of early industrial societies actually worked.

At its inception, the most radical feature of English industrial society was its philosophical underpinnings rather than its political structure. As industrial society first emerged in England (and later in the United States and Canada), it was still decidedly anti-democratic. What distinguished early industrial England from its predecessors was its liberal not its democratic character.[4]

By the middle of the eighteenth century England had become a society in which mercantile and manufacturing interests had taken their place as part of the governing classes. Coincidentally, the business of production, commerce, and the affairs of state had become increasingly secularized. As religion slowly withdrew or at least moderated its focus on the economic and political affairs of men, a new morality, grounded in an old tradition of the liberty of the individual Englishman, gained ascendancy as the governing theory of social organization.[5] While there were several versions of this moral vision, common to them all was the idea that the well-being of the community and each of its members would best be promoted if the individual were permitted – indeed required – to be responsible for his or her own personal development.

In some circles there was widespread scepticism with the idea that an invisible hand could effect a perfect congruence between the interest of each individual pursuing her or his personal purposes and the well-being of the community as a whole. Nevertheless, the idea that each man was the best judge of his own interest lay at the root of the reigning philosophical doctrines of the day. For radical utilitarians no less than for conservative adherents of doctrines of natural law and natural rights, the freedom of the individual to establish the priorities and plans for his life, to be free from the strictures of status and customs that had affected earlier forms of social organization, was the touchstone of their theories of personal morality and social justice. Individual autonomy, both moral and political, the right, indeed the obligation, of every person to govern himself, became the ideal against which the major institutions and systems of social organization were measured.

As a predicate for personal behaviour, theories of individualism manifested themselves in admonitions of self-discipline, self-reliance, and personal responsibility for the choices one made.[6] As the premise for political theories of social organization, individualism naturally allied itself with the tradition of the social contract into which the members of a society were understood to have voluntarily entered. The community thus created would respect and honour the voluntary choices each person made. In the world of work and economic exchange, the ethic of individualism gave rise to the principles of free will and contract as the primary, if not exclusive, source of legal obligation. Consent of the individual rather than the command of the sovereign or the custom of the social order would define the vocation one would pursue and the conditions on which one would practise it. The workplace, in addition to the home, was a place where neither the king's nor Parliament's writ was meant to run. By the method of contract these were the places in the community where a thousand lawmakers, if that was the number employed, were meant to bloom.

Arising as it did in a "natural," demographic environment so hospitable to it, the ethic of individualism (or liberalism as it has come to be known), manifested itself in a variety of ways in the labour code of the late eighteenth century and through at least the first half of the nineteenth century.[7] Most dramatically, during the first third of the nineteenth century virtually all the central principles of the earlier labour code were swept away as being coercive and paternalistic intrusions upon the individual's right of self-determination. The wage-fixing system was struck down in 1813. If individuals were to be free to pursue vocations of their own choosing, then it followed that they would know best what value their services were worth. The idea of a just wage or fair price set by some third person not party to the relationship could no longer be accommodated within this new, competitive model of social relations. One year later, the apprenticeship requirements fell, and the previously regulated trades were organized around the principle of competition.[8] For those who had enjoyed whatever modest protection was provided by the earlier codes, this massive movement of deregulation was perceived as an injurious and inequitable debasing of their work. In the ethic of liberalism, however, the previous legislative restraints were themselves regarded as serious and unjust encroachments on both the liberty of the subject to make use of her or his labour and on the freedom of others to employ workers on terms that were mutually acceptable.

The settlement laws,[9] which had restricted mobility, as well as the Poor Law,[10] which had guaranteed the individual the resources to survive, were also swept away as further impediments to the realization of a society in which all a person's obligations and rights were to be fixed by his own free will. Indeed, the ethic of individualism was so strongly felt that, for a brief period in 1824, the logic of liberty contributed to the repeal of the Combination Acts, which up until that time had rendered unlawful associations of workers as well as political activists. Although there were a variety of forces and motives at play in freeing workmen, amongst others, from the most severe strictures of the earlier Combination Acts, the statutory enactment which allowed workmen the freedom to associate with anyone they chose were partially supported as following naturally and logically from the liberty of the individual. If a workman was free to enter an agreement to render services for another on terms and conditions to which he consented, there was nothing, as a matter of principle, which could distinguish and invalidate agreements with fellow workers to market their services collectively.[11]

The influence of the liberal ethic of individualism also permeated much of the "common" law of work relations of the period. Most significantly, because the courts remained generally true to the formalist conception of individualism and personal responsibility which underlay the rules of contract, they did not inquire into the fairness of the labour exchange. As a matter of contract doctrine, a court would inquire into the adequacy of consideration only in the most exceptional circumstances. Whatever terms had been agreed to was the best evidence of the fairness of the exchange precisely because they had been established by the parties. The worker, like everyone who entered a contractual arrangement, was presumed to know better than anyone else, including the courts, the value of his own services. The basic assumption that the individual was in control of the development of his or her own life precluded a court from inquiring into, let alone remedying, the indecently inadequate remuneration the least advantaged workers were able to command. The logic of the (common) law of contract required the courts to ignore the abusive and inhuman outcomes it generated.

In theory, the courts could have focused on the gross disparity in the bargaining power of each of the interests that are party to the labour exchange as the basis on which to protect the workers' interests. The courts might have rejected the assumption of the common law that the labour contract was the product of an unfettered and freely given expression of consent. They could have characterized the power of consumers and employers to deny workers access to the opportunity to work as constraining, coercive, and menacing as an authoritative government command.[12] They could have – but they didn't.

Instead, by and large, the courts remained true to the reigning laissez-faire version of individualism in which force and fraud were the only grounds (apart from certain extreme personal disabilities such as infancy or mental incapacity), accepted as vitiating a person's consent.[13] Rather than recognize degrees of freedom and coercion, the common law saw consent operating in the manner of a light switch. The law of contract refused to give any legal recognition to the vast disequilibrium in power that actually characterized the working relationships of those whose services were in the most abundant supply.

Other common law principles of employment relations also reflected this formal, minimalist definition of equality and liberty. Thus, in this era courts generally treated restrictive covenants, "voluntarily" agreed to by employees as part of their contracts of employment, like parallel covenants attached to the sale of business. Where they were reasonably restricted in their reach, they were declared to be valid and enforceable commitments of the worker's free will.[14] Similarly, that part of the labour code formulated by the courts to govern industrial accidents caused by the negligence of a co-worker was strongly influenced by the same idea of individual responsibility. If individual workers were competent to settle the wages they required to compensate them for the degree of risk they faced in the performance of their work, it followed that they were equally competent to determine the degree of risk to which they were willing to expose themselves from the negligence of their co-workers.[15] Finally, it was also partly the ethic of individualism, and the freedom of the individual to pursue his or her projects as a producer, that motivated the courts in their development of the doctrines of criminal and civil conspiracy. With these doctrines courts were able to prohibit what were perceived as coercive attempts by one group of workers to force others to conform to their rules. From the courts' perspective, such constraints, which limited a person's right to settle the place and conditions of work, were deserving of no greater respect than those which, in the earlier legal regimes, had been enforced by the governing classes.[16]

Taken together, then, there was a good deal of legislative and judicial activity which reoriented the system of labour relations and reversed two hundred, and in some cases four hundred, years of social regulation. Rather than governing the workplace with a set of statutory enactments, administrative processes, and customary practices, derived by a ruling elite from ancient theories of ethics and law, the thrust of the new legal order was in the direction of a public commitment to private or self-regulation. According to the new theory, an employment relationship, like friendship, was assigned to the sphere of private autonomy and beyond the reach of social control. Although, as we shall see, these laws never stood by themselves and never constituted a comprehensive code of work relations, they did come as close to creating a completely free market in labour as any legal system ever has. In the late eighteenth and early nineteenth centuries this was deregulation with a vengeance. It was a labour code that looked to private contract rather than public institutions and enactments to regulate employment relations.

Of course, a perfectly free market in labour never actually existed.[17] However, it will assist our understanding of the next phase in the evolution through which our labour codes have passed if we pause to examine the character of work relations which tends to be developed within this legal paradigm. Although the market principle is no longer the foundation of our own system of work regulation, it does still function as an important pillar that upholds and shapes our labour code. Probing the balance that a purely laissez-faire model of work relations develops should shed light upon our own model of labour relations, which remains essentially a modified contractual arrangement in which many, though obviously not all, obligations are grounded in consent.[18]

Perhaps the most obvious, but often the most forgotten, feature of this legal model of labour relations is that it represented as conscious and as deliberate a collective decision of society as any that could possibly be made.[19] It is important to keep this social, public dimension of the "private" model in mind.[20] Although a contractual model does not explicitly use public, legislative instruments to regulate the performance of work, that should not obscure the fact that the model itself would be the product of and enforced by a collective, not an individual, choice. Laissez-faire liberalism could not become the organizing principle of the law of the workplace unless a society, acting collectively, decided to make it so.

Certainly, as a matter of historical fact there was nothing at all natural in the translation of libertarian theories of liberty into legal codes of work relations. To the contrary, the chronology we have been following confirms that it came to dominate the structure of early industrial organization so completely as a result of massive government intervention. Indeed, all the historical evidence reveals that the artisans whose interests were protected by the pre-industrial model of work regulation, as well as many of the unskilled populace, were generally opposed, or at best indifferent, to such a shift to a purely private, decentralized system of work relations.[21]

It may be, as its adherents believe, that a laissez-faire model of work relations can be justified over all its competitors. Still, the fact remains that such a system necessarily entails a social choice to use principles of competition[22] rather than alternate criteria (for example, medieval ideas of just prices/wages or modern theories of fair procedures) to govern the structure and substance of the rules which regulate relations at work. If only by the state's enforcement of the contracts which specify the terms and conditions of work, there is an inevitable and integral public and coercive dimension to what is now commonly described and thought of as a private, contractual system of work relations. Moreover, because many individuals like the artisan and labouring classes of early industrial society opposed this method of social order, it could not even be said that, in a society organized primarily on a market principle, all obligations and all limitations on a person's freedom and liberty were based on consent.

So, while the laissez-faire model of work relations was radically different in form from the pre-industrial model, the two share the common characteristic that each was chosen and put in place by their societies' sovereign law-making institutions. However, for the purpose of tracing the broad development in the legal regulation of work relations, there is a second, more important, feature which these two systems had in common. The balance that each of these legal regimes struck between the competing interests of purchasers and producers was substantially the same. Even though it might be expected that a purely laissez-faire system of labour relations would promote the worker's purposes by freeing him from social structures inimical to his well-being, in fact it did not.[23]

History shows that this model proved as insensitive to the interests of large numbers of workers as those labour codes promulgated in pre-industrial England by the sovereign herself. For workers who were among the least advantaged in early industrial society, contract could never be the "horizontal," consensual process of making law that classical economic theory held it out to be. Indeed, as the many unskilled workers who petitioned Parliament to retain the wage-fixing system of the pre-industrial code well understood, the shift to a market model of labour relations meant the legal system was even less sensitive to their needs and purposes than it had been in the past. Only for the elite, for the most gifted and advantaged members of the workforce, would the adoption of a private, decentralized model of labour regulation sub-stantially enhance their freedom and opportunities of personal self-government. In Polanyi's classic turn of phrase, if the pre-industrial code of work relations threatened large sections of the working class with "the rot of immobility," in the new market model, "the peril was ... death through exposure."[24]

The evidence on this point is depressingly conclusive. The brutal and abusive exploitation of child labour stands as a permanent indictment of the kind of imbalance that the market model of work relations is capable of striking. Where competition was fiercest, conditions were worst. Historians still debate the extent to which others in the working population suffered similarly degrading and inhuman treatment; whether their circumstances were very much worse than what workers had traditionally endured in pre-industrial society; and whether, regardless of the cause, there was anything the governing institutions of society could have done about it.[25] They do agree, however, that for large numbers of workers the adoption of a contract model of labour regulation threatened their very existence. No one denies the horrible reality of the sweated labourer who "agreed" to work on terms so meagre as to imperil her life. All of the classic descriptions, of the Hammonds, Engels, the Webbs, Thompson and even Ashton,[26] portray large numbers of persons whose most basic biological needs were not given adequate consideration when English society moved to the market principle. For these individuals, a labour code organized on a principle of contract was just as "vertical" and coercive a system of social ordering as the feudal model it replaced.

The strong empirical evidence of the serious imbalances in this model of work relations only confirms what the theory predicts will occur in conditions of perfect competition. From the beginning, Adam Smith was quite clear that in the legal environment of a free market of labour, the consumer, not the worker, would be sovereign. Indeed, that was precisely why the market was proposed as the most appropriate social institution to regulate work. For Smith and all subsequent proponents of a perfectly competitive system of labour relations, work was to serve the consumer's not the producer's interests. Smith said it all when he wrote:

Consumption is the sole end and purpose of all production; and the interest of the producer ought to be attended to, only so far as it may be necessary for promoting that of the consumer. The maxim is so perfectly self-evident, that it would be absurd to attempt to prove it.[27]

The reasons why a market model of labour relations is so solicitous of the consumer are not difficult to explain. In circumstances of pure and perfect competition there is a gross imbalance in the bargaining power of each of the parties to the labour exchange to control and realize their competing objectives in the performance of work. The closer any market for labour replicates the paradigm – where, for example, there are a sufficiently large number of independent workers – each becomes, in the professional parlance, a "price (wage) taker." Each loses all control over the terms and conditions on which he or she will work. Each approximates the economist's favourite metaphorical sheaf of wheat destined for a futures market wafting to the whim of the consumer's preference. According to the classical theorists, the natural price of unskilled labour, at least in the demographic circumstances of the earliest industrial societies, was a bare subsistence wage.[28] As a group, it was the large pool of unskilled labour, of which women and children were most often a part, whose circumstances most closely approximated the market ideal. For these workers, the sovereignty of the employer and consumer was virtually absolute. The services that each of these persons could offer to their communities were, by definition, of relatively inconsequential value. Given the dramatic increase in the size of the population in this period, the kind of work they were able to perform was abundant and readily available from others. They had no basis on which to demand that, in exchange for their work, employers and consumers must provide them with wages and working conditions of sufficient value to guarantee their physical, let alone spiritual, well-being.

The circumstances of consumers and employers were exactly the opposite. Regardless of the number of persons to whom workers might sell their services, in every exchange employers controlled and could withhold from workers the means of survival.[29] Holding a good (the opportunity to work) of such immense and immediate value gave every employer an enormous bargaining advantage. Being in control of the means of another person's livelihood meant that as a group the employers and consumers had vastly more bargaining power than the workers, which enabled them to acquire the services of workers on terms that were most favourable to their interests. In the circumstances of the unskilled labourer at the dawn of the Industrial Revolution, when competition was at its keenest, the disparity in bargaining power was at its greatest and the model worked as its theorists predicted. Rather than an instance of market failure, the indignities visited on the most vulnerable workers in early English industrial society confirm that the sovereign authority of the consumer will show as little concern and respect for the projects of those under its control as the earlier monarchies it replaced. The empirical evidence simply corroborated the model's hypothesis that conditions for large numbers of workers will be worst when their economic and social circumstances come closest to replicating a perfectly competitive environment.

But it would be a mistake to leave the impression that the legal code governing employment relations in early English industrial society was exclusively grounded in the market conception of individualism and formal equality. Just as we had to remind ourselves not to be overly romantic about the legal regime governing the workplace in pre-industrial society, there is a risk of being unduly negative about the labour code of its industrial successor. Like the labour law of the pre-industrial period, the rules of industrial England were not entirely one-sided. Both the legislative and judicial branches of government did initiate legal rules which qualified the laissez-faire model of work relations.

For their part, in the industrial period courts enunciated and supported rules which encouraged employers to provide a safe working environment.[30] As well, they insisted that employers pay wages to their workers for the duration of the contract, including periods when there was not sufficient work for them to do,[31] or when they were too sick or incapacitated to work.[32] As with the law the courts contributed to the pre-industrial labour codes, some members of the judiciary were at least sensitive, even in the heyday of laissez-faire liberalism, to the most basic physiological needs workers pursue through their work. These principles of the common law of employment were undeniable instances of rule-making by courts which insisted that certain interests of workers be given some minimum degree of concern and respect. Together with the rules the judiciary inserted in the pre-industrial labour codes, they offer some basis to be optimistic that, in our time as well, courts can contribute legal rulings to our labour code which will be equally sensitive to the most important purposes each of us has in our work.

In a similar way, although the laissez-faire model of employment relations formed the basis of the labour code legislators insisted early industrial society must embrace, exceptions and modifications were made by them as well. Even in the early years of the nineteenth century, departures from the pure contract model of work relations were legislated, especially when considerations of public morality and community health were at stake. By and large these initiatives were restricted to relieving the most glaring injustices which scarred the social landscape and they were extended only to children and subsequently to women who were compelled to work for a living. In the totally male and highly paternalistic parliaments of the day, women and children were not regarded as free agents, either morally or legally. So motives of "parental" responsibility as well as self-interest could incline legislators to subordinate their own interests as consumers to protect the physical integrity of these individuals.[33] Acting by and large pragmatically and on an ad hoc basis, Parliament responded to circumstances of critical need, first in the cotton mills, then gradually to other sectors of the economy.[34] Throughout the nineteenth century the practice of Parliament was to "act" incrementally both in the scope of protection afforded and in the groups of workers who would benefit thereby. While adult male workers did benefit from some of this factory legislation in the last quarter of the nineteenth century – for example that pertaining to sanitation, safety, and accident prevention – it was only after the turn of this century that legislators in England (as in Canada and the United States), began to systematically regulate their hours of work and wages as well .

FOUR

Labour Relations Laws: Post-Industrial Society

Since the turn of the century, the scope and substance of labour law has changed dramatically. As the working classes have been able to participate more fully and effectively in the democratic processes of government, they have used that opportunity to secure legislation much more favourable to their interests.[1] In the last eighty years, English, Canadian, and American societies all have increasingly returned to the legislative instrument to regulate the relations of people at work and to limit, though not eliminate, the sovereign authority the consumer wields in the marketplace. In both volume and detail the regulation of work by legislative and administrative mechanisms rivals that of pre-industrial English society. But in nature and purpose it is radically different. Whereas the earlier regulation was directed primarily to securing a balance of interests favourable to employers and consumers, in our own time legislators have been more concerned to promote and protect the interests a worker has in his or her job. Instead of procuring labour peace in the community by legal sanctions of criminal and civil liability, in more recent times it has been purchased by legislation aimed at enhancing the opportunity for self-control.[2]

Taken together, all the laws we have come to rely upon to regulate and coordinate work activities in our community, can be seen as providing more extensive forms of protection for workers against arbitrary authority. Increasingly, legislators have added principles and rules to our labour code which endeavour to establish how some individuals in our community can control others. In contemporary liberal jargon, our legislative record could be said to promote the political ideal that everyone's interest as a worker be shown some basic – and in that sense, equal – concern and respect.[3] It tends to enhance the liberty and autonomy which each of us is entitled to enjoy. It strikes a quite different balance between the interests of workers and their employers from that brought about by the feudal and laissez-faire codes it replaced. Interestingly, it borrows two quite dissimilar techniques from each of them.

One strand of our present labour code continues the tradition of the early factory legislation. It guarantees, essentially on the same motivations of health and morality, an expanding set of entitlements pertaining to the physical, economic, and occupational security of the person. This is the method of our employment standards and human rights legislation. In the same manner that the earliest pieces of factory legislation required the processes of production to be carried out in ways that did not threaten the physical security of the person, modern legislation also proscribes other terms and conditions of work which we now recognize as being equally deleterious to the autonomy of the worker. Minimum wage legislation was enacted primarily to ensure that all who worked would earn enough to make a decent living – something beyond the minimum that would merely keep a person alive.[4] Legislation regulating hours of work and rest, vacations, holidays, and periods of leave guarantees people the opportunities to pursue other activities they value. Notice and just-cause clauses, restricting the power of unilateral termination, provide a measure of economic and occupational security upon which a worker's control and direction of his or her life ultimately depend. And the general injunction of our human rights legislation – that decisions affecting the organization and processes of work be made rationally and on relevant rather than discriminatory bases – tries to ensure that each worker's purposes and projects will receive some equal measure of respect from the rest of the community.

In each of these enactments, society shows increasing sensitivity to the connection between a person's physical and mental well-being as a worker and his or her ability to define and control his or her own destiny. In expanding the set of entitlements which attach to industrial citizenship, we can be seen to have continued the gradual evolution of our labour law. We have moved from protecting the most basic concerns of the worker for her or his physical safety and survival, to enacting a set of rules that accommodates the more human aspirations most people have in their work. Gradually, by stipulating more of the essential features of the legal arrangements within which people work, we have come to make a meaningful commitment to our equality as humans who want to control as much of our own lives as possible.

In addition to establishing a set of minimum, substantive conditions to which most workers are entitled, our legislatures have employed a second method to permit workers to protect their own interests more effectively in the private processes of law-making. It is here where the more detailed rules governing their working lives are expected to be settled. Rather than relying exclusively on substantive prescriptions to constrain market outcomes, our legislators have turned to procedural devices through which those who are the weakest and most vulnerable to the competitive forces of the market can join together to better protect their personal ambitions in their work. As Mr Justice Holmes long ago observed, legislation promoting a system of collective labour relations is intended, inter alia, to establish the equality between individuals on which liberty in contract depends.[5] Paraphrasing the words of another advocate of our system of collective bargaining, our legislators substituted a model of work relations predicated on the rule of law for one based on the fiat of man.[6] Contemporary labour legislation has even extended the logic of this legislative method by making similar structures available to employers when the conditions of the market make them especially vulnerable to those whom they wish to employ.[7]

This strategy, of adapting the market method of work relations to collective or democratic processes of decision-making, parallels the technique of enacting standards to prevent the most egregious substantive solutions which markets are capable of generating. Both date back to the early nineteenth century and both reflect the same pattern of evolution in which gradually the rules and laws show an increasing amount of concern for the interests workers have in their jobs. The earliest enactments of this type – the repeal of the Combination Acts (1824), and later the Trade Union Act (1871), Criminal Law Amendment Act (1871), the Conspiracy and Protection of Property Act (1875), and the Trades Dispute Act (1871)[8] – had as their primary objective the removal of various legal impediments imposed earlier, by courts and commons alike, on workers' freedom to associate with each other. These early legislative initiatives, promoting systems of collective labour relations, gradually removed the various institutional and legal arrangements which had interfered with the workers' freedom of association and capacity to participate meaningfully in the settling of the legal rules under which they worked.

It is in this tradition of making procedural adjustments to the market model of regulating work that our contemporary collective bargaining laws belong. Collective bargaining statutes, as well as more recent federal and provincial initiatives establishing health and safety, and redundancy committees,[9] are designed, inter alia, to overcome additional social impediments to workers' opportunities to join with each other in common cause. Collective bargaining legislation addresses the serious "private" obstacles which the modern forms of corporate organization can place in the paths of workers who want to associate together. Such legislation also signals a recognition that the freedom of workers to form associations needs more than neutrality and tolerance by the state in the legislation it enacts. It requires active state support to counteract the obstacles which the market and the private institutions of production can themselves create. Therefore, collective bargaining statutes characteristically prohibit any outside interference with the formation of unions, and require their recognition when they are chosen freely and according to due processes of law. In legislation of this modern type, the legislature is attempting to ensure that the power of private property, which may otherwise be used in making decisions in the market, cannot be invoked to interfere with workers' initiatives to form their own associations. Together, collective bargaining and the earlier conspiracy legislation endeavour to put the workers' freedom to associate beyond the reach of both public and private centres of power.

Viewed in its entirety, the legal practice by which our society now regulates the performance of work can best be understood as endeavouring to provide fairer processes of decision-making, through which the competing interests of workers and those who purchase their services can be reconciled more equitably. Essentially the market model, which emerged with the development of industrial society, has been adapted so that the balance is more sensitive to the needs and the purposes people pursue in their work. On the one hand, setting minimum standards of safety, security, and physical well-being provides a check on the tyranny which, as we have seen, is the potential of this decision-making process.[10] On the other hand, insisting that everyone in the community respects the freedom of workers to associate with whomever they chose ensures the latter will possess a sufficient measure of countervailing power to enable them to have a more significant input in the final balance that is struck. Modern labour legislation, taken as a whole, insists that all sources of power and influence be used in a way which respects the equal entitlement of everyone to the conditions which are necessary to be meaningfully involved in the decisions which determine how they will live out their lives.

As we observed when we chronicled the shift from the pre-industrial to the laissez-faire model of work relations, there are a variety of causes to which this latest transformation can be attributed. Certainly sociological, political, philosophical, technological, and economic factors have all played an important part in influencing the legal rules we have developed to govern the workplace. It is not necessary again to detail the various forces that have influenced this most recent shift. Suffice it to observe that prominent among them is the political climate in which our rules and labour regulations have grown. Unquestionably, the formal enfranchisement and increasing influence of all segments of the labour force in the legislative and executive processes of government is one of the most striking features of our social landscape.[11]

Certainly early democrats such as Mill and Bentham recognized that universal suffrage could have a profound impact on the substance of the rules which governed social, including work, relations. Workers, like all who participated in the processes of government before them, were expected to act in their own self-interest and to protect themselves from the excesses and injustices of the earlier labour codes. There was never any doubt that the working classes would use their newly acquired authority to redress the incidents of servitude and the unequal bargaining power under which they had laboured so long. And that is precisely what they have aspired to do.

Consistent with the hypothesis Mill advanced, as workers have been able to represent their own interests in the executive and the legislative branches of government, their interests were not so easily ignored or filtered through distorted lenses. With their formal inclusion in the process of politics, workers have lobbied for rules and regulations which could constrain the sovereignty employers and consumers exert in the market place. As workers have been able to participate more effectively in the public processes in which law is made, through unions and organized political parties, they have insisted on legislation that would allow them to participate more fully in the private processes of law-making as well. More equal freedom in the political sphere has led logically, not paradoxically,[12] to greater equality of participation in the marketplace as well.

Interpreting our own legal model of work regulation as an attempt to invoke fairer processes to reconcile our differences as employers, consumers, and workers is instructive, then, in offering additional support for the connection drawn by Mill between accessibility to the institutions of government and the substance of the rules which find their way into our labour code. Describing our labour laws in this manner is also helpful in offering another perspective[13] on why, notwithstanding the emphasis in recent times on the legislative instrument, our society is still very much within what Henry Maine characterized as the progressive tradition. On the interpretation we have been following,[14] our own contribution to the history of work regulation continues the evolution away from status toward consent as the principle governing the regulation of work relations. Most of the legislation we have enacted since the turn of the century can be understood as instances of social control over the ways in which and the extent to which some (employers and consumers) in our community are empowered to exercise legal authority over others (workers).

Human rights legislation is perhaps our most explicit denunciation of status as a relevant basis on which an individual's interests in his or her work can be settled. Other components of our labour code, including collective bargaining and more recent initiatives of worker participation (for example, health and safety and redundancy committees), can also be described as furthering that evolution. In a sense, legislation of this type simply insists on a more rigorous and sophisticated definition of consent.[15] By bargaining collectively, workers are able to avoid, or at least ameliorate, the social, economic, and personal disadvantages which as much as force or fraud may drain their agreement of consent. The expectation that collective bargaining will redress the enormous inequalities in bargaining power that derive from the social, economic, and personal circumstances of each worker is what justifies the claim that workers will be able to participate in formulating, rather than passively accepting, the terms and conditions under which they will work. Like an employment standard of procedural justice, collective bargaining is ultimately defended by its advocates as intrinsically valuable as an experience of industrial self-government.[16] It is said to offer opportunities for self-determination and self-discipline which, certainly for the least advantaged workers in our community, are unavailable in pure market or contract models of work regulation. Interpreted as a whole, our contemporary labour code can be seen as shifting the priorities which this body of rules has traditionally been used to achieve. Rather than striking a balance in favour of the interests of consumers or employers or the well-being of the community in the aggregate, now individual autonomy and personal self-government has become the dominant characteristic of the legal practice we have developed to regulate the employment relationship. Slowly, over time, our labour code has endeavoured to protect the purposes which work has come to serve for both the individual and the community alike.

Two Principles of Constitutional Review

The existence and validity of human rights is not written in the stars.
Albert Einstein

FIVE

Law, Politics, and the Least Advantaged

This is an appropriate place to pause and survey the path we have travelled. As one reflects on the past six hundred years of work regulation, there are three characteristics which stand out. Unquestionably the most striking feature of the legal regulation of work activities is the virtually uninterrupted commitment of successive societies to subject this vital form of human behaviour to detailed social regulation. At no time during this chronology have labour relationships been governed exclusively by rules and regulations settled by the persons who are parties to the relationship. Rather, the balance that was eventually struck between the competing interests of the producers and consumers of labour was one that was strongly influenced by the collective efforts of all three branches of government.

Almost as conspicuous is how the balance in these labour laws has gradually shifted to show increasing sensitivity to the producer's interest in his work. We saw how the first statutory interventions by the sovereign were prompted by a concern to ensure that the consumers' and employers' interests were not overwhelmed by the bargaining power of the workers which had been suddenly and artificially inflated by the Black Death. Over the past two hundred years, by contrast, much of the social regulation has proceeded in exactly the opposite direction. Now our laws endeavour to enhance the opportunity each person has to realize an identity he or she chooses through work. Fundamental human rights and equality of treatment are among the distinguishing characteristics of the Canadian system of regulating work relationships.[1] Equality of autonomy or personal self-government can be described as the deep principle of justice which connects and underlies our labour code as a whole. In this sense, there is some truth in the popular claim that labour legislation has become increasingly one-sided in its focus. What remains to be decided, and what the analysis that follows will endeavour to explore, is whether this bias has gone on too long or whether it still has not gone far enough.

The third outstanding feature of this chronology of labour codes is the manner in which it has evolved. While it is true that the legislative process has shown itself to be increasingly sensitive to the vital functions work serves for the human condition, the way in which labour law has developed also underscores the real limits that constrain this branch of government. The larger lesson of history is surely a confirmation of how susceptible the legislative and executive branches of government are to the influence of what today we call pressure group politics. The chronology we have traced offers compelling evidence to support Mill's hypothesis linking the concern and respect that a community shows for the interests of various individuals and the ability of the latter to adequately represent their needs and ambitions in the processes in which the collective will of the community is expressed.

As a matter of procedural fairness, the record of the legislative (as well as the judicial) branch of government in enacting and declaring the laws making up our labour code still leaves a good deal to be desired. Rather than the outcome of a principled program of legislative decision-making, the chronology we have just reviewed is the product of ad hoc, pragmatic, and frequently self-interested compromises of various social, economic, and political forces of the day.[2] Thus, in the period preceding the Industrial Revolution, when working people were denied any influence in the processes of government, laws were enacted establishing ceilings on wages and floors on the hours they must work. The labour code of the pre-industrial period was for the most part quite insensitive to the workers' interests and ambitions. Again, during the latter part of the eighteenth century and the early years of the nineteenth century, the deregulation movement, which shifted the labour code toward a competitive, laissez-faire model of work regulation, was largely promoted by, and coincident with, the emerging political influence and ethical values of the industrial class. Then, as more and more working people obtained the franchise, the legislative history of labour law becomes one of sporadic and pragmatic compromises which endeavour to accommodate conflicting objectives. Even in our own experience we see how the bulk of recent legislative initiatives directed to the needs and aspirations of female workers (for example, laws promoting equal opportunity, equal pay, and affirmative action) generally have followed, rather than preceded, women organizing themselves as an important and influential political force. Clyde Summers, one of the pre-eminent labour law scholars in the United States, has summarized the parallel history of the legal regulation of work relationships in his country, as the product of "political eruption," not "rational evolution."[3] Labour legislation, perhaps more than any other area of social policy, is still peculiarly the product of legislative compromise of sharply divergent views.

Against that historical backdrop it should not be surprising that our own substantive rules of labour regulation are still very much a function of the relative influence which the competing interests of consumers, employers, and producers (or, more accurately, organized segments within these groups), are able to exert on the political processes of government. While certainly less pervasive than it was when relations at work were first subjected to social control, those who have the fewest resources, both material and personal, with which to influence the legislative and executive branches of government still receive the least concern and respect from the state. As we shall see, agricultural workers and domestics – who have been excluded from much of the legislation we have just reviewed – provide a most explicit example of how the least advantaged and influential members of our society can be ignored by those who now control the processes of government. Although the general evolution in the legal regulation of work relations has been increasingly sensitive to the aspirations of workers, that same chronology suggests, and the analysis we shall follow in this part confirms, that we still have not gone far enough.

The risk that the interests and aspirations of the less advantaged workers in our community will be ignored or sacrificed by more powerful forces in our political institutions is probably as acute today as at any stage in the past. Contemporary political debates are dominated by those who argue that we have already gone much too far in preferring the interests of labour over those who employ and ultimately consume their services. They see in the history of work regulation a broad and persistent bias that unfairly favours the worker. They point to the same chronology of laws regulating work and claim, with some accuracy, that workers' interests are now better protected than they have ever been and, in their view, ever should be.

Indeed, for some who hold this view all social intervention of the past two hundred years is open to serious question. They ask why, if a person saves rather than spends the resources he has earned and/ or inherited so as to pursue an economic venture of his own choosing, he should not be able to associate with whomever he wants, on whatever terms he is willing to offer to others who want to join him in his enterprise. What right, it is asked, has the state to prohibit such a person from refusing to hire individuals he does not like, even if his hostility is based on racial or religious grounds? Critics of our labour code challenge the basis on which a majority of persons in our society, acting through their elected representatives, are entitled to interfere with their "rights and freedoms" by stipulating minimum terms and conditions at each phase of the employment relationship and by prescribing a collective decision-making process through which every other detail of their relationship with their workers must be settled. According to this view, human rights codes, employment standards legislation, collective bargaining laws, affirmative action programs, constraints on mandatory retirement, can all be characterized as serious violations of peoples' freedom to do as they choose and to associate with whomever they please.

If that is a fair representation of the climate of the current debate, it can be seen that while the momentum may have shifted, we are not in a very different position from that which has existed in the past. We face an obstacle which seems endemic to the terrain. The issues and even the terms of the debate are depressingly similar. Yet though the current controversy parallels earlier struggles, there is at least one difference of enormous significance in our present political and legal environment. By and large, most of the rules that made up the different labour codes of the past were formulated in our legislative and executive branches of government. Although the courts have, from time to time, formulated legal rules which protected some of the most basic attributes of economic security for workers, judges have never been given a particularly broad mandate in the definition of the legal principles which have made up our labour codes. Nor at any time in the past were the courts given the constitutional authority to review the substance of the rules enacted by the other two branches of government.

Traditionally, the best labour code was the one finally chosen by the people themselves – or more accurately by those anointed or appointed to govern them. However imperfect or inequitable the legislative and executive processes might have been, the will of the sovereign (be it monarch or a majority of the people), was generally accepted as the final arbiter in choosing the form in which and the extent to which work relationships should be regulated. Although the courts did not always subscribe to the principle as faithfully as they might have, by and large the will of the sovereign legislative institution was understood to be supreme.[4] The debate between consumers and producers was held almost exclusively according to the rules of the political processes of government.

In our present circumstances, if, as much of the evidence seems to suggest, the will of a majority in our legislatures supported more deregulation, favoured allowing individuals greater freedom to choose for themselves the terms on which and the people with whom they would work, then majoritarian democratic theory would argue for the integrity and legitimacy of that determination. According to that theory of democracy, that would be the "right" resolution simply because that is where we as a society, acting through democratic procedures of decision-making, would choose to be. Regardless of how adversely it might affect those already least advantaged in our community, the political authority of the majority would be the decisive criterion for its "acts." If any group of workers wanted to resist that conclusion, wanted to strike a balance more favourable to their own ambitions, they would be obliged to do so through the same political procedures arrayed against them.

Since 1982 that is no longer the case. As of that date workers who had little access to and influence on the political processes are no longer constrained by such a procedural disadvantage. What is unique about our current legal environment is, of course, the fact that the political processes are neither the exclusive nor the final forum in which the debate may be continued unless a legislature expressly asserts such a monopoly on "power talk."[5] On 15 April 1982 our constitution was patriated and radically amended. Beyond doubt, the most dramatic and significant part of that constitutional moment was the entrenchment of a Charter of Rights and Freedoms which assures a list of fundamental personal freedoms for everyone in our community. By this guarantee a new process of legal validation of social policy has been added to our system of government. Whatever else is may come to imply, it is apparent, just from the act of entrenchment, that a new avenue of participation – a kind of conversation of justification – is now available in which the debate we have been following can be pursued. In the judicial branch of our government, however, the debate will take on an entirely different cast. In this forum the dialogue about what rules and laws should be included in our labour code will be decided much more as a matter of reason and right than on the possession of material and political influence than ever before. The Charter will make it impossible for any interest group in the debate to prevail simply by virtue of having secured the support of a majority of representatives in the legislative process. In the words of our Chief Justice, "We have moved somewhat away from pure parliamentary sovereignty."[6] A new opportunity to participate in the processes of government, in what Ronald Dworkin has called the forum of principle,[7] is now available to test the appropriate limits of, and balance within, the social policies we use to regulate relationships in the places we work.

In this second part of the book I want to explore the basis on which and the extent to which those workers, who are among the least well-off members of the labour force, can make the Charter work for them. I want to inquire whether through our third arm of government they will be able to resist and even roll back the siege under which they and their supporters believe themselves to be labouring. My objective is to explore how, if at all, this constitutional rearrangement will affect the way in which our society resolves the ongoing historical debate. I want to think out loud about the most probable effects of this fundamental change on the substantive rules regulating our affairs when we are at work. If the chronology we have been following teaches us anything, it is that shifts in the opportunity to participate in the processes of government of this dimension, like extensions in the right to vote, will have an important impact on the content of our labour code. The agenda here, then, is to see whether the processes of judicial review will present a real opportunity for those who have had the most marginal impact on the legislative and executive branches of government to participate in a way which will ensure that their interests are no longer ignored.

Any attempt, at this point in time, to analyse the impact of the Charter on the entitlements that working people can validly claim is an undertaking fraught with risk. All "Charter jurisprudence" is at the earliest stages of its development, and the Supreme Court has yet to even pronounce upon the constitutional validity of any of the major enactments we currently use to regulate the work relationship. There is a real shortage of the legal stuff lawyers rely on to effect such analyses. Proceeding now, before that jurisprudence is available, aggravates the possibility that any method of inquiry one chooses can be characterized – and dismissed – as the product of the writer's own favourite and entirely arbitrary theories of constitutional law.

I suspect this is a hazard which can never be completely avoided when a study of this kind is attempted so soon after the legal event being examined has occurred. Yet it seems to me, from the state of constitutional law and theory in the United States, that this charge can probably be levelled at all manner of constitutional theorizing, and indeed all methods of interpretation, whatever the nature or vintage of the document being probed. Moreover, it is a contingency which, I believe, can be substantially attenuated, even in the earliest attempts at understanding a new constitutional order, if one proceeds from the weakest and least controversial assumptions possible. Sticking to very cautious and conservative principles of interpretation would be in keeping with the Canadian judicial tradition[8] and would enhance considerably the credibility of the conclusions the analysis yields.

In the end, of course, any principles we choose to invoke will involve some normative dimension, as well as a positive description, of our law and system of government. All interpretation has some creative aspect to it and constitutional interpretation is no different in this respect. Every principle of judicial review involves some choice of a political theory which can locate it and justify it in the larger constitutional structures of the state.[9] But this is a feature of constitutional law we ought to welcome. Being at the earliest stages of the development of the constitutional order of our society, we enjoy a unique opportunity to reflect and write judgments from first principles dealing with the most basic rules we have created to govern peoples' relations at work. We live in a time in which we can write opinions and essays about constitutional law and political theory less constrained by the often awkward rulings of earlier precedent than succeeding generations ever can be. We enjoy a unique moment in history which allows us to bequeath a principled theory of the Canadian political/constitutional order which will organize our own and future societies for generations to come.

SIX

Interpreting the Charter: Two Principles of Judicial Review

If we apply a strategy of caution and conservatism to the project at hand, we would be safe grounding our analysis on the assumption that the basic focus of an entrenched bill of rights is to constrain the powers of the legislative branch of government. Constitutional theorists of virtually every stripe perceive the Charter as providing, at a minimum, some check on the will of the majority, acting through its elected representatives, to accomplish whatever social objectives it wants to pursue. It is, to some degree, a limitation on what otherwise would be (and until now has been) the absolute sovereignty of Parliament to pursue whatever social policies it has devised. Although there is a lively debate on whether the Charter can affect the actions and behaviour of individuals when they act privately,[1] everyone agrees that the Charter must apply to programs initiated by the state in its legislative and administrative capacities. Unless a legislature expressly declares (pursuant to s.33) that the Charter is inapplicable to a statute, or brings itself within the purview of s.1, the constitution specifies a set of substantive criteria – our fundamental rights and freedoms – which must be respected if our governments are to "act" constitutionally.

Although a consensus has yet to emerge on the extent to which the scope of the Charter goes beyond the legislative institutions of government, both the language and logic of our new constitutional rules argue for its being applicable equally to the executive and the judicial branches. Regardless of whether it applies to the behaviour of individuals acting privately, it seems clear it controls all the activities and institutions of our three branches of government. S.32 explicitly states that it applies to "the Parliament and government" of Canada and each province. On the broad and liberal interpretation most people agree should be brought to our understanding of these new constitutional rules,[2] government would naturally refer to both its executive and judicial institutions.

There is certainly nothing in the text or political philosophy underlying the Charter to support the narrower reading, which some would give it,[3] of "government" to mean only the executive institutions and structures of state.

Any ambiguity that the word "government" entails dissolves when it is read in the context of the Charter as a whole. In particular s.52 points strongly to the conclusion that all three branches of government must respect our new constitutional constraints. That section states clearly and unequivocally that, as part of the constitution, the Charter is the supreme law of Canada and *any law* which is inconsistent with its terms has no legal force or effect. To read the language in s.32 to refer only to the legislative and executive but not the judicial arm of government would entail, as a matter of consistency, a parallel interpretation of s.52, thereby excluding the common (that is, "unwritten," "judge-made") law from its terms.[4] If, in s.52, "any law" means what it says, and embraces the common law as well, s.32 would logically be understood to be comprehensive in binding all, not just two-thirds of the legal structure, which is characteristic of our liberal-democratic state. If the Charter is superior to law which is adjudicated as well as that which is legislated, s.32 must of necessity embrace all three branches of government.

It is difficult to imagine how any counter-argument could possibly be sustained. Limiting the application of the Charter to the executive and legislative institutions of government would mean the courts which have been assigned the function of infusing our constitutional values into the structures of state could themselves ignore, or even worse, deliberately violate, its terms. It would mean that in defining and fleshing out the principles and rules which make up our labour code, legislators, members of the executive, and their subordinate agents (for example, labour boards and arbitrators[5]) would be obliged to respect the rights and freedoms of every individual in our society but judges would not. Their rules, the traditional common law of the shop, and not the constitution, would become the supreme law of those aspects of the workplace that they regulated. Adopting such a narrow interpretation of the language of s.32 would mean that, in establishing the rules of tort and contract which govern many of our most characteristically human activities, the coercive authority of the state would be grounded in the rule of men and a few women rather than the rule of law.

It is perhaps wise to leave this issue to one side; there is, it turns out, no need for us to take a final position on which branches of government the Charter constrains. In almost all of the cases it will be self-evident that it is the legislature which has declared the law we will scrutinize. In the two instances where the reach of the Charter is in issue, the only question will be in determining what constitutes a legislative "act" and we can consider that question at those times.

With the scope of the Charter set, we can turn our attention to the nature and object of the legal constraints – the rights and freedoms – it establishes. Here the text is not so explicit and unequivocal and it will be necessary to spend some time fleshing out the objectives those rights and freedoms seek to achieve. In the end, I want to say that subjecting social policies, such as those which make up our labour code, to the scrutiny of the Charter ensures that when any majority gets control of the legislative process it will respect the equal authority of each individual to participate in and ultimately to maintain some control over the various decision-making processes through which his or her life is governed. With the entrenchment of the Charter, some conception of the equal autonomy and dignity of each person is guaranteed unless, pursuant to s.33, a legislature quite explicitly declares its intention to deny that entitlement or unless, pursuant to s.1, its policies can be demonstrably justified in a society which organizes its social structure on principles of freedom and democracy. That is, in essence, what the Charter is all about. Whether one invokes this liberal ideal of personal self-government in the service of some larger political theory of human rights or the democratic process itself, the right of self-determination will, for a variety of reasons I will come to momentarily, be at the core of what the Charter protects. In language more familiar to lawyers, the Charter guarantees a set of civil liberties which are thought to be conditions precedent to the freedom and dignity of the person.

Another way of expressing the basic ideal the Charter captures is to say it secures for each Canadian a basic equality in the extent to which she or he is able to govern or control her or his own destiny. Reduced to its simplest terms, the Charter is grounded in the quin-tessential liberal idea that the state must respect the fact that, regardless of the unique talents and merits of each person in our society, regardless of the distinctions in our persons and personalities, all individuals in the society share a will and a capacity which makes each of us desirous of directing the most basic aspects of our lives.[6] In effect, the entrench-ment of the Charter demands that in constructing the processes through which (for example, collective bargaining) and formulating the rules according to which (for example, mandatory retirement) each person must organize and pursue his or her own purposes, society will respect this basic equality in our liberty. In the coordination and reconciliation of the competing ambitions of each individual, the Charter requires our legislatures to respect some basic equality in a person's right to self-government – what I will call equality of liberty for short.

I recognize that for many such an attribution of the underlying purpose of the Charter will not be immediately self-evident, so I want to spend some time explaining why this depiction of the political theory which infuses the Charter is, in the final analysis, as straightforward and unproblematic as the scope of its reach. Let us start with the document itself. Both in its structure and text, the Charter makes it clear that some evolving definition of equality in personal self-government is the most basic ideal on which our political and legal order is grounded.

As one reads through the document, one can see that two different techniques have been employed by the drafters to realize this overriding constitutional objective. First, the Charter guarantees a certain degree of physical and intellectual independence which is taken to be a precondition for an individual to be autonomous and in control of his or her own development. It marks off a space in each person's life free from the intrusions of others, in which the individual may determine the most basic aspects of his or her separate existence. Thus, in its guarantee of the integrity of our physical persons against unreasonable search and seizure (s.8), arbitrary arrest and detention (ss.9–11), cruel and unusual treatment (s.12) and the associated legal rights to counsel (s.11), to interpreters (s.14), and against self-incrimination (s.13), we see the Charter protecting the conditions of human freedom which have the deepest roots in our legal system. Simultaneously, in guaranteeing (in s.2) the fundamental freedoms of conscience and religion, of thought, belief, opinion, and expression, of assembly and of association, the Charter protects the corresponding intellectual independence which is equally essential and a precondition of individual autonomy and self-control.[7] Together these rights, to our physical and intellectual independence, mark off an area of privacy and personal responsibility in which each of us is entitled to be equally (but not absolutely) free from the interference of others.

The Charter's commitment to the political ideal of equality of liberty is not, however, a concept which is exclusively negative or anti-social in character. It has a positive, social dimension to it as well. In addition to requiring our legislators to respect a private sphere within which all individuals may govern and choose for themselves, free from the interference of others, the Charter also extends its commitment to equality to the public arena. Thus the democratic rights set out in ss.3–5 and the equality rights provided in s.15 together guarantee that each person has a right to participate as an equal in, and be treated as an equal by, the legislative processes when the community collectively settles the rules which govern its affairs. Where conditions of conflict and scarcity prevail, where our ambitions as individuals collide and must therefore be reconciled by rules jointly and publicly determined, the Charter's guarantee of our democratic rights and equality rights ensures that each person can participate to some minimum (and therefore equal) degree (to vote, stand for office, and so on) in the formulation of those rules and will benefit from and be protected by their equal application. It guarantees the integrity of the democratic process itself.

To summarize, then, the principle of equality of liberty guaranteed in the collective expression of the rights and freedoms specified in the Charter can be characterized as our first principle of social justice. "Ordered liberty," as it is sometimes described,[8] is in a sense our most basic political ideal. With respect to those conditions our society regards as essential to being able to choose a lifestyle for oneself, each individual is guaranteed equal protection against all forms of social coercion. And, in the processes and institutions which settle the rules of social cooperation to which everyone's life plans must conform, the principle insists on a further dimension of the equality that derives from membership in a common community. Together the political, civil, legal, and equality rights entrenched in our Charter commit our legislatures to, and constrain them by, what Ronald Dworkin has called a "general requirement of justice." As defined by him, such a requirement entails that

... government must treat its citizens as equals, as equally entitled to concern and respect. Of course this general requirement is very abstract ... But we can nevertheless speak of a general duty of government to treat its citizens [as equals] and derive from this two distinct and more concrete responsibilities. The first is the responsibility, in creating a political order, to respect whatever underlying moral and political rights citizens may have in the name of genuine equality. The second is the obligation to extend whatever political order it does create equally and consistently to everyone.[9]

The idea that an equal right to self-determination is the first principle of social justice to which our Charter is committed seems to follow directly from the structure of the Charter and from the specific enumeration of the rights and freedoms it contains. However, even if that were not the case, there are other grounds, both within and beyond the text, which confirm that some specification of the principle of equality of liberty is the ultimate constitutional ideal to which the Charter commits us. There is considerable additional evidence to support the conclusion that this characterization is accurate as a positivist description of our constitutional practice.

The most compelling piece of corroboration is to be found in the preamble to the Charter itself. In its opening words the Charter makes reference to this constitutional ideal. Through its preamble the Charter introduces and explains the rights and freedoms we have just identified by proclaiming that the Canadian method of organizing social relations is predicated on the "supremacy of God and the rule of law."

Now the concept of the rule of law is simply another formulation of the political ideal I have characterized as the equal right of everyone to dominion over themselves. While it is undeniably true that, over time, numerous conceptions of this political ideal have been formulated, at its core the concept has always been grounded in some formal specification of an equal right to liberty or personal freedom. Like the Charter, the rule of law is ultimately founded on the liberty and dignity of the individual and has as its object the reconciliation of each person's freedom with the public order and the common good.[10] It is recognized as an instrument or principle of "an organized society whose objective is the creation of a community in which a person is enabled to fulfill himself by the full development of his capacities."[11] Theorists as divergent as Dworkin, Hayek, and Raz all have understood the rule of law as constraining, morally if not legally, the exercise of the coercive power of the state by some specification of a principle of equal personal dignity and freedom.[12] Whether the rule was formulated in terms that the law must be made up of general rules, announced beforehand and consistently applied,[13] or as requiring that all individuals be subject to only one law,[14] or that government itself was subordinate to law,[15] the ideal that was being promoted was an equality in the human dignity of individuals, in their freedom from and protection by the legal order which held the community together.[16]

While obviously each of these precepts by which the "rule" came to be described secured different degrees of equality in a person's power of self-government, they were all grounded in that essentially liberal conception of social justice. Even Dicey, who would formulate one of the weakest versions of the rule, was quite clear that the rule of law was the root, not the result, of constitutional theory and legal order.[17] Even though he focused his attention on the rule of law in constraining the subordinate, administrative processes of government, rather than on the sovereign authority of the legislature itself, he was quite insistent that the right to personal freedom was the basis, not the result, of the law of the constitution.

So in the preamble, as well as in its text and structure, we can see how the principle of equality of self-determination permeates the Charter. Indeed, it would not misrepresent the substance of the Charter to describe it as marking an extension in or an intensification of our commitment to this egalitarian corollary of the liberal ideal. Thus it could be said that before the entrenchment of the Charter, the rule of law insisted that the principle of equal concern and respect was applicable only to the administrative agencies of the legislative arm of government. After its coming into force, however, the other two branches of government as well as the legislature itself are bound to proceed in conformity with the more general principles of constitutional law which the Charter now guarantees. Even if it is premature to attempt to flesh out the extent to which the Charter will eventually be applied to the different processes and institutions of government, it is certain its reach extends beyond the administrative apparatus of the state.

The textual evidence for the Charter's commitment to the principle of equality of freedom for all individuals could hardly be more explicit. It was hardly surprising, then, that our courts should give it immediate recognition in the constitutional jurisprudence they developed. Early and often the Supreme Court has insisted that "respect for the inherent dignity of the human person, commitment to social justice and equality, [and] accommodation of a wide variety of beliefs"[18] are among the values and principles which are the "genesis" of the rights and freedoms the Charter guarantees.

Moreover, beyond its positivistic powers to accurately describe the substance of our constitutional law, the principle of equality of liberty also provides a very powerful account of how law and legal order justify the exercise of coercive authority by the various governmental institutions of the state. Regardless of which version of liberal theory one chooses to explain and legitimate the process of judicial review, the principle of equality of liberty will be a vital and integral part of it. Whether one assumes that the ultimate purpose of judicial review is to ensure fidelity to the text of the Charter as it was understood by its drafters, to the rights and freedoms considered the natural and inviolable entitlement of every human being, to the democratic character of our processes of government, or to some specification of the moral code of the community, the ideal I have called equality of liberty will be an important and central ingredient of that theory. Whatever version of liberal democratic political theory one accepts as best explaining a constitutional order of government which includes an entrenched bill of rights,[19] a commitment to some degree of autonomy for every individual will have to be made. However one ultimately reconciles equality and liberty, integrates freedom with democracy, the entrenchment of the Charter requires that some specification of individual autonomy is beyond debasement by the society at large.

For theorists who advocate that the courts must give effect to the original intentions of those who designed the constitution and brought it into creation,[20] there is ample evidence that the interpretative principle I have just proposed will do just that. Protecting the equal freedom of the least influential Canadians from government's insensitivity and indifference is a theme which is manifest in the writing of those who were instrumental in the proposal of an entrenched bill of rights.[21] Similarly, for those who conceive of declarations of human rights as instruments by which entitlements which are fundamental to or irreducible in the personhood of every individual are protected and guaranteed, the principle of equality of liberty would be central if not essential to their analysis. As H.L.A. Hart has logically demonstrated, if recognition of general human and civil rights means anything, it must, above all else, "imply the recognition of the equal right of all men to be free."[22] Equally, theorists who justify judicial review by focusing on its capacity to ensure the fairness and integrity of the legal processes of democracy, also recognize that an equal right to be free from the arbitrary or coercive intrusions of others is essential to their account.[23] If judicial review is justified on the basis that it secures rights and privileges – for example, of speech and association, of privacy and the person – "which are prerequisites to the existence of democracy,"[24] a principle of equality of liberty would be integral to that justification. Finally, constitutional theorists who instruct our courts to hold legislatures to their communities' moral and/or legal ideals, at least when invoked in liberal societies such as our own, would be similarly committed to this ethical principle.[25] Although each of these competing conceptions of what liberal theory entails will define very differently the extent to which the autonomy of the individual constrains the legislative process, all of them begin with the person and her freedom to pursue whatever goal or objectives she chooses so long as she recognizes a reciprocal right in every other member of society. Equality of self-government is an essential value in all liberal theories of constitutional law.[26] The principle represents a political ideal through which the tension that is implicit in the liberal and democratic strands of our method of social relations could be substantially attenuated if not completely harmonized.

Though we have avoided controversial assumptions about either the positivist or normative character of our constitutional law, it is not clear that our conclusions can advance our project very far. To say the Charter guarantees some equal entitlement to benefit from, as well as participate in, the law-making process we use to settle the rules which coordinate our competing goals tells us nothing about what the precise nature and extent of that equality should be. By itself a principle like equality of liberty can never provide a blueprint of how courts should rule when they come to review the major statutory schemes we have enacted to regulate our employment relationships.

Even conceding the force of this observation, it is important to see that, as part of a larger political theory, the principle of equality of liberty can organize the structure of arguments which are appropriate in the process of judicial review.[27] It can and should guide the court in its assessment of the constitutional integrity of any legislative enactments it might be asked to review. As a principle of interpretation it can provide a larger focus, a richer understanding within which the Charter can be applied. It can, and indeed already has.[28]

Moreover, as a principle of validation, it clearly does identify at least one ground on which governments can begin to defend any challenge which is made to their constitutional authority to "act." If a particular rule or regulation being challenged promotes the equal freedom of those who are among the least advantaged people in our community, that would seem to be, if anything is, a constitutionally valid purpose on which any restriction such a regulation entails on the rights of others can be justified. There has never been any doubt that considerations of justice – as opposed to utility – can justify limitations on the rights and freedoms set out in the Charter and it is hard to imagine how there ever could be.[29] So, in the case of our labour code, even from the very brief description we saw in Part One, we can sense immediately that it will, in large measure, be found to be consistent with our new constitutional order. Regardless of how it affects the well-being of the community overall, its general thrust can be justified on the very same values on which our constitutional order now rests. Even if it was not the actual motivation of those who designed it, our legislators can defend most of the basic features of our labour code in this way and without having to prove that it made our society materially better off.[30] In the language of American constitutional law, "acting" to protect the equal opportunity of personal self-government is a sufficiently compelling interest to withstand even the strictest and most rigorous scrutiny by the courts.

It simply could not be otherwise. Rights and freedoms collide. When, for example, my employer terminates me from my employment because I have reached sixty-five years of age, its freedom to associate (by contract) with whomever it chooses can be seen to conflict, unavoidably, with my right not to have decisions made about my life simply because of my age. One of these entitlements – or maybe both – will have to give way. Such collisions between competing rights are, as we shall see, at the heart of the controversy over human rights legislation and union security laws. Indeed, defenders of minimum wage, health and safety, and employment standards legislation can point to the economic liberty of those they purport to protect as legitimizing some interference with the freedom of those they constrain.

But as important as this principle is to understanding our new constitutional order, it is true that by itself it doesn't tell us enough. We need to know more than what that principle says before we can carry our analysis any further. Integrity of purpose is not sufficient by itself. Even when it is pursuing objectives which are most in keeping with our new constitutional criteria, there are limits as to how far government may go. Purity of purpose is not sufficient to exculpate us from liability when, acting as individuals, we carelessly or intentionally interfere with the personal integrity and autonomy of others, and it cannot be otherwise when, acting collectively, we do the same. Means, as well as ends, must conform to some external, objective standards of constitutional review.

The Charter itself is quite explicit on this. Even in circumstances where the integrity of its objectives is secure, s.1 requires a legislature to meet a standard of reasonableness when, in the sorts of conflictual circumstances we have identified, it undertakes an initiative which entails a restriction on the rights and freedoms of some individuals. In the language of s.1, its acts must be of a kind that "can be demonstrably justified in a free and democratic society." In addition to legitimacy of purpose there are parallel constraints on the means by which those objectives can be achieved as well as on the consequences they can bring in their wake.

Much of the most important part of Canadian constitutional law will be taken up with specifying just what these additional criteria will be. Canadian courts will add their understanding of the meaning of these seductively simple words, which are so characteristic of modern declarations of human rights. As our courts examine the various pieces of social policy brought before them, they will have to identify the specific inequalities and exceptions to our constitutional ideal that can be justified within (and which will ultimately determine what is distinctive about) the Canadian conception of social organization and community.

In the performance of this avowedly creative function judges already have begun[31] and will continue to develop general principles of judicial review consistent with the particular political theory which, in their view, best explains our constitutional order of government. In addition to the protection of rights and freedoms, courts will have to specify other purposes or circumstances where legislatures can create exceptions or place limitations on the rights and liberties guaranteed in the Charter. Because our constitution does not do so explicitly (as many modern Charters of Rights do, and our earlier Victoria Charter did), our courts will have to decide whether the community, acting through its representatives, can point to considerations of public order, health, safety, morality and even its own material well-being to justify limiting one or other of the freedoms and rights it guarantees.[32] The courts will be obliged to articulate the particular standards of review they intend to apply to each of the rights and freedoms which are guaranteed.

They will have to decide whether some rights, such as freedom of association, are more fundamental than others,[33] and whether invasions of certain rights will attract higher and more rigorous standards of review. In this capacity the courts will develop a rich array of constitutional principles to mediate the application of our community's ideals to the realities of our everyday living.

Working out solutions to these complexities will be an ongoing enterprise. Given the method we are employing, it would be inappropiate to attempt to anticipate all the principles and standards the courts may formulate. Nevertheless, it is plain that we need another principle before the analysis can proceed further. If the principle of equality of liberty will be of assistance in telling us when a legislature might initiate legislation that constrains the liberty of some members of the community, we now need something to tell us when government must stop.[34]

In keeping to our strategy of caution, it will be appropriate to limit ourselves to one additional principle of judicial review. This principle I shall call the doctrine of the reasonable alternative,[35] although it can as easily be described as the maximization principle.[36] Stated in its simplest terms it says that if, *all other things being equal*,[37] there are several different policies which can accomplish a valid social objective, (for example, the protection of some right or freedom of those who are relatively less well off), one of which derogates from our constitutional commitments less than the others, that alternative would have to be chosen by the legislature to accomplish its purpose. In the face of such an alternative, the limitations and exceptions to our constitutional commitments that would be caused by all the other means of social regulation could not be demonstrably justified in a society which claimed to be democratic and free.[38]

My expectation is that this second principle of judicial review will not be any more controversial or troublesome for those who must interpret the Charter than the first. Especially when we are considering legislation which seems to prejudice those who are already serious disadvantaged, if we failed to hold our legislatures to this principle, if rights could be violated unnecessarily, the Charter would not be worth very much. The constitutional commitment to our equal right to control our own development would be drained of all meaning if our rights and freedoms could be sacrificed needlessly.

The principle is in fact one of the mildest variations of what has come to be known as the proportionality principle.[39] This is really a rubric for a number of rules. In its widest formulation, it holds that any restriction on our constitutional rights must be proportionate to the public interest that is served thereby. The more serious the limitation or invasion of a right or freedom, the more compelling the justification must be. The principle of the reasonable alternative is a narrower rendition which stipulates that a limitation cannot be justified if it can be shown less stringent measures are available to accomplish the social purpose at hand. Both are examples of the criterion of reasonableness to which governmental restrictions on rights and freedoms must now conform.

Both the narrower and wider versions of the principle have already received a good deal of recognition from our courts and commentators,[40] as well as by those in other free and democratic societies which have had considerable experience in identifying when and explaining how limits on constitutional rights and freedoms can be justified. Indeed, even before the entrenchment of our Charter, the Supreme Court had already shown its familiarity with the values which underlie the criterion of the reasonable alternative means. This is especially true of the principles it employed to interpret the division of power sections of our constitution. In its practice of "reading down" statutes to apply only to the circumstances clearly within the authority of the enacting government,[41] and in its rulings that one level of government might invade the authority of the other in circumstances in which it was "necessarily incidental" to the exercise of some power to do so,[42] the court has consistently shown its commitment to the overbreadth criterion – which is what this proportionality principle is all about.[43] In addition, the court had suggested, albeit infrequently, that exceptions to and derogations from our earlier Bill of Rights had to be "necessary departures" for the attainment of valid social obligations.[44]

Moreover, since the entrenchment of our Charter, a large number of courts, including the Supreme Court, have signalled their approval of the proportionality principle to assess the constitutional validity of legislation which infringes rights and freedoms set out in the Charter.[45] In one of the clearest examples, the Ontario Court of Appeal invoked the principle to cut down a complete prohibition on public access to juvenile trials as being unnecessarily broad for the reason that an alternative rule involving a discretionary ban could have accomplished the public's purposes just as well.[46]

The European Commission and Court of Human Rights and the United States Supreme Court have also turned to this principle when they have tested the validity of legislative initiatives which constrain the rights and freedoms set out in the European Convention of Human Rights and Freedoms and the American Bill of Rights respectively. In the case of the latter, it is a fixed principle of American constitutional law that "strict scrutiny" (which includes but is not exhausted by the principle of reasonable alternatives), will be given to any governmental initiative infringing on any of the specific rights, such as freedom of speech and assembly, explicitly set out in the American Constitution.[47] Thus, in a leading case already incorporated in our jurisprudence, the American Supreme Court invalidated an Arkansas law which required disclosure by each teacher of every group with which he or she was affiliated. The court ruled such a law was a violation of the teachers' freedom of association because less drastic alternatives were available to the state to accomplish its purposes of evaluating the capabilities of its teaching staff to discharge their duties.[48] It is worth noting that the court invoked this standard of review even though freedom of association is only a derivative right and is nowhere explicitly recognized in the American Bill of Rights. Indeed, the American Supreme Court even applies this principle when it invokes an "intermediate" standard of review to evaluate social policies which distinguish between people on the basis of their sex.[49] In a parallel fashion the European court, interpreting language which substantially parallels the words we have used in s.1, has consistently applied both the broader proportionality principle and its derivative of least drastic means.[50]

It is not surprising that this principle of constitutional validation was incorporated into our Charter jurisprudence as quickly as it has been. It is, after all, integral to the ideals of justice which are at the base of our constitutional system of government. It is a central tenet of most liberal theories of justice that equality of liberty should be secured, all other things being equal, at the highest degree possible. Described in this way, the principle of reasonable alternative means might more aptly be characterized as the maximization principle. As Gregory Vlastos, a contemporary liberal philosopher, has put it:

... if a legislature has before it two bills B(L) and B(M), such that B(L) would provide for greater personal freedom than would B(M), then, other things remaining equal, they would be voting unjustly if they voted for the second. They would be violating the human right to freedom of those affected by the legislation. A vote for B(M) would be tantamount to a vote for the needless *restriction* of freedom. And since *freedom* is a personal (or individual) right, to equalize its restriction would be to aggravate, not alleviate, its injustice.[51]

A variation on this theme is at the root of the second of Rawls's two principles of justice and it has also been routinely invoked by utilitarians. Bentham, for example, relied on the principle in his discussion of proper principles of punishment.[52] In a sense one might say the principle is the natural derivative of an interpretation of the rule of law as the commitment to a paramount law of reason.[53] In a society which professes to be organized around liberal democratic principles, reason cannot be restricted unnecessarily by law. A society which claims to be free, democratic, and governed by the rule of law must be able to offer some coherent explanation and justification when it departs from the ideal of equality by which it is defined.

Moreover, integrating this principle of constitutional interpretation into the fabric of our Charter jurisprudence accords with our image of the institutional competence of the courts. It meets our understanding of procedural fairness and the integrity of the judicial process. Not only is the principle consistent with the language of the text and the ideals of justice underlying the Charter, but as well the principle only asks the court to do what we think this branch of our government does best. It avoids the difficult issue of specifying the extent to which courts should evaluate the legitimacy of legislative ends. Instead the principle focuses exclusively on the means adopted by the legislature to accomplish its purposes. Rather than declaring to the democratically elected forums of government that they are prohibited from pursuing a particular substantive result, the principle merely requires those institutions to pursue their constitutionally valid objectives in the most egalitarian, liberal way. As a principle of judicial review it interferes least with the policy-making function of the legislative and executive branches of government and in doing so accords with the tradition of our courts to respect the will of the peoples' representatives to formulate such matters of policy.

Indeed, considerations of justice as well as procedural fairness argue strongly for our courts to turn to this principle of judicial review before employing any others which entail a more activist, interventionist relationship with the other two branches of government. The Supreme Court has already demonstrated its intention to assess the proportionality that holds between the ends and means of a particular legal rule or policy before it turns its attention to the more complex relation that holds between the social benefits and constitutional costs the same law entails.[54] Assessing the proportionality of any part of our labour code along the latter dimension entails a court balancing the benefits of the law against the costs it imposes on the constitutional fabric of our labour code. Such a review is potentially much more invasive of the decisions of the other two branches of government than the principles to which we will confine our analysis.[55] As the more cautious principle of judicial review, courts have accorded this principle of reasonable alternate means priority and should be expected to continue to do so. Because it involves a much more passive and conciliatory role for the courts in their relationship with the other two branches of government, the principle of proportionality relating means to ends would be said to be lexically prior to the broader, more intrusive one which balances constitutional costs against social benefits.

The second principle, then, like the first, seems certain to figure prominently in any fully elaborated theory of Canadian constitutional law. It captures directly a central though not exhaustive meaning of the written text of s.1. It is, to use the conventional phrase, an interpretation the language and law of the Charter reasonably bears. It is also faithful and gives effect to the political ideals which, as we have seen, can explain and mediate the practice of judicial review. Both in substance and in structure, the principle of the reasonable alternative ensures that we will enjoy the benefit of our constitutional commitment to equality in our liberties to the highest possible degree. And finally, the principle calls for our courts to operate within their own sphere of competence. Focusing exclusively on the means employed by the legislature to accomplish its social purposes, the principle implies an institutional concern which accords with our tradition of judicial restraint.

Taken together, the two principles we have enunciated provide us with a sufficient standard against which to measure the competing claims that are voiced in our political conversations concerning the appropriate balance that ought to be struck in our labour code. To avoid misunderstanding, it should be emphasized again that the principles we have derived from the Charter do not represent a complete or comprehensive statement of judicial review. They are clearly only part of that theory. On some issues they can provide final answers, on others, as we shall see, they cannot.

In exploring the effect that our two principles will have on our laws of employment, it makes good sense to begin by considering those judgments and laws we feel most certain about and which we hold in the greatest confidence.[56] One is able to get additional confirmation of the strength and integrity of our principles by considering the easiest cases first. If the process and principles of judicial review do not lead us to results that are consistent with the convictions we hold most strongly, there will be little point of proceeding further. If the principles produce legal outcomes that offend our most basic intuitions about how work should be organized, they will not likely have much, if any, force in cases where our present arrangements are more controversial and problematic.

Proceeding on this strategy, the next sections of the book are organized in the following way. First we will consider what role our two principles of interpretation will likely play in the event a constitutional challenge is made to the validity of our minimum wage or anti-discrimination laws. For most of us, these parts of our labour code are thought to be essential to the freedom and autonomy of all workers in our country. Next, we shall examine ways in which particular occupational groups, such as agricultural workers and domestics, might invoke our principles to counter what seem to be the most blatant and offensive instances of injustice still imbedded in our legal code of work regulation. Then we will move on to analyse how, if at all, our two principles of constitutional interpretation might force our legislatures to draw distinctions between workers on the basis of personal attributes such as their age or sex in a more sensitive and sophisticated way. We will conclude by holding those rules which require or authorize compulsory membership in unions up to the same test of judicial review.[57]

The structure of the analysis will be simple and straightforward. In each case the method remains the same. Each of the rules and laws of our labour code that we have identified will be tested for the constitutional validity of their ends as well as the proportionality of their means. Each of these constituent parts of our labour law will be evaluated to see whether it can be said to promote the autonomy of those who already have the least control over the legal rules which govern their lives and whether it does so in a way which shows the most concern and respect for the rights and freedoms of those it constrains.

Now before we start off on this exercise I want to pause here one last time to make it clear that, as an exercise in exploring the theory which underlies our system of government, my ambition is to rely only on the most obvious and least problematic principles of constitutional interpretation. I have deliberately constrained the analysis in this way in order that we can be certain of the minimum role the Charter will play and the results it can be expected to achieve.

The two principles we have derived from the language and the theory of the Charter suit these analytical needs. Separately and together these principles of constitutional review ground the project in premises which are very cautious and conservative in two important and quite distinctive ways. First, both principles are embedded securely in our most conventional sources of law. Both have their roots deep in the structure and substance of the text. They have been recognized early and often by every level in the judicial branch of government. As a positive statement of our constitutional law, the principles accurately describe the body of rules they are intended to organize. Indeed, not only are they already an integral part of the constitutional practice whose meaning they are intended to illuminate but as we saw in the first part, they are also manifested in and offer a powerful justification for many of the most important parts of our existing labour code. Secondly, and of equal importance, these principles provide the beginning of a very cautious account for a political theory that can justify how the practice of judicial review fits within our larger processes and institutions of social organization. They express and can be derived from principles of procedural fairness and substantive justice which have widespread allegiance in all liberal, democratic societies such as our own.

As a matter of substantive justice, as the analysis unfolds we will observe that these principles of constitutional interpretation will validate virtually every important part of our existing labour code on the ground that the plans and projects of those who are protected by them and secure their benefit are entitled to our equal concern and respect. As the chronology we followed in Part One made clear, virtually all the basic rules of our labour code can be justified as enhancing the autonomy of those who are among the least privileged in our community.

Equally, as a matter of procedural fairness, employing the principles we have just derived will mean our courts will interact with the legislative and executive branches of government in a way which respects the sovereignty of Parliament and the will of the people. Courts will invalidate expressions of the popular will only when they are satisfied there are alternate means to accomplish the objectives of the legislative in a way that is more consistent with our constitutional guarantees. Rather than second guessing whether a rule or statute is in the best interests of the community as a whole, courts will restrict their focus to determine whether it can be justified on the basis of how it reconciles the conflicting rights at stake.

In the result, both in the method and framework of analysis they will employ, the role the courts will play in the development of a constitutional labour code will parallel the function they perform in their declaration of our common law. All the conclusions the courts will reach, and the gains of social justice they will be able to achieve, will be effected within our legal and political traditions of judicial caution and restraint. In all of the cases we will consider, the courts will inquire whether the rule or law under consideration does promote our constitutional commitment to equalize people's opportunities for personal self-development in the most sensitive way that it can. In essence, on the principles we will use, the role of the third branch of government will be to ensure that whenever a group of individuals gains control of the law-making powers of the state, they do not use that coercive authority to unfairly limit the opportunities of others to develop their faculties and pursue their projects in ways they have chosen for themselves.

PART THREE

The Components of a Constitutional Labour Code

We know a few things that the politicians do not know.
Albert Einstein

SEVEN

Equal Opportunity

We will begin our analysis of the constitutional validity of our labour code by focusing on the least problematic rules we use to regulate employment relationships. There are a variety of rules one might select, but the one I think most people support as enthusiastically as any is that which outlaws most forms of arbitrary and invidious discrimination. Although, paradoxically, these human rights or fair employment laws are of relatively recent origin,[1] insofar as they insist that every person qualified for a position must have an equal opportunity to be hired in, promoted to, and treated with concern and respect while in it, they would seem to be one of the least controversial parts of our labour code.

While many would say that commitment is no longer sufficient,[2] few would now dispute the justice of the principle itself. Careers open to talents is a fixture of our (liberal) moral and legal universe. Rules or legal regimes that tolerate and/or sanction racial, sexual, religious discrimination in the distribution of opportunities to work are taken by just about everyone as being fundamentally unjust within the predicates of a liberal democratic state. None of these laws are at issue in the current political and constitutional controversies over what principles should be included in our labour code. If our interpretation of the Charter jeopardized this part of the legal structure within which we organize people at work, it would create a strong presumption that one of our principles of constitutional review was simply wrong. A written constitution is supposed to be a confirmation of the deepest values a society holds in its rules of social organization.

To some it might seem that examining whether anti-discrimination laws satisfy our principles of constitutional review is really not much of a test at all. It might be thought that there is no theory of constitutional interpretation which could put such legislation in doubt. Apart from anything else, s.15 of the Charter seems to authorize, if not require, the enactment of laws of precisely this kind, guaranteeing the right to be free from such invidious treatment.[3]

Yet the matter is not quite so simple, because the Charter also guarantees each of us the freedom to associate with whomever we choose. Even if laws prohibiting discrimination in employment satisfy one part of the Charter, it may still be questioned how that justifies the invasion of rights protected in another.[4] To return to a question I raised earlier, if our rights do collide, on what basis does your entitlement to be free from discrimination override my right to associate exclusively with members of my own sex, colour, religion, age at my place of work? Why can't a person in our society, perhaps with a group of colleagues with whom she shares a particular faith or world view, refuse to hire a person as a receptionist because he is a male of Palestinian descent? Why shouldn't our constitution be interpreted to respect the tradition which has tolerated a certain amount of discrimination of this kind?

While these questions may not, in the final analysis, be particularly difficult to answer, neither are they rhetorical. They have been raised in the past, and one still hears echoes of them in our own communities today. On our theory of the constitution, they deserve an answer, and while there are several that might be given, the principles of equality of liberty and reasonable alternatives can together supply at least one of them.

The response that our two principles of constitutional interpretation would give to those who think we must tolerate such racial, sexual, or religious discrimination is simple and direct. First, the objectives that anti-discrimination rules seek to accomplish fall squarely within our first principle of judicial review. Anti-discrimination laws are intended to promote the very equality between persons on which the Charter itself is grounded. As their preambles make explicit, human rights codes insist, so far as laws can, that in the workplace each member of our society must treat everyone else with some minimum – and in that sense equal – concern and respect. They stipulate that a person's immutable characteristics (e.g., sex, age or race) cannot be used as criteria on which such scarce and important resources as jobs may be distributed if these features would have little or no effect on the employer's legitimate business interests.[5] These laws insist that each of us, no matter what our personal views, extend to every other individual the same liberty to control his own fate which we claim for ourselves. Equality of opportunity, which human rights codes are designed to promote, is the means by which individual freedom and autonomy is achieved. Anti-discrimination rules do exactly for the private processes of decision-making what the constitution does for our public processes of law-making. They simply translate our constitutional values to this more local level of formulating the rules by which we must live our lives.

In the result, those who benefit from this part of our labour code need not advance the more controversial claim that such initiatives enhance the public order, morality, safety and well-being of the community in order to justify the restriction such laws impose on others' freedom of association. While such arguments may be available to support such legislation (that is a matter a full theory of the judicial review will eventually have to address), they do not satisfy the constitutional criteria we are employing. If we are to keep to our commitment of a very cautious and limited role for our courts, we must leave aside questions of whether such utilitarian goals will be regarded as constitutionally valid and, if so, in what circumstances they would justify limitations on the rights and freedoms they entail. Those questions involve an element of balancing and second guessing of legislative assemblies which lie beyond the scope of our analysis. Balancing such constitution costs and social benefits requires a court to invoke the broader, more activist principles of proportionality that we are endeavouring to avoid.

It seems certain then that the anti-discrimination principle in our labour code satisfies our first principle of constitutional review. Like the idea of deriving just inequalities from the concept of equality itself, anti-discrimination rules justify limitations on the freedom (of association) of intolerant individuals on the richer conception of liberty which underlies and unifies the Charter. Indeed an argument can be made that, had our legislators not already done so, the entrenchment of the Charter would have obliged the courts to reformulate the common law of employment to include an equal opportunity rule.[6] In the absence of our human rights codes, the weakest and most vulnerable individuals in our midst could be (and historically often were) denied equality of access to the opportunity of work. For whatever reasons, and however regrettable it may be, our courts were not able to develop a rule outlawing discriminatory treatment by one person of another. As the Supreme Court of Canada recently reminded us, there is in the common law governing work relations no prohibition against discrimination; no obligation to confer an opportunity or benefit on a stranger or to treat such a person the same as everyone else.[7] If the common law had prevailed, our personal relations in the workplace would always fall short of our constitutional ideal. There would always be some in our midst, the weakest and most exposed groups, who could be denied that very equality in personal autonomy our system of government was intended to promote. In those circumstances our courts would have violated the spirit, if not the letter, of the constitution if they had consciously refused to rectify this failure of the common law to ensure equal access to the places in which people work. A deliberate decision to allow the common law rule to govern the workplace would undermine our constitutional order in the same way that a law to repeal the existing human rights code would offend our constitutional commitment to respect the equal autonomy of every person in our community.[8] Just as some provision of legal aid seems essential to satisfy our constitutional commitment to a fair trial and legal counsel for all,[9] so, it could be claimed, our courts would have had to insist that the anti-discrimination principle be included in our labour code if our legislators had not recognized it already.

Workers who are protected by and benefit from this legislated rule of our labour code can also claim that the anti-discrimination principle is itself a "reasonable" means by which government can seek to accomplish its constitutionally valid objectives. Not only is such legislation constitutionally justified in terms of objectives which no one who claims his freedom is limited can consistently deny, but these laws accomplish their purpose by interfering as unobtrusively as possible with his freedom to associate only with people he chooses. To the extent these laws infringe upon the freedom of association of employers and employees, they do so only to a minimal degree. To be faithful to our constitutional commitment to construct a legal regime which respects an equality in personal autonomy, there is no alternative policy available which interferes less drastically with the freedom of those it constrains. Human rights codes, at least in their conventional form, are the least drastic, and therefore most reasonable, means by which the equality to which the constitution commits us can be realized.

None of these laws, at least to the extent they are implementing the anti-discrimination principle, actually compel anyone to associate with anyone else. Nor do they specify the range of criteria on which a choice between candidates may be made. The only constraint legislation of this type entails is to deny the freedom – the licence – of some people not to associate with others or treat them as equals simply because of their race, sex, religion, etcetera.[10] Rather than stipulating which reasons are relevant in determining who should be selected for a job, our human rights codes adopt the less invasive technique of declaring specific factors irrelevant to that choice. These legislative rules simply say one person's preference not to associate with another because of some immutable characteristic of the latter cannot count as a valid basis on which to award a position. To accept this would deny to those others the very equality of liberty from which the freedom (of association) that is being claimed is itself derived. By itself, a person's preference (or prejudice) can never be an adequate justification for excluding others from the opportunities of survival and self-development which work provides; it denies the very reciprocity that the Charter insists be part of our rules of social regulation.

In the result, if governments are ever called upon to justify the equal opportunity principle, it turns out that the two principles we are testing will be invoked in aid of their validation and not their negation. Legislation of this type meets the constitutional criteria both in the objectives it pursues and the means it employs. Our two principles will provide no support to those who would endeavour to undermine this policy of legal protection that our legislators have seen fit to provide. They could not, in short, be used to the disadvantage of those who are, even with the benefit of this law, among the most vulnerable in our midst.

EIGHT

Economic Security

Being able to justify equal opportunity laws is an important, though hardly difficult, test for our principles. This is not the type of social initiative which is at the centre of the controversy about the appropriate balance that our labour code ought to effect. A slightly more rigorous test is to see how our two principles would figure in a challenge to the constitutionality of those laws which govern minimum wages, maximum hours, and employment standards. These laws are very much part of the current debate and are frequently cited as showing how the pendulum has swung too far in favour of workers or certain segments of that group. They have been challenged, often by public-spirited lawyers and economists,[1] who worry that such laws, in discouraging incentives, may ultimately injure many of those they are intended to benefit, such as minorities and our youth. This challenge of the political right, which is serious and sophisticated, demands an answer to the question of how these laws, which seem to "forbid capitalist acts between consenting adults"[2] and which deny people their constitutional "freedom to associate" together on terms and conditions which are mutually agreeable, can ever be justified.

The full force of this challenge can best be sensed when it is recalled that when the United States Supreme Court was first confronted with this question, it was unable to formulate an adequate theory of constitutional interpretation to support their validation. The result was that most of these laws, except in narrowly defined circumstances, were struck down as violating the commitment in the American Bill of Rights to liberty in general and freedom of contract in particular. In the view of the majority of the judges who sat on that court for the first third of this century, a minimum wage law was simply and exclusively a price-fixing law. In their judgment, the law was unconstitutional because:

It forbids two persons having lawful capacity ... to freely contract with one another in respect of the price for which one shall render service to the other in a purely private employment where both are willing, perhaps anxious, to agree, even though the consequences may be to oblige one to surrender a desirable engagement and the other to dispense with the services of a desirable employee ...

To the extent that the sum fixed exceeds the fair value of the services rendered it amounts to a compulsory exaction from the employer for the support of a particular indigent person, for whose condition there rests upon him no peculiar responsibility, and therefore, in effect, arbitrarily shifts to his shoulders a burden which, if it belongs to anybody, belongs to society as a whole.

The feature of this statute which perhaps more than any other puts upon it the stamp of invalidity is that it exacts from the employer an arbitrary payment for a purpose and upon a basis having no causal connection with his business or the contract or the work the employee engages to do.[3]

So challenges to this component of our labour code would seem to present a more serious and more realistic test for a set of interpretative principles which claim to be an integral part of a larger theory of our constitution and political order. They have a professional and legal pedigree to them which suggests that they must be taken more seriously than challenges made to our anti-discrimination laws.[4]

And yet, on reflection, that turns out not to be the case. Governments can advance precisely the same answer here as the one they used to silence the bigot. Employers who challenge our minimum wage laws on the ground such enactments violate their freedom to associate commit the same inconsistency. They fail to recognize an even more basic right to economic security and physical well-being in others which, in asserting their freedom of (contractual) association, they assume for themselves. They claim an absolute liberty to do as they please even if, as happened at the beginning of the Industrial Revolution, such freedom inflicts serious damage to the physical and spiritual well-being of those (especially women and children) whose circumstances compelled them to work for a living.

So on the constitutional principles we are applying, legislatures should have little difficulty defending these rules against challenges of this kind. Although they may be problematic as policies designed to serve goals such as the eradication of poverty or the efficient allocation of resources, they can always be justified in a constitutional regime grounded in an ideal of equality in personal autonomy.[5] Minimum wage laws, like anti-discrimination rules, can easily be validated as serving the same end as that which is enshrined in our first principle of judicial review. They promote a measure of economic security which is a precondition for anyone to be free.[6] Although they limit the freedom of some to contract with whomever they wish, they do so to secure the conditions on which, for many workers at least, the very system of contract depends.

As we saw in Part One, these laws have deep roots in the feudal, pre-industrial labour codes. At their inception these laws guaranteed the necessities of our physical existence. Tying the level of wages to the price of basic provisions, the earliest versions insisted on the payment of a "living wage." Later they were intended to reduce, if not eliminate, the subjugation and domination that infected the practice of "sweating" in which workers who were the most vulnerable could be "persuaded" to labour on terms insufficient to meet the bare cost of living. In their modern and more sensitive versions, these laws are justified not simply because they are critical to our physical well-being but also because legislators came to recognize, as one of them put it, that "necessitous men are not free men."[7] Now these laws are intended to promote that degree of economic freedom which is essential to participate as an equal in a contractual process of labour regulation.[8]

Ultimately, the United States Supreme Court recognized that the liberty of a person depended directly on his or her economic security and physical well-being, reversed its earlier judgments, and upheld the constitutionality of minimum wage laws. In its landmark decision of *West Coast Hotel* v. *Parrish*,[9] the Supreme Court explicitly justified the limitation that minimum wage laws imposed on freedom of contractual association by pointing to the greater and more basic equality of freedom that these laws secured for all. In its reasons for judgment, the court made repeated references to the plight of the weakest and most vulnerable workers in the community whose wages were otherwise insufficient "to meet the very necessities of existence, [and] ... the bare cost of living." Limiting the liberty to contract for some was justified by the provision of a more basic and fundamental liberty to survive for all.

When minimum wage laws are analysed in this way, it can readily be seen how they function in precisely the same manner as our equal opportunity laws. Paralleling that part of our labour code, the legislated rule against sweating responded to another fundamental deficiency in the common law. By that law, at least since the middle of the sixteenth century, courts were committed to the principle of almost never inquiring into the fairness of or the equivalence in any exchange.[10] By ignoring the economic and social realities which denied any equality of bargaining power between the most disadvantaged members of the workforce and those who might employ their labour, the fiction was maintained that the self-interest of each of the parties was the best guarantee of a fair bargain. The extension of the principle of contract law, that the courts would never inquire into the "adequacy of consideration," to examine the terms under which people worked, meant society would be committed *by law*, to tolerating the payment of starvation wages. In consequence, if our society was committed to guaranteeing that every individual in the community was paid a wage sufficient to live on, it was necessary for our legislatures to "act." In the face of the courts' inability or unwillingness to break free from the strictures of the doctrine of consideration, it fell again to the legislators to ensure that the "unscrupulous and overreaching" amongst us could not threaten the physical survival of those in our community whose social and economic circumstances made them most vulnerable.

So even though minimum wages rules clearly interfere with the freedom of some people to associate by contract on terms of their own choosing, they do so in the cause of objectives which are at the heart of our constitutional order. Minimum wage laws, in particular, and employment standards in general, all can be comfortably accommodated within our first principle of judicial review. In addition, in the method it uses to accomplish its objectives, a minimum wage law, like our equal opportunity laws, involves the least drastic invasion of the freedom of those who claim the right to contract for labour on whatever terms they and their workers agree. In formulating rules of minimum compensation, the legislatures have constrained their law-making powers as narrowly as possible. There is simply no other way these objectives could be accomplished which would constrain fundamental freedoms less. Neither income support and welfare programs nor government wage subsidies could be regarded as reasonable alternatives to our minimum wage laws. While the former can obviously provide the same degree of material support as a minimum wage law, they plainly cannot promote all of the other psychological and associational purposes that people pursue when they work. Wage subsidies can be rejected as reasonable alternatives because, as the lessons of Speenhamland[11] made abundantly clear, they set off incentives in which increasingly larger shares of the wage package come out of the public purse.

Like our human rights codes, standards legislation of this type does not actually require anyone to enter any association at all. It does not tell a person whom he must hire or the criteria on which such decisions must be made.[12] Nor, as Mr Justice Holmes observed, does it compel anybody to pay anything to anyone else. As he wrote, "It simply forbids employment at rates below those fixed as the minimum requirement of health and right living."[13] It just says that *if* one enters a labour relationship, one must do so on terms which respect and provide for the physical integrity of the worker. The only freedom that is constrained is entering into an association in which the equal freedom of the worker is denied by the payment of something less than a "living wage."

Neither minimum wage laws in particular nor employment standards in general should be vulnerable to a challenge by employers in the courts if the judiciary sensitively applies our two principles of judicial review. In a constitutional conversation to evaluate their validity, our principles would defend, not defeat, rules of this kind. Standards legislation is entirely consistent with and, in the context of our judge-made law, essential to each of the principles of social relations that the Charter now requires our legislatures to meet. All legislation of this type can be interpreted as ensuring that the legal code which regularizes relations in the workplace does not itself interfere, in the way the common law did, with the equal right of every person to that degree of security which is a precondition for people to be able to control their lives. And it accomplishes this objective in a way which interferes least, both qualitatively and quantitatively, with the freedom of the rest of the community to organize their lives in such ways as they see fit.

When it comes to opposing politicans bent on standardizing the most important conditions of employment through legislation, a challenge on constitutional grounds will require stronger principles of judicial review than the two we are using. To argue, for example, that economic free zones are constitutionally superior to the labour code we currently have means courts must be prepared to differ with our legislators' judgment that the social and constitutional advantages such policies produce warrant whatever costs in our constitutional order they may cause. However, so long as courts focus their inquiry on whether such legislative initiatives maximize the equality of freedom that workers in our society will be able to enjoy, minimum wage laws will be constitutionally secure.[14]

Thinking through the way in which the Charter will be involved in future debates about the constitutionality of either the anti-discrimination or anti-sweating principles should provide an additional measure of confidence in the way the analysis is proceeding. Our first two examples show that, properly interpreted, the Charter can be invoked by the weakest and least advantaged in our society to protect their autonomy and integrity against further encroachments by those who are more intolerant and overreaching than our political ideals encourage Canadians to be. These examples demonstrate that, even when it is read according to quite cautious and conventional principles and when it is applied in a very defensive and non-threatening way, the Charter can insist that we live up to the ideals we have now entrenched in our constitution.

Having said that, it must be conceded that the conclusions to which our two principles have directed us are hardly radical. In both instances the Charter simply confirms what a majority of our community have long recognized – that two of the most important components of our labour code are predicated on a set of values that have been imbedded in our legal culture over a considerable period and which we have now entrenched in our constitution. Yet even if that were the only contribution the Charter made to the ongoing debate about what a proper labour code should look like, it would not be a trivial accomplishment. At the very least, it would be an improvement on the interpretative principles and theory of liberal democracy the United States Supreme Court pursued at the turn of this century. Interpreting the Charter according to the two principles we are employing would allow us to avoid a legal and social result which is considered by the vast majority of American legal scholars as one of the darkest moments of American constitutional law.[15] It would entail a clear recognition, in the words of a leading constitutional scholar in the United States, that:

The suffering of the underprivileged, including the misery of the underpaid, overburdened, or unemployed workers [would be] seen not as an inescapable corollary of personal freedom or an inevitable result of forces beyond human control, but instead as a product of conscious governmental decisions to take *some* steps affecting the affairs of economic life – punishing some people as thieves, awarding damages to others as the victims of trespass or breach of contract, immunizing others through concepts of corporate law – while *not* taking *other* steps that might rescue people from conditions of intolerable deprivation. Indeed it [would be] to see such preventable harm as a kind of violence – different in form and source from more conventional types of human violence, perhaps, but violence none the less.[16]

As conclusions of constitutional theory or labour law neither of these results is, on one level, especially significant. Decisions upholding the constitutionality of a human rights code or minimum wage law, while an improvement on the American experience, would not in any way challenge the sovereignty of Parliament. The judgments in these cases would not provide any evidence of how the judiciary could promote the democratic quality of decision-making in our processes of government on its own initiative. They would confirm, not controvert, the integrity of the rules and principles that were chosen "by the people," or at least a majority of their representatives, to govern the places we work. The Charter would be used in defence, not in defiance, of the popular will.

So while these examples of how the Charter will validate anti-sweating and anti-discrimination rules give us additional confidence in the integrity of the principles that we are employing, we still cannot make very strong claims about the force of the Charter as an instrument of social justice. Neither of the first two examples we have considered allow us to consider the extent to which the third branch of government and the principles of constitutional interpretation we are using can advance the cause of the less advantaged on their own.

To do that it is necessary to invoke the Charter in aid of less defensive purposes. We must inquire when, if ever, an individual can successfully resist the legislative will when the latter deviates from the ethical ideal which is entrenched in our constitutional rules. It is only when the Charter is put forward by the weakest and most vulnerable members of our workforce against rather than in aid of the majority's will that the strength of the Charter, as an instrument of social justice, can be fully measured. It is only in those circumstances that we will be able to see the extent to which the judicial branch of our government can promote the autonomy of the least influential members of our community on its own initiative.

Our project, then, is to canvass those circumstances in which the least powerful members of our society might be able to successfully invoke the Charter to resist "acts" of social injustice even when they are committed or sanctioned by one of the branches of government. As we embark on this next step in our analysis, it is important to underscore again the limits of its ambition. We will not be seeking final answers to all the questions still alive in the current debate concerning the role of law in the regulation of work relations. At this stage of the analysis our focus will still be on the process of judicial review. As much as assessing the validity of various components of our labour code, my ambition here is to get a better fix on whether, with our two principles of constitutional interpretation, the courts can provide those who have been least influential in the formulation of particular laws with a forum which will allow them to participate more effectively in our community's processes of collective decision-making. In this part, then, I am still interested in confirming the integrity and exploring the reach of our two principles of constitutional review. Only in Part Four, when we consider the principle of employee representation in a system of collective labour relations, will we follow a conversation of constitutional justification through to its logical conclusion.

Even within these limited objectives, however, we will be able to assess whether the Charter can enhance the justice of our labour code in important and meaningful ways. We know that in filling out the details of our labour code our legislators have generally been motivated by the ethical and political values that are enshrined in our Charter. That consistency of purpose is what best explains the validity of the laws we have just reviewed. However, we also saw how, on occasion, legislators exercised their sovereign authority in highly pragmatic and on occasion acutely partisan ways. One of the lessons that the chronology of our labour codes teaches is that because of the nature of the decision-making process in our legislative and executive branches of government, instances of legislative tyranny or inconsistency have almost certainly been committed by our representatives as well. On the basis of the history we followed, one would expect the interests of those in our own communities who traditionally have not been well represented in the political process would also have been sacrificed to some degree to those who are more organized and more powerful. It would be surprising not to find our own legislatures had worked the occasional injustice on the least influential in our society in effecting the compromises which characterize so much of our labour code.

Holding different features of our labour code up to our principles of constitutional interpretation provides an especially important opportunity to reassess the role of the judiciary in our system of government. If the Charter and the process of judicial review are to be important instruments in enriching the quality of justice that our system of social relations provides, then it would be expected to do so in this area of law. If the Charter were unable to secure any improvements in the social justice of the relations between people in the places they work, it would be difficult to be optimistic that it could reconcile our differences more fairly anywhere else.

In fact, it turns out nothing so nihilistic will occur. Even on the uncontroversial understanding of the Charter that we have been applying, we will be able to identify in the remaining sections of Part Three a variety of persons who are among the most disadvantaged and most poorly represented in our society, who can call on our third arm of government to ameliorate, if not eliminate, some of the grossest instances of social injustice which depreciate the quality of their working lives. We will see how, in the kind of debate a court conducts, those individuals and groups of workers most prejudiced by decisions authorized in the name of the popular will can participate much more effectively and secure the respect for their equal entitlement to personal autonomy that the majority has denied them for so long. In the effective dialogues they are able to initiate in the third branch of government we will gain an understanding of how the judiciary can substantially enhance the democratic character of our processes of policy-making.

Domestics and agricultural workers are perhaps the most obvious groups of persons who can point to the provisions of the Charter to enlist the support of the judiciary to call for an end to some of the most blatant and crudest forms of occupational discrimination which

still infect our labour code. With our two principles, the judiciary will
not allow statutory restrictions and exemptions which unequally and
unfairly constrain the freedom of these people to lead lives of their
choosing to continue. Women, along with some of the oldest and youngest
members of our workforce, are others who will also be able to put
the Charter to work to enhance their opportunities for personal self-
government. Members of these groups, who make up a disproportionate
share of our poor and unemployed,[17] will be able to use the Charter
and our third branch of government to secure a measure of social justice
which our legislators and their executives have as yet been unwilling
to provide. With the Charter in their hands, all of these groups will
be able to insist our legislators be a good deal more sophisticated and
sensitive in discriminating between workers in the extent to which they
will benefit and be protected by the rules adopted to govern the workplace.

However, it is those who some have called the unskilled, unlucky,
and unorganized[18] who will be able to put the Charter to work with
the greatest and most dramatic effect. In their cause and on the cautious
and conservative reading we have been giving it, the Charter should
provide the vehicle through which the historical evolution in our labour
laws can be taken to its next logical step. The entrenchment of our
Charter of Rights will mark the occasion on which those persons most
prejudiced by our current system of collective bargaining will finally
be able to insist our legislators design alternative systems of collective
labour relations around principles of participation which conform more
closely to our constitutional ideals. They will be able to move the debate
about the content of our labour laws to the judicial branch, where
they should be able to demonstrate that our commitment to principles
of liberalism and democracy – of freedom and equality – must be reflected
in the institutions we use to govern the places where we work in addition
to those where we live and play. Even when the meaning of the Charter
is much more fully developed, democracy in industry may be the most
important legacy it will leave in the gradual liberalization of labour
laws that we have seen evolve over the past six hundred years.

NINE

Occupational Discrimination

A. AGRICULTURAL WORKERS

The most straightforward situation in which the judicial branch can secure a measure of social justice on its own is when it aims the Charter at social policies that endorse what might be called occupational discrimination.[1] Take the case of agricultural workers, who are among the most economically exploited and politically neutralized individuals in our society. Because they are heavily drawn from a migrant and immigrant population, these workers face even more serious obstacles to effective participation in the political process. Typically, these workers have not been covered by many of the most important parts of our labour code, including our collective bargaining legislation.[2] Denying agricultural workers the benefits of this rule of law means that the legal processes which enable much of the rest of our workforce to be involved in decision-making at the workplace in a realistic way are unavailable to the farm workers. Thus a group of workers who are already among the least powerful are given even less opportunity than the rest of us to participate in the formulation and application of the rules governing their working conditions.

The blanket exclusion of farm workers from our collective bargaining laws is comparable to our earlier hypothetical example of a legislature repealing our fair employment laws. At a minimum, it is a deliberate decision of the legislative branch not to show the same respect for the farm workers' freedom of association as that shown to their brothers and sisters who work in the industrial and service sectors of our economy. Refusing to extend "the protection and benefit" of our Labour Relations Acts to agricultural workers means their freedom to associate is governed by the common, judge-made law. However, as the courts in the nineteenth century made painfully clear, any attempt by agricultural workers to form associations would expose them to civil and criminal liability.[3] In addition, denying them the protection of the statutory scheme has left them vulnerable to a wide variety of actions by their employers designed to obstruct the formation of a union.

The practical effect of excluding farm workers from our Labour Relations Acts is to create two separate legal superstructures, which entail radically different degrees of worker participation in the settlement of the rules which govern the workplace. Farm workers are assigned to the one which offers substantially less protection for their opportunities for personal self-government. Legally, that is discrimination of the most blatant and explicit kind. Can such a gross inversion of our constitutional order be defended? In the language of the Charter, the legitimacy of such apparently discriminatory treatment reduces itself to a question of whether such statutory exclusions can be "demonstrably justified in a free and democratic society."

In the case of agricultural workers, two arguments are conventionally advanced to justify this failure to respect their constitutional rights. The first asserts that to allow the system of decision-making which we use in our factories to be employed on our farms would cause labour costs to rise to the detriment of consumers or to the farmers (employers) themselves if the increased costs could not be passed on.[4] The second argument is more narrowly focused and contends that collective bargaining would substantially interfere with, and ultimately jeopardize, the existence of the family farm.

However successful the first argument has been in debates in the legislature, it is clear it would have little force in a conversation in our courts. It directly contradicts our constitutional commitment to respect a basic equality between individuals in the control they retain over their lives. If indeed collective bargaining increases the costs of labour to the overall detriment of society, then our legislators should repeal the legislation in its entirety rather than selectively exclude those most in need of its protection. The legislature has not given credence to this argument for the rest of the workforce. Workers who are in similar circumstances are able to choose collective bargaining as the process by which they will participate in decision-making in the workplace and settle, for example, the amount of remuneration they will receive.[5] Our constitutional commitment to respect each person's opportunity to control his or her development and secure the equal benefit and protection of our laws requires that agricultural workers be given this opportunity as well. The argument from financial consequences, while obviously a powerful one in a legislative process, where the farm lobby is strong, offers no principled basis on which the differential treatment of agricultural workers can be defended constitutionally. If anything, their already inferior economic status would demand that agricultural workers receive more, not less, protection from the law.

The second argument, however, is a principled argument in the way the first is not. It can be argued, I think, that the family farm implies a way of life, a form of social organization, which is distinguishable from that which prevails in our factories and office buildings. The types of personal relationships implied by each are sufficiently unique to suggest that different decision-making processes may be appropriate to regulate the distinctive relations in each of these social spheres.[6] Thus, if it can be established that collective bargaining is actually antagonistic to the way of life that is carried on in a family environment, the equal freedom of those who desire to pursue the pastoral path may provide a principled basis on which to limit the reach of collective bargaining statutes. These circumstances parallel those we considered when we examined the constitutionality of our anti-discrimination and minimum wage legislation. Here, as there, rights collide and in such circumstances some limitation on personal freedom is inevitable. In this situation the freedom of those who choose to experience their lives in such non-commercial, self-sustaining ways may justify restraining the freedom of others who would wish to associate with them in a way which would threaten or deny them the opportunity to realize their choice.

It is not necessary to finally determine whether the exclusion of individuals who labour on family farms from collective bargaining legislation would, on the principles we are using, ultimately be sustained. Like the contest between workers whose autonomy is promoted and those who are prejudiced by our minimum wage laws,[7] we need additional principles to the ones we are working with to determine how this conflict of rights would be resolved. It is sufficient for our analysis to observe that even if such an exemption were determined to be constitutionally valid, on the basis of the Charter's commitment to respect an equality in people's opportunity to control their own lives, that would be the limit of the exemption which could be justified. If the object of excluding agricultural workers from our system of collective labour relations is to protect the way of life and the equal liberty of those who operate family farms, the least drastic means to accomplish that objective would be to confine the exclusion, as some legislatures have, to those who actually work in such settings.[8] The claim of preserving a unique social institution like the family farm, while a principled one, could never justify excluding all agricultural workers as the Ontario legislation, for example, does. The latter enactment is an instance of the grossest kind of over-inclusion which the principle of the reasonable alternative would effectively proscribe. A blanket exclusion of the kind enacted by Ontario is a needless and therefore unreasonable restriction of the freedom of workers who labour for larger and more commercial agricultural enterprises.

B. DOMESTIC WORKERS

Agricultural workers are not the only group denied the protection and benefit of important rules in our labour code. Domestic workers[9] present an equally dramatic illustration of how our legislative and executive branches of government can deliberately deny a group of persons, who traditionally have been among the least effective and influential participants in the processes of politics, the equal concern and respect to which they are now constitutionally entitled. These individuals are commonly denied the full benefit and protection of those standards in our labour code pertaining to wages, hours of work, overtime, paid vacations, as well as workers' compensation and occupational health and safety legislation.[10]

Having just confirmed that legislation which standardizes the most fundamental rules of work is constitutional, it is difficult to imagine what rational, let alone reasonable, basis there could be to justify laws that allow the poorest of our workers to be paid less than what we consider, for others, to be a living wage. If in the cause of personal autonomy a legislature outlaws the practice of sweating and the subjugation and domination that it entails, our constitutional commitment to equality of liberty requires that it banish it for all.

In a society constitutionally committed to principles of freedom as well as democracy, there is no principled basis on which such exclusions from minimum wage and maximum hours legislation can be justified. Defenders of the existing legal regime could not mount an argument based on privacy or equality of liberty like the one which might single out some definition of the small family farm. The way of life and rules of social interaction in such an environment are entirely independent of and not threatened by the wages a person is paid or the hours he or she works. To justify such differential treatment, supporters of the status quo might be expected to claim that if coverage of those parts of our labour code were extended to domestics, it might well have an adverse effect on their employment opportunities. But as we have already seen, this is not a principled justification for singling out specific classes of workers for such special treatment. As in the case of farmworkers, if those arguments were relevant, they would call for the repeal of this legislation in its entirety and not for the selective exclusion of those very groups who are most in need of its protection.

The constitutional claims that agricultural and domestic workers can effectively mount provide the simplest examples[11] of how the Charter makes it possible for individuals who have traditionally been relatively ineffectual in debates in the political arena can rectify injustices imposed on them by legislatures. In the more constrained and principled conversations our courts allow, unless it can be established that such discrimination serves a valid social purpose (such as protecting the equal rights of others) and is drawn in a way which minimizes the infringement of the constitutional rights of those adversely affected by the classification, laws of this kind can no longer figure in our labour code. Farm workers and domestics provide clear and unequivocal evidence that the Charter can be used by groups of workers whose weakness in the political process may have been exploited or abused in the past.

But their circumstances are by no means unique. There is more evidence of that kind readily at hand. The Charter's commitment to equality and autonomy is much broader than these examples show. On the interpretation we are following, the Charter insists that our legislatures respect a basic equality between each individual person as an autonomous agent and not just between occupational groups. Distinctions drawn on the basis of an individual's personal characteristics, no less than those relating to his or her occupation, must conform to our two principles of judicial review to be validated constitutionally. Once again, legislators will be able to justify rules they enact which classify people on the basis of some aspect of their personal identity only if those distinctions can be shown to serve a valid purpose and are drawn in a way to do the least possible damage to the constitutional entitlements of those they affect.

TEN

Age Discrimination

Let us now consider those rules in our labour code which purport to distribute benefits or impose burdens on the basis of a person's age. To take a topical example, we can focus on the legitimacy of those rules and regulations which compel people to retire involuntarily and simply on account of the number of years they have lived. Whether it is proper to distinguish between people in this way is a good test for our rules of judicial review. Because it is not associated with past discrimination against a particular group,[1] and because the number of people affected by the rule appears to be small,[2] the issue presents a relatively neutral example through which we can work our principles of judicial review again. It is generally free from the emotion and rhetoric which so often clouds discussion on the propriety of using other immutable characteristics of the person, such as his or her sex, in making decisions about workers' rights and responsibilities. Framing the issue as a court might phrase it, the question would be whether mandatory retirement is a legitimate rule of work regulation in a society that espouses principles of liberty and equality as the foundation of its legal order.

To answer this question we will employ the same method we used when we examined the other components of our labour code. The reasoning will be the same. Prima facie mandatory retirement is a form of discrimination between individuals because of age and therefore a violation of the Charter's explicit equality guarantees. However, like any occupational exception, it can be justified if it is dedicated to constitutionally valid objectives and kept within proper bounds.

Now, before we follow the analysis which leads to these conclusions, it is probably wise to pause for a moment to deal with a preliminary matter which, I suspect, may cause some to wonder how the issue of mandatory retirement would be brought within the purview of the Charter at all. Some will question how persons who, for example, were retired according to pension policies instituted by their employers, or collective agreements signed by their unions, would be able to mount a constitutional challenge against their mandatory retirement.[3] It might be said their claim fails to raise any allegation of governmental action which, we have assumed from the outset, is a necessary ingredient of any valid complaint brought under the Charter. Their remedy, if any, it might be asserted, would be under the human rights legislation which to varying degrees and in varying circumstances outlaws discrimination on the basis of age between individuals in their private affairs.

The effective reach of the Charter is an issue which will be of central importance when courts come to consider the constitutional validity of much of our collective bargaining legislation and in particular the status of the collective agreement and the arbitration process. Consideration of what our courts eventually decide constitutes governmental action is probably one of the most controversial questions confronting our constitutional law. Legal academics and courts in Canada are already divided on the matter, and the state of jurisprudence in the United States is one of hopeless inconsistency and disarray.[4] If we are to adhere to our strategy of avoiding controversial questions, it would seem that this is a challenge we ought to take seriously and perhaps put to one side.

In fact, it turns out, that need not be the case. First, and most obviously, certain individuals such as public servants, who are compulsorily retired by an act of the legislature, will clearly be able to satisfy the "state action" requirement.[5] There it is the act of government itself that fixes the tenure of their employees on the basis of their age. However, even those who are retired from their employment in the private sector, pursuant to provisions in collective agreements to which they have not consented, should also be able to satisfy this threshold requirement of any constitutional challenge.

At first blush, it may seem difficult to see how government is involved in any way in the circumstances of persons who are not public servants who are terminated from their employment on account of their age. These claims seem to be contests between private persons and beyond the scope of the Charter. That has certainly been the overwhelming conclusion of those courts which have considered the extent to which the acts of trade unions, and the collective agreements they sign, can be brought within the focus of constitutional review.[6] And yet, on further reflection, one can see that government is involved in the retirement of any person against their will.

In the first place, even if one treats collective agreements like any other contractual arrangement, the state is unavoidably involved in every case in which compulsory retirement is resisted by a worker simply in virtue of the political and legal fact that our courts do constitute the third arm of our government. On each occasion that such a provision of a collective agreement or contract is enforced by a court or some subordinate agency of the legislature (e.g., a board of arbitration), government's neutrality and impartiality is lost. Just by enforcing the rule which allows for the retirement of workers against their will, government sanctions the coercive exercise of legal authority such terminations entail.

Although both law and logic can be invoked to support treating a collective agreement simply as a variant of our normal contractual regime, and locating the requisite government action in the enforcement of their terms, such an analysis would be quite controversial. If the American experience is any guide, this theory of state or government action will be hotly debated by our courts and commentators for a long time to come. We will therefore focus on those features of collective agreements which owe their validity directly to the legislative and executive branches of government and which distinguish them from the more conventional two-party contracts which are the staple of judge-made law.

Shifting our focus from the judicial to the legislative branch of government is not difficult. As every student of Canadian labour law is taught, but for the enactment of our labour relations statutes both the status of trade unions and their collective agreements would be of dubious validity. Over a quarter of a century ago the Supreme Court of Canada recognized that it was these legislative initiatives by the state that removed the disabilities trade unions and collective agreements suffered under common law.[7] It is only because of the extensive legislative support contained in our Labour Relations Acts that a collective agreement is binding on the parties who sign it as well as on the third parties (the employees) who are governed by it.[8]

Canadian judges have been much less creative than their American counterparts. The latter were able to validate contracts which had been settled in processes of collective decision-making by devising rules to overcome their common law disabilities.[9] By contrast, in the eyes of the Anglo-Canadian judges, collective agreements were regarded at worst as being unlawful in restraint of trade, and at best as unenforceable gentlemen's agreements in which no one had any intention to create legal relations.[10] Moreover, according to the Anglo-Canadian version of the third-party beneficiary rule, any attempt to burden or benefit employees who were not "privy" to the contract would be utterly ineffectual.

So there can be little doubt that the ultimate source of authority by which the legal interests of individual workers are recognized and/ or lost in collective agreements lies in the legislative enactment of our collective bargaining system. Statutory schemes promoting rules of collective bargaining are like an amendment which repeals or limits some part of our human rights code. These expressions of legislative will do much more than tolerate the enforcement of contracts against persons who are not privy and do not consent to them. They make such assertions of legal authority possible by repairing the deficiencies of the common law. Unless the legislature acts, none of the conditions set out in a collective agreement would have any legal force. Collective bargaining, and the rules and regulations of employment it generates (including those pertaining to retirement), should be seen as the product of a delegated law-making power. As the courts in the United States have explicitly recognized, in the enactment of systems of collective labour relations, legislatures have seen "fit to clothe the bargaining representative with powers comparable to those possessed by a legislative body both to create and restrict the rights of those it represents."[11]

The European Court of Human Rights has also considered the question of whether any governmental responsibility could be ascribed for a union security clause which was negotiated as part of a private collective agreement. It concluded: "Although the proximate cause of the events giving rise to this case was the 1975 agreement between British Rail and railway unions, it was the domestic law in force at the relevant time that made lawful the treatment of which the applicants complained."[12]

It is precisely – indeed only – because our legislators have delegated to unions and employers the legislative and adjudicative functions of settling the legal rules on which people will work (and retire) that collective agreements (and enforced retirements) have any legal force. Understanding that the legislature has given unions, in cooperation with employers, the legal authority to legislate (by bargaining) and adjudicate (by arbitration) the rules that will govern all work relations should satisfy even the most cautious interpretation of what degree of governmental action needs to be involved to qualify for constitutional review.

Against that conclusion, two rejoinders have been made.[13] First, it has been argued that if the Charter were applied to a collective agreement just because someone's right or freedom could be adversely affected, the same could be said of any private contractual arrangement. On this view, the entire system of freedom of contract would be threatened with the prospect of detailed judicial regulation against our new constitutional norms. It would become a relic of our past. Secondly, the claim that trade unions function like administrative agencies or arms of government in regulating the rules which govern the lives of people in the workplace has been met with the simple denial that unions are in any respect a branch or extension of government. Here it might be pointed out that unions can be controlled and even abolished by government. So, by definition, they cannot themselves be considered in any way like or part of government. On this view, unions are more like private religious organizations and corporations and therefore are beyond the reach of judicial review.

Each of these arguments rests on a common fallacy. Both fail to see the non-consensual, public dimension that distinguishes trade unions and the agreements to which they are signatory. Collective agreements are not simply private contracts between consenting individuals (members) precisely because, by statute, they bind third parties who otherwise do not consent to them. Mandatory retirement or union security rules are not terms each individual agrees to. To the contrary, each may be imposed on her by an organization acting solely on the authority delegated to it by the state. Rules in collective agreements compelling termination from employment on account of one's age are governmentally (publicly), not personally (privately) determined. Mandatory retirement contrasts sharply with early retirement which is chosen voluntarily by the individual worker.

Moreover, even if collective agreements were properly regarded as being the same as any other contract, mandatory retirement rules would still seem to come within the purview of constitutional review. While it is unquestionably an exaggeration to say the entrenchment of the Charter renders freedom of contract a thing of the past, it is equally mistaken to assume no term of a contract can be subjected to judicial review. Many terms and conditions of even the most conventional contracts, including rules of compulsory retirement, are uniquely the product of a cooperative law-making enterprise by our legislative and judicial branches of government. Actually, when one examines how mandatory retirement rules come to be included as part of Canadian employment law one sees an integrated process of public and private law-making which is quite typical in our society. In the first instance, consideration of mandatory retirement as a social policy for sharing work is given to the legislature – to the people – to debate. In the end, the extent to which mandatory retirement will be considered a legitimate way workers can be severed form their employment is determined by our most conventional democratic decision-making criterion of majority rule.

And rule the majority has. In fact, different majorities in the eleven Canadian jurisdictions have come to a variety of conclusions. Several of them, including Ontario, decided that each industrial or occupational community should choose for itself whether a rule of coerced retirement would be used in the places they work. In effect, the will of the majority in Ontario, for example, was that local autonomy and free choice should determine whether this particular policy was an appropriate method by which employment would be shared. In essence, the decision of whether mandatory retirement will be operative in our community was delegated by the legislators to the workers and their employers to decide for themselves.

The legal process by which this method of decentralized decision-making was effected involved three separate stages. First, after some debate, the legislature deliberately refused to extend the protection against discrimination on the basis of age in its human rights codes to persons under eighteen and over sixty-five.[14] In terms of the extent of the legislature's involvement, limiting the protection the human rights code affords against discrimination on the basis of age is exactly the same as the hypothetical amendment repealing some part of our equal opportunity rules which we considered earlier. As a consequence, whether workers can be discriminated against on the basis of their age is left to the judges to determine. In turn, the judiciary have held that whether people could be terminated from their employment at age sixty-five against their will would be up to the workers and their employers to negotiate. It has been the position of the judiciary that, in the absence of statutory prohibitions, there is nothing in our legal system which prohibits one person from discriminating against another simply on account of that person's age, sex, or race, etcetera. In a landmark decision of only a few years ago, seven judges of the Supreme Court of Canada unanimously held that, in the absence of prohibitions in our human rights codes, there was nothing in the common law that prevented Seneca College from refusing to hire a woman of East Indian descent, who was in all material respects qualified for the job, simply on account of her race. In the professional jargon of lawyers, the Supreme Court held there was at common law, no "tort" (civil wrong) of discrimination.[15]

Thus the explicit legislative decision to exempt people over the age of sixty-five from the protection of their human rights codes, together with the common law's tolerance of discrimination in general, makes it possible for each group of workers, together with their employers, to negotiate a legal rule to retire people at age sixty-five as a means of distributing employment opportunities in their offices and factories. These decisions of our legislative and judicial branches have delegated to workers and their employers the legal authority to impose on certain individuals what most people consider to be severe social, economic, and psychological burdens, without fear of incurring legal liability of any kind.

And, finally, it also misses the mark to say that trade unions are not governments because they depend for their very existence on the exercise by the state of its legislative powers. Of course a trade union is not a government. It is the creature of government. That is precisely the point. But a union is an agency of government, like any administrative tribunal, which performs functions which are at the heart of what modern government is all about. It is precisely because they have been given the legal authority by the state to participate in the (legislative) process of setting binding rules of employment, and to adjudicate disputes over their meaning and application, that trade unions are more like governmental bodies than they are like religious or corporate bodies whose membership is entirely voluntary and whose purposes lie beyond the traditional functions performed by government.

Both the major activities performed by unions have historically been the prerogative of the state. As we saw in Part One, throughout the past six hundred years the legislative and executive branches of government have assumed the primary role of regulating the principal terms on which work is performed. There has been no period during this time when the legislature and executive did not actively discharge this rule-making function. And the role of dispute resolution is one which is still exercised both by the third branch of government and by subordinate agents of the second. Controlling access to the administrative tribunal (arbitration) which has exclusive control over the resolution of disputes about virtually every term and condition of employment, involves trade unions in the performance of what is one of the most characteristic functions of government and the state.[16] Unlike religious and corporate bodies whose purposes are spiritual, social, economic, and so forth, trade unions have been empowered to exercise substantial control over the legislative and adjudicative functions which lie at the core of our conception of the state.

Notwithstanding the early judicial pronouncements, we can, I think, fairly assume that the threshold requirement of establishing governmental action can be met by a person who challenges the constitutional validity of being forced to retire from work under the terms of a collective agreement. A rule of compulsory retirement is, in fact and in law, the product of a law-making authority granted by the cooperative efforts of two branches of the state. The question that remains is, how will such initiatives fare on their merits? On both a literal interpretation of s.15 of the Charter, as well as on the deeper reading of its purposes, it seems that cutting people off from their livelihood when they turn sixty-five is, prima facie, a violation of their constitutional rights when it is done without their consent and without regard to their ability to continue to work. Terminating people from their employment in such a fashion seriously discriminates against them by denying their equal freedom to pursue their vocations. A worker aged sixty-five is no different, qua worker, than his colleague who is sixty-four. For most academics, legislatures, and courts[17] the discrimination seems plain. The only serious issue is whether, in a free and democratic society, such a distinction is one whose reasonableness can be "demonstrably justified."

When we turn to our now standard, two-tiered analysis, it is immediately apparent that there are a large number of different objectives which mandatory retirement schemes seek to promote. Economic analysis identifies a wide range of possible justifications for the implementation of mandatory retirement rules. Rationalizing long-term, deferred-compensation packages, harmonizing standardized public and private sector pension plans, and minimizing administrative and monitoring costs of employee performance are among the more commonly cited benefits mandatory retirement schemes are said to accomplish.[18] In addition, making more job and promotion opportunities available to younger workers, as well as reducing risks to health and safety that may be caused by employees being unable to discharge their duties on account of their age, are almost always offered in the catalogue of objectives this long-standing rule of our labour code has been said to promote.

We need not concern ourselves with the economic rationales of mandatory retirement. To continue our strategy of ensuring the courts show the maximum respect for the sovereignty of the popular will, we must not judge whether the economic returns mandatory retirements are expected to secure justify including such rules in our labour code. To make that judgment would require a court to undertake a balancing exercise and employ a utilitarian method of decision-making which our two principles of constitutional review cannot accommodate. As we saw in our analysis of minimum wage laws and the treatment of agricultural workers, that kind of judicial review involves the broader proportionality principle and a more activist posture by the courts toward the two other branches of government than our analysis allows.

So we can focus our attention on the other two objectives which figure most prominently in the defence of legal rules which compel retirement at a specified age – opening up positions in the workplace for younger workers and considerations of health and safety. The second of these actually parallels the one we considered in assessing the constitutionality of the equal opportunity rule and applies to people who work in occupations where age can legitimately be characterized as a relevant, occupational qualification. In these circumstances, where there is sufficient evidence to establish the relevance of the age qualification to the individual's capacity to perform the work,[19] there will be a constitutional basis on which mandatory retirement rules can be defended. In theory, it is possible to justify mandatory retirement in a limited number of occupations, on the basis that the limitation it imposes on the freedom of some people to work as they choose is effected for the equally basic liberty of those (fellow employees, members of the public, etc.) whose health and safety could be put at risk if such people were allowed to remain at work beyond a specified age. Once again, one can always justify an exception or limitation on a right or a freedom when it is derived from the very value which supports the right or freedom itself.

However, this justification is of very limited scope. Like the exclusion of agricultural workers from our system of collective labour relations, compulsorily retiring people against their will would be constrained by the principle of reasonable, alternative means. It would apply only in those vocations, such as police officer, fire fighter, pilot, military person, where age may be shown to be a bona fide occupational qualification. It could have no application for the vast majority of persons in the workforce who are routinely retired just because they have reached the age of sixty-five.

For this group, retirement rules may be justified as legal instruments by which work, when it is scarce in the community, can be shared. The argument is that although these schemes obviously do discriminate on the basis of age, they treat workers equally because, assuming they are uniformly applied, all who reach this age will be affected by the rule. All of us, or at least those of us who live to sixty-five, are said to benefit from or be burdened equally by the rule. Michael Perry has put the justification in these terms:

What does the choice to retire persons by age imply? Most persons need to be engaged in "work", in the sense of productive activity that contributes, in some fashion, to the material or spiritual well-being of the community. Certainly this is a need older persons have as well as younger persons. But older persons have had their chance – their turn – to satisfy that need (which ought not to be confused with financial need, which is a distinct matter). Surely it is not unreasonable, or morally improper, to think that younger persons ought to be given their chance too.[20]

As a derivation of our principle of equality of liberty, this is certainly an argument which can fairly be advanced in the kind of dialogue the courts permit about the constitutionality of the different features of our labour code. For the same reason that it is legitimate to distinguish between workers in their termination from employment on the basis of their age when it is a bona fide occupational qualification, so justifying mandatory retirement as part of a work-sharing policy fits squarely within our first principle of constitutional review. Whatever other objectives it may or may not serve, mandatory retirement clearly enhances equality of liberty in our community by protecting an equal opportunity to work for every member of our society.

Against this latter justification it might be said that it rests on a common and fatal mistake. Coined by economists as "the lump of labour fallacy," the argument is that it is both logically and empirically incorrect to assume that forcing older workers to retire will increase the number of jobs and promotional opportunities for younger members of the workforce. The thesis is one which seems to have the general endorsement of the economics community at large, although in any given case its application is still a matter of some debate and dispute.[21]

For our purposes it is not necessary to explore the coherence of this theory. Again, on the principles and strategy of judicial review to which we are committed, it is not for the court to judge the wisdom or effectiveness of a rule or policy which a legislature has chosen to pursue. Such an argument might be pertinent under a proportionality principle, in which the benefits of a social policy are weighed against the cost to our constitutional order.[22] It cannot, however, be invoked when the only question before the court is whether a particular rule enhances our constitutional commitment to equality of liberty in the most reasonable way that it can.

In this respect a compulsory retirement rule is like a minimum wage law. Regardless of the scepticism with which economists may view the allocative efficiency of this long-standing rule of termination in our labour code, it can still be justified as an attempt by the legislature and/or its agents to meet the commitment in the Charter to our equality as autonomous, human beings. Predicated on the vital importance of work to the human condition, mandatory retirement purports to distribute work opportunities equally by identifying, through the proxy of age, those who have already had their share.

But against our second principle of interpretation, the proxy is too crude and clumsy to be a valid part of a constitutional labour code. It is an instance of insensitive and ultimately invalid stereotyping. It is at one and the same time over-inclusive and under-inclusive. Even though mandatory retirement rules can be defended as serving constitutionally valid objectives they do not do so in a manner which shows sufficient respect for the rights and freedoms of those they infringe.

If the legislature's justification for its authorization of mandatory retirement rules is to provide each individual an equal turn at work, at least two fundamental features of the existing schemes would have to be changed. First, to meet our second principle of reasonable alternative means, the relevant criterion of distribution would have to be years of work rather than years of living. Limiting the number of years a person can occupy a (scarce) opportunity to work is more reasonable as a job-sharing device than the standard formulation of mandatory retirement at sixty-five. It does less violence to our constitutional commitments than the rule we now use. For large numbers of workers – especially females who for family and related reasons often choose to enter the workforce and pursue their occupational ambitions at a later phase of their lives – the conventional rule of retirement does not guarantee the same equality of liberty and freedom of association as one which is predicated on years of service. Given the very different stages in their lives that people begin to work, basing termination on years of service rather than years of living makes more equal the opportunity each person has within the places which are so integral to our dignity and self respect.[23]

A second, quite radical, change in the current formulation of mandatory retirement schemes would also be required for these rules to be justified in this way. Thus, if the state (or those to whom it has delegated its authority) in justifying the rules of involuntary retirement, claims to be creating a legal environment in which each person has an equal opportunity to engage his or her talents productively, then it would also be bound to demonstrate that it had taken whatever complementary initiatives were necessary to ensure that the employment opportunities created by the retirements did not disappear.[24] As part of a job-sharing policy, a rule of mandatory retirement cannot be effective by itself. In order to establish its bona fides it would be incumbent on the legal authority imposing the rule to implement whatever complementary policies were necessary to ensure some sharing of jobs was actually achieved. Moreover, with a commitment of that kind, the economists' concerns that mandatory retirement rules do not achieve their objective of sharing work would be alleviated. Without it, it cannot simply be assumed that rules of compulsory retirement will function as the job-sharing instruments that they profess to be.

If a program of mandatory termination from employment at a specified age failed to satisfy conditions of this kind,[25] it could not be validated by our two principles of constitutional review. Incorporation of both of them would, by contrast, immediately qualify rules of mandatory retirement for inclusion in a constitutional labour code. With those conditions attached, a program of systematically retiring people after a maximum number of years of service would be consistent with the principles of interpretation with which we have been working. As amended, it would complement other work-sharing policies such as laws which regulate the amount of overtime that can be worked or which integrate unemployment insurance benefits with shorter work weeks. It would further the constitutional objective of equalizing access to the work opportunity by imposing a ceiling on the quantity of work a person could reasonably expect to claim over the course of his or her life just as these other parallel standards do for the day and week.[26]

In the event, we have another example of how groups who traditionally have not been well represented in our political institutions can invoke the process of constitutional review to claim a greater measure of concern and respect. Retirement by years of service would relieve the hardship and injustice suffered by those (predominantly female) workers who have had relatively short careers and who will have few pension credits on which they can live after they turn sixty-five. Conditioning enforced retirements on a commitment not to reduce the employment opportunities which are created by such a rule would also promote a more equal opportunity for the youth in our workforce to embark on the careers they have planned for themselves than their present circumstances realistically allow.

ELEVEN

Sex Discrimination

Women are perhaps the most visible and vocal group of workers looking
to the Charter and the process of judicial review to remedy injustices
which they believe can be traced to their relatively disadvantaged position
in the political process. Female workers have been quite clear about
their intention to require our legislators to be a good deal more sophisticated and sensitive in their reliance on immutable characteristics such
as a person's sex in the enactment of laws regulating work relations.[1]
It is not my intention to review, let alone resolve, all of the ways in
which the Charter will advance the cause of equality between the sexes.
The subject is much too large and the issues far too complex and
controversial.[2] For our purposes two examples will suffice to show how
women, like other relatively disadvantaged groups, will also be able
to use the process of judicial review to engage our legislators in a
conversation concerning whether various laws the latter have enacted
show them that degree of concern and respect which is now their
constitutional due.

A. HEALTH REGULATIONS

Government regulations which control the use of certain toxic substances
in the workplace, by fixing different levels of acceptable exposure for
men and women, provide one of the least complicated and most topical
illustrations of how women can invoke the Charter to demand our
legislators respect their equal right to personal self-government. One
of the most controversial regulations of this kind has been promulgated
by the government in Ontario, which establishes limits of acceptable
exposure to lead. The levels of exposure set for men are much higher
than those for women who are capable of bearing children. No one
disputes that this kind of differential standard has a detrimental impact

on the employment status of women. At the very least, if they are removed from the workplace because the lower threshold for them has been passed, they stand to lose financially. Worse, because of the costs to the employer of complying with standards for their protection, they may never be hired at all.[3] Once again, we seem to be faced with a rule in our labour code authorizing discriminatory treatment of precisely the kind the Charter was designed to prevent. Requiring women to bear such additional burdens denies them equality in the workplace.

Against such a charge of inequity, defenders of these differential standards generally respond that there is no invidious discrimination here at all. They argue that there is certainly no arbitrary discrimination on the basis of sex, which is one of the specific kinds of differential treatment that s.15 and s.28 of the Charter explicitly proscribe. Supporters of the status quo claim that there is a relevant distinction, apart from the sex of the individuals involved, which justifies the differential treatment such standards prescribe.[4] That difference is, of course, the potential hazard to a fetus of being exposed to certain toxic substances and the resultant legal liability of an employer and social obligations of the state that may arise if a more rigorous standard is not applied to all women.[5] It is the protection of the fetus, not the sex of the worker, which is said to justify what otherwise would seem to be a clear violation of the Charter.[6]

Whatever other purposes such rules may promote, protecting the life of the fetus should qualify as a constitutionally valid objective of the state. Justified as serving that objective, such rules fit squarely within our first principle of judicial review. Assuming that at some stage of its development a fetus is sufficiently similar to the human condition to be capable of bearing the rights to life and liberty which the Charter protects,[7] its future autonomy is as compelling an interest for the state to protect as any we have considered so far. In the result, once again the constitutional validity of these regulations can be reduced to a conflict of rights. The task confronting our courts will involve an evaluation of the manner in which the legislature has reconciled the competing liberties at stake.

Proponents of the status quo will have to demonstrate that there are no alternative means by which the legislature's objective can be accomplished so as to infringe less the constitutional rights of women.[8] However, if the experience in Ontario holds true, that may not be an easy position to prove. Even though it might seem that such an exercise would be a simple and straightforward task, it apparently has not proven so. At the present stage of the debate, it is not at all clear that differential standards are the least drastic means by which a legislature could accomplish these objectives.

In the first place, it has not yet been established that prescribing a uniform standard to apply to all workers (i.e., at a level which would be safe for a fetus), is an unreasonable method for legislators to achieve their objectives. So far no evidence of that kind has been forthcoming.[9] However, on the interpretation of the Charter we are employing, unless it could be established that it was unreasonable to fix a single standard of exposure for all workers at a level which would protect the most susceptible person in the workplace, differential standards like these could not be defended under the Charter.[10] Moreover, even if differential standards for the most vulnerable workers could be justified,[11] it would still be incumbent on a legislature to consider protecting the life and liberty of the fetus by means of protective equipment for individual workers or by temporarily reassigning them to a less hazardous position before removing them entirely from the workplace.

Either of these alternative programs would seem to provide the same protection to the life of the fetus in a way which is demonstrably more sensitive to the liberty of the worker who is or is endeavouring to become pregnant. By comparison, differential regulations seem unnecessarily invasive of the equal autonomy of this group of workers. Only if such alternatives did not exist could the present legislation be justified as the least drastic policy available to the government to meet its objectives.

Ultimately, of course, it may well transpire that our legislators could make out that case. They may be able to establish that the alternatives we have considered are not reasonable substitutes in certain important and fundamental respects. In that event there would be no basis on which a court, applying our two principles, could interfere. If a legislature is able to demonstrate differential regulations are the most effective policy instrument available to guarantee a fetus complete protection against exposure to toxic risks in the workplace, it would, at least on our principles of review, be entitled to insist on the sovereignty of the parliamentary process.

In this example there would be no opportunity for those whose rights and freedoms are constrained by these rules to advance an argument that differential regulations are over-inclusive. This component of our labour code is not vulnerable to an argument of overbreadth in the same way as were the rules excluding farm workers from collective bargaining legislation or retiring people against their will because of their age. The regulation must cover all women who are capable of reproduction and not simply those for whom pregnancy is a desired and/or existing condition, since even the most sophisticated methods of birth control may fail. However remote this risk may be, if the object of a legislature is to provide each fetus with full protection, it would not be possible to define the classification more particularly to apply only to women capable and desirous of bearing children.

But even in bringing the debate that far, it is apparent that our two principles would have an important heuristic effect. Generating a dialogue like the one we have just rehearsed would make it clear that the judgment which motivated the legislators' choice of policy was either ethical or political and was not, as is often claimed, based on scientific theory or fact. There would be no doubt that the legislature was requiring women to bear this burden because of its intense commitment to protecting the fetus from toxic risks in the workplace, however improbable and remote these dangers were, and however many other hostile environments it allowed a fetus to inhabit.[12] On such a scenario we obviously could not claim that our principles of judicial review were sufficiently strong to prevent a legislature from adopting rules of differential treatment. Nevertheless, forcing a legislature to face the prospect of justifying such policies in a forum of principle may ultimately have precisely the same effect.

Regardless of the ultimate result, women would be given the opportunity for a more rigorous debate than the Ontario legislature afforded them when it initially adopted the regulations in question.[13] Reasons, which would be subject to close cross-examination, would have to be advanced to show why the legislature failed to adopt one of the other available policies. And if ever defenders of differential standards were unable or unwilling to advance such reasons, such standards as a means of protecting the life of the fetus could not survive. In those circumstances, legislators would have failed to discharge their burden of proving that the limitation they imposed on the rights and freedoms of the women was demonstrably justified.[14]

So the challenge that can be made against differential standards governing exposure to toxic risks at the workplace presents yet another relatively straightforward example of how, in this case, women will be able to invoke the Charter to secure a measure of respect some legislators are apparently still unwilling to show them. Although our principles cannot, by themselves, hold differential standards unconstitutional, they can force a debate, the very possibility of which may ensure that that result is achieved.[15] The potential for participation that judicial review offers to women may be so effective that, consistent with Mill's hypothesis, the other two branches of government may consider on their own initiative alternate policies which are more sensitive to the equal opportunity of women.

B. AFFIRMATIVE ACTION POLICIES

The other set of social policies of particular importance to women that warrants brief consideration are affirmative action programs. Given the great expectations for affirmative action and the complexity of programs of this kind, it is important to underscore again that the analysis we can fashion with our two principles of justice will of necessity be incomplete. Other principles will be developed by the courts which will have an important impact on the constitutional validity of these programs. Moreover, the Charter will likely be put to less offensive purposes when it considers these policies than it was than in the cases we have just considered. Its role will usually parallel the one it played in our assessment of the constitutional validity of minimum wage and fair employment legislation. However, even with those caveats, the question as to the integrity of affirmative action plans is of such central concern to disadvantaged groups in our society that even if our two principles cannot provide final answers to these questions, it is important to know how they would respond. For many the persuasiveness of our principles will be strongly influenced by how they assay the constitutional purity of this most recent, and most controversial, addition to our labour code. Canadian human rights legislation now routinely accommodates programs of affirmative action [16] and the Charter itself explicitly sanctions their constitutional validity. Section 15(2) provides that the Charter's conception of equality ". . . does not preclude any law, program or activity that has as its object the amelioration of conditions of disadvantaged individuals or groups, including those that are disadvantaged because of race, national or ethnic origin, religion, sex, age or medical or physical disability."

At the outset we can say that there is nothing in our two principles of interpretation which is at odds with this popular and constitutional commitment to affirmative action programs. There is, I trust, widespread recognition in our community that women are one of those groups of workers who have been discriminated against in the past, and who will remain disadvantaged in their work opportunities unless additional programs of affirmative action are initiated to reverse the effects of the injustices they have been made to endure.[17] The position of many women in the labour force is not unlike that of an individual whose life is threatened. The classic example is the New Yorker "who gets a note from Murder, Inc., that looks like business."[18] In circumstances such as these liberal theories of justice call for additional police protection for that person on the basis that her right to her physical security is equal to those of others who live in New York. Inequality of resources is justified by, and derived from, the deeper value of equal worth that liberal theory insists holds between all individuals.[19] It is the conditions which are necessary to provide some modicum of physical security (on which autonomy depends), and not the allocation of police resources, which are the focus of the liberal's egalitarian ideal.

The same principle of justice is implicit in the constitutional theory we have been using and supports policies of affirmative action designed to reduce conditions which interfere with the equality of personhood which the Charter guarantees.[20] Programs that confer special benefits on female workers who have been discriminated against in the past, such as special training and apprenticeship programs or financial support (e.g., pregnancy leave) or day-care centres, can be justified on the same basis as the additional police security that is provided to someone whose life is threatened. All of these are, ultimately, policies of equal opportunity and not of preferential or special treatment.[21] They endeavour to bring women up to the starting line. Like the protection given to the New Yorker, an unequal distribution of certain resources (e.g., fringe benefits such as pregnancy leave, occupational training) can be justified as a legislative policy necessary to secure the deeper equality on which our whole theory of social organization is based. To treat individuals in these circumstances equally it is necessary to treat them differently. Just as liberty does not mean licence, so equality is not sameness.

Most people no longer consider legislative policies of this type controversial.[22] The credibility of our theory of the constitution would be seriously weakened if it could not accommodate such policies. More contentious are programs of stronger affirmative action intended not just to secure some equality of opportunity to engage in productive, remunerative work but, in addition, to award positions to these persons even when others are available and more qualified on all of the relevant criteria. It is important to know how the constitution, at least as we are interpreting it, responds to such programs which purport to rely on a person's sex or race as the ultimate basis on which certain jobs will be distributed.

As a matter of both principle and textual interpretation, these are much more difficult cases to resolve. On the one hand, strong policies of preferring one person to another for a position because of her sex seem to offend both the explicit language and underlying premises of the Charter. Such policies seem to deny the entitlement of every person in our community to be able to pursue a life they have chosen for themselves on an equal basis with everyone else.

For many people, such strong rules of affirmative action are seen as reverse discrimination. The law seems to tolerate an asymmetry in the rule against giving preferential treatment to anyone on the basis of characteristics which have no relation to their moral worth. In this view, strong policies of affirmative action simply result in a redistribution of injustice.[23] All that changes is that now it will be other individuals (men, whites, etc.) who themselves may have played no part in the past discrimination and who may have suffered similar or even more damaging forms of injustice, who will be treated differently simply because of their sex or race.

Against this, supporters of strong policies of affirmative action begin from the idea that these policies are altogether distinguishable from the arbitrary and invidious treatment tolerated in the past. Now differences in race or sex are being acted on for entirely different (and in their view, legitimate) reasons. To their proponents, strong affirmative action programs do not entail the systematic denigration of a race or class as being morally inferior.[24] Rather, these policies are practised to promote the equal opportunity of self-development of persons who belong to a group which has suffered serious disadvantages in the past. Distinguishing between individuals on the basis of their sex is said to be a benign form of discrimination when, as it is claimed on behalf of the programs we are now considering, it is done to secure the equality between individuals to which we are now constitutionally committed.

Whether the distinction drawn by advocates of strong affirmative action will carry the day depends, in the first instance, on the specific purposes which such programs are said to promote.[25] Ultimately, the constitutional validity of these policies will turn on the reasons advanced to distinguish such "well intentioned" acts from the abusive and invidious discrimination of the past. Once again, it is not necessary for us to consider all of the objectives these stronger forms of affirmative action are said to promote. Like almost every other component of our labour code which we have held up to judicial review, the inequality of treatment that is entailed by these programs can be derived from and justified by the concept of equality which underlies our constitutional framework of social relations as a whole.[26]

The simplest illustration of when our principles of interpretation would validate policies of this type occurs where it can be shown that a person's sex is a relevant characteristic by which his or her suitability for a position may be judged. Paralleling cases where a person's sex might be described as a bona fide occupational qualification, a person's sex may also be a relevant criterion against which his or her personal abilities and qualifications may be judged. As the California Supreme Court suggested in the now famous case of *Regents of University of California* v. *Bakke*[27] and as individual justices in the U.S. Supreme Court have also acknowledged,[28] if an individual has had to endure the effects of past discrimination because of her race or sex, those factors will be relevant considerations against which her qualifications should be assessed. On the relevant criteria on which a job or position is assigned a female applicant may have had a lower score than the males who competed against her. However, if her performance was handicapped by the discrimination women have generally suffered in the past, it may be quite appropriate to conclude that her qualifications are actually higher than her objective scores would indicate. In these circumstances, consideration of an individual's sex would be entirely compatible with the theory of the constitution we have been employing. If our laws are to satisfy the conception of equality of personhood which our Charter embraces, we cannot always be sex or colour blind.[29]

A related, though larger, circumstance in which stronger programs of affirmative action could be justified within our new constitutional constraints arises where the effects of past discrimination are such as to effectively preclude a person from ever being in a position of competing as an equal. Here policies of preference may be necessary as the only form of compensation available to remedy the past discrimination and to secure the equality to which we are constitutionally committed.[30] More generally, we may say that whenever it can be established that the weaker policies of conferring special benefits on traditionally disadvantaged individuals or groups are unable to accomplish their purpose, when they do not result in women being able to enter particular vocations or to secure promotions to more senior ranks in an organization, strong affirmative action programs may be the only (that is, the least drastic) means of acting consistently with our constitutional ideal.[31]

It is clear from these examples that some programs of strong affirmative action can be accommodated within the Charter if it is interpreted according to the principles we have proposed. It is also clear, however, that our principles cannot tell us whether all the variations such programs can take are likely to pass the constitutional test. The principles we are using are only part of the theory. They show that some of these additions to our labour code will be constitutionally valid when they are enacted to promote the ideal of our equal autonomy and to compensate for past injustices, when other less drastic alternatives have been found wanting. They cannot tell us whether other programs, for example quotas for the appointment or promotion of members of disadvantaged groups, can withstand the rigours of judicial review.

At first blush, our two principles would seem to put what are unquestionably the strongest form of affirmative action in some jeopardy. From the perspective we have adopted, quotas seem to be a glaring example of a social policy badly overdrawn. If the purpose of affirmative action is restricted to promoting our constitutional commitment to equality of liberty, quotas seem to be a crude and insensitive means to that end. They do not appear to provide a very close fit between ends and means because they make no attempt to assess the individual circumstances of those they benefit. Quotas unavoidably and frequently confer advantages on persons who may have suffered the least serious effects of past discrimination themselves. They may, for example, give jobs to women who have been raised in economically and psychologically secure environments, who have acquired special skills and educational qualifications, and who generally have been able to compete as equals in all of the relevant competitions with their male classmates and colleagues. Indeed, the logic of quotas would seem to argue that the most sensible policy of appointment is to choose those individuals from the disadvantaged group who themselves had suffered least from the discrimination borne by the group as a whole. Those are the people who would likely perform most effectively and so would provide the best role models quotas are said to foster.[32]

On this view, quotas seem contrary to our commitment to equalize opportunities for personal self-government. They confer benefits on some individuals who already enjoy relatively more advantages than the persons whose liberty they constrain.[33] To respond to this challenge, supporters of compulsory quotas would argue that all that needs to be done, in order to get a better fit between means and ends, is to expand the objectives of affirmative action to include a time dimension. Instead of simply saying that affirmative action is designed to overcome some disadvantage an individual has suffered in the past, a new objective is set to realize the ideal of equality of liberty – of a fully integrated, assimilationist society – as expeditiously as possible.

It is true that when they are dedicated to these more ambitious purposes, quotas should meet the principle of proportionality linking means to their ends. Even though quotas may confer benefits on individuals who are already relatively more advantaged, quotas do so to secure a society in which sex is not an impediment to equal opportunity more quickly than any of the other programs of affirmative action can. Once the governmental objective includes a timetable for its realization, quotas can be put forward as the least drastic means available to meet it. By definition all of the other policies would have failed to reach the desired result.

Nevertheless, even though quotas may achieve the ideal of equality more quickly than the other forms of affirmative action, whether they will be included as part of a constitutional code of labour will not be possible for us to say. To make that judgment, more activist and controversial principles of judicial review are required. A court will still have to determine whether the extra speed with which the ideal can be realized justifies the compromise in the constitutional fabric of our labour code that quotas seem unavoidably to entail. In terms of the constitutional law that is already on the books,[34] validating the constitutional integrity of quotas would require a court to assess the proportion between the temporal advantages quotas enjoy and the costs they impose on those whose equal opportunity they deny.[35] Balancing the costs and benefits of quotas in that way means courts would have to apply a more activist, demanding standard of scrutiny than the one we are committed to use. In addition to making some assessment of the degree to which quotas foster the assimilationist societies they are intended to promote, a court would also have to make some judgment as to whether the benefits that are thought to distinguish such communities justify infringing the freedoms of those they prejudice.[36]

Applying such utilitarian calculations to quotas raises controversial questions about how deferential our courts should be to the other two branches of government. We have been able to avoid these issues so far and there is no reason to change our strategy here. It is sufficient to conclude that even if they cannot provide final answers to all of these questions, our principles are able to accommodate programs of affirmative action as part of a larger constitutionally valid system of work relationships when that is a "reasonable" way of helping those individuals whom law and politics have disadvantaged in the past.

TWELVE

Rules of Collective Decision-Making: Compulsory Union Membership

We have now spent a considerable time sifting evidence for the thesis that, with the Charter as their mandate, the courts can be enlisted in aid of the least powerful in our community. And so far we have kept to our commitment of proceeding with an interpretation of the Charter which is both cautious and uncontentious in the relationship it envisages between the courts and the other two branches of government as well as in the principles of justice it applies. If the analysis is open to criticism, most likely the charge would be that the conclusions we have derived are by and large so confined and localized that they do not support my initial claim that in the debates and conversations it structures and supervises, the judiciary may be the most democratic of all our institutions of state. It might be said that what gains have been identified so far have been limited to groups which have traditionally been among the most exploited, and they have been confined primarily to correcting anomalies in existing legislative regimes. Even in the case of affirmative action programs, the results we have generated are not as progressive as they might conceivably be.

There is no doubt that other theories of our constitution, richer and more radical than the one I have been developing, are and will be available to generate more dramatic results. It would be very misleading, however, to leave the impression that even with the principles of interpretation which have confined our analysis, our courts are only capable of enhancing the democratic character of and social justice in our community in marginal and interstitial ways. If the results we have derived so far strike some readers as being unexceptional, that is only because it has been my strategy to be absolutely certain of the integrity of the principles I have been using. By examining the easiest cases first, I have intended quite deliberately, to avoid contentious conclusions.

It is now time to see whether, their inherent conservatism notwithstanding, our principles of constitutional interpretation are capable of advancing the cause of justice and democracy in our social relations in much broader and significant ways. To accomplish this final objective I want to consider the question of the constitutional validity of the principle of exclusive representation of employee interests in our system of collective labour relations. This legal rule, which is known as the principle of exclusivity, controls how the interests of all of the employees in an enterprise or some division thereof will be represented collectively in the bargaining process. Its procedural character makes it an ideal candidate for constitutional review. Because it is quintessentially a rule of procedure, it addresses directly a subject which, as modern theorists such as Rawls have made explicit, is at the heart of our liberal democratic tradition of justice. Certainly for those who believe judicial review can best be reconciled with our democratic processes of government when the courts perform a "representation reinforcing" function for those who traditionally have had little influence in the decision-making processes, it is hard to imagine a subject more appropriate for close constitutional scrutiny.

When this principle, which is perhaps the most distinctive characteristic of the North American models of collective labour relations, is brought within the focus of the Charter, the results are spectacular indeed. It turns out that when the Charter is aimed at the principle of exclusivity, a claim can be made on behalf of the working class as a whole, and especially on behalf of those who are among the most disadvantaged members of that group, that a change in the processes of industrial government is now constitutionally required. Using the same principles of interpretation we have employed throughout, an argument can be advanced that in building our system of collective labour relations around a principle of exclusive representation, our legislators have not been as attentive to the principle of equality of liberty as they could have been. With the entrenchment of the Charter, working people will be able to insist that when legislatures establish or authorize processes of collective decision-making to govern the places in which we work, they must design institutions which are more democratic and compatible with the Charter than collective bargaining has ever been or can ever hope to be.

The outline of the argument is easily summarized. The method of the analysis remains unchanged. The principle of exclusivity stipulates that when a group of employees – or, more properly, a majority of them – choose a union to bargain on their behalf, that union becomes the sole and exclusive agent for all the employees in prescribing the terms and conditions under which each of those individuals will work. In virtue of this principle, the employer is forbidden to deal with any other person or union without the consent of the exclusive bargaining agent.

As with so much of our labour code, this principle of employee representation can be defended, within the kind of conversations which are conducted in our courts, as promoting objectives which justify some limitation on the rights and freedoms of others. In its purpose, the exclusivity principle is entirely consistent with our constitutional commitment to respect each person's equal opportunity of personal self-government. The deficiency, it turns out, is that this principle of employee representation is not the "least drastic" means available to legislatures to accomplish the objectives they pursue when they design systems of collective labour relations. In fact, there are alternate principles of employee representation which are more consistent with the rights and freedoms our Charter now guarantees and around which different models of collective decision-making in the workplace can be organized. These models – which provide the same degree of worker solidarity as our system of collective bargaining and operate in one form or another in most of the free and democratic societies in Western Europe – are grounded on principles we might characterize as voluntary and/or plural representation. As we shall see in the next part, both these principles show greater concern and respect than collective bargaining can for our freedom to associate with whomever we please. Additionally, they are more sensitive to our right to "benefit" equally from, and to be "protected" equally by, whatever laws our legislatures choose to enact. In short, both these principles of employee representation, which operate through works councils and multiple union bargaining structures, secure a greater equality of freedom than collective bargaining, and on that basis must be constitutionally preferred.

Even with the assurance that the method of analysis that leads to this conclusion is the same one we have been employing throughout, the consequences for our system of collective bargaining are so controversial that it seems prudent to rehearse the principles and the conversation they support one last time. Fortunately, there is another feature of our system of collective bargaining closely related to the principle of exclusivity which can be – and in fact already is being – held up to judicial review. This is the part of our labour code which requires or authorizes[1] some form of compulsory union membership in every collective bargaining relationship. In particular, these rules require that every employee in a group which has chosen to bargain collectively, must be associated in some way with the union that is certified to represent him or her. For our purposes this is an especially pertinent feature of our labour code. First, it is a rule which, unlike many of the others we have considered, potentially affects the rights and freedoms of all workers and not simply a particular group. Secondly, it is illuminating for us because it underscores how far our labour law has travelled in its treatment of associations of working people. In sharp contrast with the labour codes which regulated work in earlier times, in which the (common) law of criminal and civil conspiracy made even voluntary associations highly problematic, our law now authorizes some form of compulsory, formal association between those who work in a common enterprise. Examining this part of our labour code is especially relevant to the current debate of whether, in the laws we have included in our own labour code, we are still proceeding in the right direction or whether we have travelled too far.

Although there are many varieties of compulsory membership, in most collective bargaining relationships three forms of association are most common.[2] First, there is the agency shop, known in Canada as the Rand formula, which calls for the payment of union dues. In many jurisdictions, this form of association is required by statute.[3] The second arrangement is known as the union shop, which insists that each worker join the certified union within a specified number of days after being hired. In most enterprises which have been organized, this kind of formal association will be required by the applicable collective agreement. Finally, there is the closed shop, which obliges every person to join the union even before he or she is employed. This is common in a variety of occupational sectors, including construction, entertainment, teaching, and the professions.[4]

Each of these formulations of union security is intended to enhance the bargaining power of the employees as a group.[5] That is their primary and most immediate purpose, although frequently the closed shop serves an additional function of work-sharing as well.[6] To different degrees, each of these rules is intended to provide for a measure of solidarity among those for whom a union has won the right to bargain. Each insists on an increasingly strong commitment between persons who work together. They call for a tighter and tighter association among members of the work group.

In theory, more solidarity and greater cohesion within the association translates into more bargaining power and ultimately a greater capacity for self-government for the group as a whole.[7] The Rand formula, which binds the employees together only by a financial bond, provides the least degree of solidarity of the three. It derives from the idea that many of the benefits secured by unions in the workplace – for example, a safety program, promotion policy, or a grievance system – are "public goods," whose cost should be borne equally by everyone who benefits from their provision. Financial obligations of this type prevent anyone from being a "free rider" and enjoying the benefits of the institution of self-government without meeting their pro rata share of the costs required to sustain it. By ensuring that everyone meets his or her financial responsibilities, rules such as the Rand formula mean the union will have the maximum resources available to discharge the bargaining functions for which it was certified and accorded its law-making powers.

The union and closed shop varieties of union security arrangements go beyond simply insisting on some measure of financial solidarity within the workforce. They create a much tighter association among workers. When a person joins a union, as he or she is required to do under either of these forms of compulsory membership, he or she enters into a set of reciprocal relations with every other person who is a member of that association. Membership in any organization carries with it the responsibility to live up to the rights and obligations that joining with others in a legal organization entails.

In law, people who join unions are taken to have entered a contract with every other member of that association, the terms of which are set out in the constitution of the organization. In this way, as a matter of contract law, joining a union means each person is bound to the terms of the constitution. In the case of most unions, that invariably means members must conform to its decision-making rules which usually provide that on most questions, including whether the workers should go out on strike, the wishes of the majority will prevail. By binding all members to decisions taken by the majority, union security clauses of this kind provide the union with the power to discipline any member who might otherwise be inclined not to accede to the will of the collective.[8] With this socially authorized grant of legal control, unions are effectively able to ensure that the "strikebreaker" (who by endeavouring to secure the gains of collective bargaining without paying the costs of withholding her labour is "free-riding" in a different way), is made to respect the decisions of the majority so that the solidarity and bargaining power of the group is protected from dissension and division.

So described, there should be little doubt that collective bargaining statutes which specify or authorize[9] such legal rules are pursuing constitutionally valid objectives. Union security rules serve the same constitutional values as those which underlie all of the other major principles in our labour code. Like fair employment laws, or legislated standards of wages and hours, solidarity is an objective which, in addition to its expected utilitarian accomplishments,[10] endeavours to promote our constitutional commitment to respect the equal autonomy of each individual in important and vital ways.[11] By requiring employees to act collectively, union security arrangements foster an equality of participation in the rule-making processes both between employers and their employees, as well as between the individual members of the workforce themselves.

With respect to the relationship between employers and employees, everyone agrees that union security rules try to ensure that workers can form effective associations with those with whom they work so that they can have a bigger say in the decision-making processes governing their workplace. Leaving aside the question of means, there can be no doubt of the constitutional validity of that purpose. If workers were not constrained to act in unison, some of them would not be able to participate at all in the formulation of their terms and conditions of employment and the ability of others would be substantially diminished. Without some legal protection of the solidarity ethic, the (positive) freedom of a large number of workers to form associations and to bargain collectively would be substantially impaired. The history of employment regulation that we followed in Part One teaches us that unless employees act collectively as a group their opportunity to participate meaningfully in the negotiation of the detailed terms and conditions of work may be effectively denied.

In addition to equalizing the opportunity of workers to participate in the rule-making process with their employers, rules of compulsory association promote an equality between workers themselves. As the "exit-voice" analysis developed by Hirschman and applied by Freeman and Medhoff so clearly illuminates, rules requiring some commitment to processes of collective decision-making ensure that the goals of each worker are weighed more equally because the union typically formulates an "average preference" when it tables its position in negotiations.[12] Such rules contrast sharply with those which govern the settlement of individual contracts between an employer and each of its employees. Under the latter regime, the preferences of the marginal worker, who is generally a younger and more mobile member of the workforce, are afforded a disproportionate weight because of his enhanced opportunities of exit. By contrast, rules of compulsory membership will make it more likely that the voice of the older, less mobile worker will be listened to as well. Rules promoting collective decision-making are therefore fairer in that they weigh each worker's interests more equally and in that sense must be constitutionally preferred.[13]

So, like most of the other pieces of our labour code that we have considered, rules dealing with union security are quite consistent with the language and underlying theory of the Charter, at least in the purpose they advance. Nevertheless, as with several of our earlier examples, a serious question remains as to whether any or all of these union security rules can be characterized as reasonable means of accomplishing their objectives. Here again, there is a valid concern whether the means are proportional to the ends. The difficulty is that, prima facie, each of these rules substantially limits, if not denies, the freedom of individuals to associate with unions of their choice. Each seems to involve a particularly flagrant violation of s.2(d) of the Charter.[14] Indeed, it is difficult to imagine a more straightforward violation of our constitutional entitlements. There is no way to avoid the fact that union security provisions, like the union and closed shops, force people to take out membership in specific organizations against their will.[15] The freedom of workers who for political, social, or economic reasons[16] do not want to join a particular union is seriously compromised by the legal enforceability of such rules.

Some might be tempted to resist this conclusion by claiming that laws which authorize compulsory membership in unions do not violate our constitutional rights because they do not interfere with a person's "positive" right to form and join associations as he or she may choose.[17] At most it might be said that compulsory membership rules violate a person's "negative" freedom to remain apart from associations to which she or he does not want to belong. That, it would be argued, is not the subject of a constitutional guarantee. Pointing to the text of the Charter itself, it might be claimed that the Charter only protects a person's freedom "of" not "from" association.

Even if such a challenge initially strikes one as plausible, on reflection, it does not seem likely it will proceed very far. In the first place, to read the Charter as protecting a person's positive freedom to form associations but not the negative freedom to remain apart from an organization to which she or he does not want to belong would be fundamentally at odds with our understanding of the concept of rights. It is now conventional wisdom that all conceptions of freedom, including both the positive and negative, are based on a single concept of triadic relations.[18] Moreover, even for those who cling to the earlier distinction between these two faces of freedom, it was the negative not the positive one which was the primary concern of constitutional guarantees in liberal democratic societies.[19]

Even more fatally, to adopt such an interpretation of freedom of association would be both incoherent and inconsistent with the larger legal environment of which it would be a part. Interpreting s.2(d) of the Charter in such a way would be incoherent because, in a liberal democratic state which we profess to be, freedom "of" association must necessarily imply freedom "from" compulsory membership as well.[20]

The logic is unavoidable.[21] Like all of the rights and freedoms we have now entrenched in our constitution, freedom of association finds its place in the Charter because of its close connection with the more basic political ideal of equality of liberty. De Tocqueville made the point when he wrote that "the most natural right of man, after that of acting on his own, is that of combining his efforts with those of his fellows and acting together."[22] For de Tocqueville and most committed democrats, freedom of association is an important means of protection against the tyranny of the majority, regardless of whether the majority's will was fixing the rules that govern relations in the workplace or in society at large. Intermediate associations such as unions are widely recognized as enhancing the opportunities for self-development while simultaneously acting as a buffer between the individual and the state.[23] Without a constitutional commitment to freedom of association it would be meaningless to speak of the liberty of an individual to organize her life and to maximize her opportunities for self-realization in the manner she chooses. People are not free to govern their lives by their own lights if they are either unable to join with others whose objects and methods are the same as their own or if they are required to join with people whose views and purposes they do not share. Freedom of association in the Canadian context can only be understood as embracing a full, robust, "bilateral" liberty which recognizes the individual's full freedom of choice. To protect one aspect of this freedom but deny the other would be a logical inconsistency of the most glaring and arbitrary kind.

This principle has not proven troublesome for most of those who have considered it. Similar entitlements providing for freedom of association in the Austrian, French, Irish, Indian, Italian, Spanish, and West German constitutions,[24] as well as in the European Convention on Human Rights, have been interpreted in this manner. Freedom of association and the liberty of the individual are seen to be restricted as much by a provision that requires people to join associations to which they do not want to belong as when they are prevented from forming associations of their own choosing. In parsing the meaning of a constitutional guarantee in the Irish constitution which was phrased even more explicitly in terms of a freedom to form associations, one of the judges who considered the constitutionality of a closed shop provision put the matter in the following way:

What the State guarantees is "liberty" for the exercise of the right of the citizens to form associations and unions. If it is a "liberty" that is guaranteed that means that the citizen is "free" to form, and I think that must include join, such associations and unions, and, if he is free to do so, that obviously does not mean he must form or join associations and unions but that he may if he so will.[25]

The concurring opinion of a majority of the judges who considered the parallel issue under the European Convention on Human Rights, in the British closed shop case, made the same point even more succinctly. In their judgment, "the negative aspect of freedom of association is necessarily complementary to and correlative of and inseparable from its positive aspect."[26] Even the United States Supreme Court, working without an explicit constitutional guarantee, has recognized that the compulsory payment of union dues has a detrimental impact on an employee's constitutional right of non-association.[27]

For many people, including most trade unionists, in addition to being incoherent, it would be grossly inconsistent to argue freedom of association does not imply freedom from coerced membership as well. For those who believe that workers' freedom to form associations of their own choosing implies an obligation on the part of the state to enact legislation to protect that constitutional guarantee from interference by employers,[28] then as a matter of consistency such persons should also insist legislatures be equally sensitive to encroachments on this freedom by a worker's fellow employees. While some may be uncomfortable with the logic of the conclusion,[29] a law enacted by a legislature which empowers some employees to compel others to join an association against their will is just as offensive to a person's freedom of association as rules imposed by employers which interfere with the ability of their employees to form unions of their own choosing.[30] If a legislature is prepared to prohibit the closed, *non-union* shop by rendering unlawful yellow dog contracts, the constitutional constraint of consistency (that is, equality) requires it to outlaw the closed *union* shop as well.[31] Respecting the freedom of association of unionists and non-unionists equally demands freedom of choice for both.

Once again, then, we find ourselves on familiar terrain. As with so much of the labour code we have analysed, the constitutional integrity of union security rules can be reduced to a conflict of rights. One group of employees asserts a positive right to form associations so they can participate meaningfully in the processes which control such important aspects of their lives. Other workers claim the freedom to associate only with those with whom they choose to join. In these circumstances, supporters of legal rules which compel association with particular unions can try and salvage their position in exactly the same way as defenders of every other aspect of the status quo have tried to respond. They can argue that even if union security rules do involve a limitation of the constitutional guarantees of some individuals, they are reasonable restrictions within the meaning of s.1.

In the case of union security arrangements of the financial kind, like the agency shop, there does seem to be a principled basis on which such a claim can be sustained. Requiring everyone who is protected by and enjoys the benefits of a public system of decision-making to bear their pro rata share of its cost is implicit in the act of joining a common enterprise. If legislatures are entitled to assign certain legislative and judicial functions to agents such as unions, principles of equality and unjust enrichment make it imperative that the related costs associated with the various institutions of collective self-government be distributed fairly among those who will benefit from them. In the same way that each of us must pay taxes to defray the costs associated with the formulation and administration of the law which guarantees our freedom and security in society at large, so in the places we work each of us must pay our fair share of the costs of the processes of industrial self-government through which our equality of liberty is recognized and preserved.[32] Even on a minimalist, "night watchman" theory of law and social organization, being a member of an industrial community or civil society carries with it the obligation to contribute one's proportionate share to the cost associated with maintaining that degree of peace and order essential to the continuation of the community itself.[33] For all workers, a safe working environment, fair processes of promotion and discipline, monitoring systems to ensure compliance with the rules, and access to independent tribunals to resolve disputes when the rules are violated or unclear are necessary conditions of being and remaining in control of one's career. Everyone, therefore, must share in the cost. Although coercing an individual to make a contribution to an association she wants no part of is clearly a limitation of her freedom of choice, it is one which is predicated on the same values as the freedom of association itself.

So the constraint imposed on a person's freedom of association by the financial obligation to pay dues to a union is another limitation which can be justified in a free and democratic society. Though they infringe on some peoples' freedom to associate, these "solidarity contributions" do so to respect the equal freedom of others. And they do so in the least intrusive way possible. Certainly the constraint imposed by the other members of the group is not very strong. It demands only accepting financial responsibility for one's proportionate share of the cost of establishing legal order and the rule of law in an enterprise. Given the close connection that exists between constitutional values and union security rules of this least restricted kind, it will not be surprising that in other free and democratic societies, including Belgium, the Netherlands, and Switzerland[34] as well as the United States, the limit on a person's freedom of association that is implied by the agency fee has been recognized to be constitutionally justified.

Nevertheless, it is implicit in this justification that there are limits on both the amount of dues a union can levy and the purposes for which such monies can be spent. Just as we saw in the case of workers who are employed on family farms, the purposes of any legal rule or policy will constrain the means that can be chosen to realize those objectives. Given the purposes that unions and union security rules are meant to serve, the coercion that is entailed in compulsory dues must be limited to the preservation and enhancement of the collective processes of industrial self-government. That is the ultimate object for which legislatures have allowed workers to act collectively. Unions can therefore only demand dues from those who fall within their jurisdiction as delegated by the legislature and then only to defray the costs which are "reasonably related" to that purpose.[35]

Justifying the first part of this claim need not detain us long. We have already encountered the idea that industrial self-government is the overriding objective of any system of collective labour relations. On any reading of the conventional collective bargaining acts in North America, the legislative objective is to foster the creation, maintenance, and flourishing of a system in which most of the rules on which people will be employed in an enterprise will be settled by negotiations between employers and their employees acting collectively. Unfair labour practice sections endeavour to provide protection to workers against employers who might otherwise try to bribe or coerce them to reject this method of governing their workplace. Certification sections set up the legal infrastructure through which the process will operate. Bargaining and strike provisions regulate the range of permissible conduct during the rule-making process and the arbitration codes provide an internal system of adjudication and dispute resolution which is expected to develop its own "common law of the shop."

Union dues are an integral part of this system of government. They are a legitimate means to fairly and fully secure the financial resources which are required to sustain the various institutions and processes which characterize this model of collective decision-making. To retain their constitutional pedigree, however, they cannot interfere with the rights and freedoms of those they constrain beyond what is necessary to accomplish those ends. They cannot be drawn in a way which is unnecessarily invasive of the rights and freedoms of those they bind. In language we have already seen the Supreme Court adopt, union dues, like any other part of our labour code, must be "proportional" to their ends.

Determining which activities and institutions fall within and which go beyond the objectives of industrial government will be a task our courts will, and indeed already have, begun to discharge. At one end of the spectrum, it seems clear that the costs for which unions could demand contributions would not be restricted to those which were incurred at the workplace. Union dues should not be limited to merely covering collective bargaining and contract administration activities.[36] Since so much of our labour code is fixed by the legislature, union lobbying activities can be justified as bearing directly on the rules and regulations under which those they have been empowered to represent must work. Government initiatives on manpower, unemployment, incomes, and overtime policy directly affect the processes and products (rules, terms and conditions of employment) of industrial government and so fall within the mandate that our system of collective labour relations delegates to unions and employers to supervise.

At the other end of the spectrum, it seems equally clear that unions could not validly insist on the financial support of those it represents for a social or political cause, such as the recognition of an independent state of Palestine, which bears no reasonable relation to the legislature's purposes of conferring legal status on trade unions.[37] Causes such as that do nothing to promote the participatory objectives legislators have in mind when they empower unions to represent workers collectively in their relations with those who employ them.

In distinguishing between those activities which fall within, and those which go beyond, the permissible encroachment on a person's freedom of association, courts will be engaged in a traditional line-drawing exercise. It would take us too far from our purposes to explore this matter in any detail here, and in any event the experience of the American courts would seem directly relevant to our own. American jurisprudence will not always be helpful in evaluating the constitutional integrity of different aspects of our labour code. Here, however, and even though union security rules have been analysed as an infringement of the first amendment's guarantee of freedom of speech, American constitutional laws can provide some guide to the competing arguments which are likely to be made.[38] For our purposes it is sufficient to observe that the compulsory payment of dues to a union can be demonstrably justified in a free and democratic society when the money is used to defray the costs of a legal system which, on the historical record at least, seems necessary to protect and preserve the equal autonomy of workers. There is simply no alternative available to a legislature to accomplish such constitutionally valid objectives in a way which would constrain individual freedom less.

There are some, however, who have argued that this conclusion is quite wrong because it discriminates unfairly against unions.[39] The claim is that in all sorts of circumstances each of us, as an individual consumer, shareholder, or member of a professional association, is frequently required to deal with one of a very limited number of institutions (banks, insurance companies, universities, telephone and utility companies, self-governing associations) who can use the money we pay or invest for causes to which we object. Indeed, this may happen to all of us when government spends resources collected from our taxes. It is conceivable the government could spend our taxes on exactly the same cause as the one we said was beyond the union's authority. In the face of this widespread practice in our community of allowing those institutions and associations to spend money in ways to which an individual contributor might object, the argument of equality is that unions should be allowed to exercise their associational autonomy just as freely and effectively.

In principle, the argument is a strong one. In theory, there is a parallel between the contributions consumers and shareholders make to corporations, or taxpayers make to government, and those contributions individual workers are required to make to unions. But in practice it does not support a charge of discrimination. When it is applied properly, the analogy does not lead to the conclusion that the situation of the dues-payer and those of the shareholder/consumer/taxpayer are treated unequally. Corporations and government have a wider authority than unions to spend the resources they collect because of the differences in the nature of the association to which each of their contributors consents and/or is legitimately compelled to belong.

The principle which governs all of these cases is that whenever a legal entity, such as a corporation or union, validly receives sums of money, whether by the consent of the individual (in the case of the shareholder or consumer of private corporations) or the force of law[40] (in the case of the taxpayer, dues-payer or consumer of some monopolistic utility), it is obliged to limit its use of those resources to those objects which justified the societal recognition of its legal status. In the case of the unions, as we have seen, the relevant objects for which unions were granted the legal authority to claim a financial contribution from those it represents relate to their mandate to collectively represent the general interests of workers in the processes under which they are employed. In the case of corporations and governments, the objects for which their legal status was established are much broader and more malleable. That, it turns out, is the crucial distinction which leads to the results some find so discriminatory and unfair.[41]

With respect to the legal status of corporations, it is generally recognized that those with the authority to direct and manage an enterprise have a mandate to pursue any activity which will further the economic well-being of the company.[42] Within such a broad legal mandate, political contributions are accepted as an inevitable part of doing business in our community. Thus, when a shareholder invests in an enterprise he implicitly, if not explicitly, consents to such expenditures being made which will further the purposes for which the corporation was formed – the making of profits. Because of the broad economic purposes for which corporations were given legal status, they will enjoy a very wide spending authority. And the same is even more true, of course, in the case of governments spending the taxes of its citizens. In their case it would seem that the objects for which governments might spend taxes are virtually unlimited. Even the principle of ultra vires in the federalism jurisprudence of our constitutional law seems powerless to constrain how a government chooses to spend the money it legitimately collects.[43]

It is important however to recognize that this is not literally the case. All laws, including those (constitutions) by which governments are formed, have purposes which will constrain the uses to which enforced contributions can be put. Consider the validity of a proposal by the present federal government to enact a law requiring a portion of our taxes to be given over to the political party it represents. Such a law would plainly violate the freedom of association of those who wanted nothing to do with (to be free from) the Tories. The political associations (countries, provinces, towns) to which by our presence we all consent to belong, do not carry with them the authorization to compel association with a particular ideology or political creed. Though we can be compelled to accept responsibility for our proper share of the cost of the legal and political system on which all of our rights and freedoms depend, we cannot be coerced to associate more intimately by paying allegiance, even if only financially, to causes which are beyond the competence of the state to control.

The significance of this example, of course, goes beyond showing how governments and corporations, as well as unions, are limited in the activities for which they can legitimately tithe the persons they have been given the legal authority to represent. More importantly, they show how the taxpayer analogy can easily be misapplied. The analogy can succeed when limited to activities that are reasonably related to the interests of workers in the rules and processes which govern their lives at work. But when unions put forward the claim that they have an unfettered authority to demand and spend the resources of those they have acquired the legal authority to represent, they are trying to justify the same kinds of acts of coercion that we would want to deny to any Conservative or Liberal or New Democrat government. They would be demanding an allegiance to an association stronger than their purposes require and their legal status would allow. To return to the language of our two principles of constitutional review, a law which recognized unions' having an unlimited authority to spend the money of those they represent would not be the least drastic means to realize the objectives legislatures have empowered unions to pursue.[44] Such a rule would be badly overdrawn.

We should now have a sufficiently clear idea of the way in which the Rand formula must be drawn in order for it to be integrated into a constitutional labour code. However, it is likely that this will represent the extent of the limitation or infringement on a person's freedom of association that will be permissible under the Charter. In the case of the two other stricter forms of union security, where the only social objective which the legislature is pursuing is preserving the bargaining power and participation of the employees,[45] there are alternative means available which can accomplish that purpose in a manner which interferes less with the freedom of workers to associate with whomever they please.

For example, instead of rules authorizing the closed and/or union shop, a legislature could simply prohibit all employees from working and/or from being paid during the currency of a strike which had been authorized by a majority of the collectivity. Alternatively, and more broadly, it might enact strike-breaking legislation of a more general kind. The first alternative has already been adopted by the legislature in Ontario, in legislation governing community college teachers.[46] The latter alternative is the means that was chosen by the legislative assembly in Quebec.[47] Either of these policy initiatives promote the same degree of solidarity among the relevant groups of employees as either the union and the closed shop, and both do so in a way which interfere less with the freedom of those who object to associating with their fellow employees in any particular union organization. Although they would be bound by the decision of the majority on the issue of withdrawing their labour, workers would remain free of that association on any other resolution such organizations typically might take. In effect, strike-breaking laws parallel the agency shop rule in offering a less restrictive form of coerced association. Rather than forcing membership and personal identification in a particular organization and the causes it supports, strike-breaking legislation requires those who would benefit financially from a strike to pay their proportional share of the costs that were expended in securing the benefits. In the same way that the Rand formula insists everyone pay their proportionate share of the costs of their system of industrial government, legislation of this type denies workers benefits they do not deserve.

On the interpretation of the Charter we have adhered to throughout, the availability and practicability of both these alternative policy instruments is a sufficient basis on which courts could legitimately require legislatures to pursue their objectives in a more focused fashion. To validate union or closed shop rules in the face of these alternate laws against strike-breaking would be the kind of needless restriction on rights and freedoms which our Charter no longer allows us to tolerate.

Perhaps we have gone on at greater length than is required to establish what is now taken for granted in most free and democratic industrial societies – that closed and union shop rules violate a commitment to equality in our opportunities for personal self-government. Indeed, I realize that there is a danger that for some the conclusion we have come to will seem surprising and even at odds with my thesis that the Charter should be seen as a powerful instrument of social justice in the hands of the least advantaged members of the working class. It may seem puzzling how a conclusion which strikes down the most effective variations of union security provisions, for which trade unions have fought bitterly over the course of the past two hundred years, could be seen as advancing their cause. Even if the result secures a greater degree of freedom of association in our society, this conclusion seems to have a vague and muffled ring of anti-unionism to it.

Such a reaction would be unfortunate. It would be wrong both as a matter of fact and as a matter of justice, and it would misconceive the purpose to which this example was put. As a matter of fact, there is simply no basis for the conclusion that union security arrangements of this kind are essential to the strength and power of any union movement. The vitality of the labour movements in western European societies is conclusive evidence to the contrary. Their example confirms that there are other principles and institutions which can preserve the solidarity of the workforce without sacrificing the freedom of workers to belong only to unions of their choice.

Moreover, to characterize the invalidation of these union security arrangements as antagonistic to the interests of workers reveals a fundamental misconception of the meaning of justice in a society which is "free and democratic." It fails to take seriously the maximization of principle, which requires legislators to pursue an objective such as worker solidarity in a way which will enhance the freedom of people in their community to the greatest degree possible. In the face of alternative means by which the same degree of worker solidarity can be achieved, continued commitment to union and closed shop union rules is a commitment for less freedom and justice overall.

So, as a matter of fact and of justice, it is inappropriate to view invalidation of these stronger forms of union security, and their replacement by legislation which constrains the rights of others to work during a strike, as a blow against the interests of the working classes. However, it is also true that holding these stronger forms of union security to be constitutionally invalid will not dramatically improve the lives of the least advantaged workers in our society. At best it will preserve the power of workers as a group, while allowing those who wish to abstain from joining a particular association to do so.

But here it must be remembered it was not my immediate purpose in raising this example to display the full strength of the Charter as an instrument of social justice in the hands of the disadvantaged. Our objective was to focus on the method, not the result, of the analysis. Our ambition was to rehearse the principles of constitutional interpretation with which we have been working one last time on an issue which, while hardly peripheral, is not vital to the system of collective bargaining as a whole.

We have now accomplished that purpose. The example of union security rules has allowed us to see again how the courts, with the constitution, can ensure that our legislators are as sensitive to peoples' equal right to make their own decisions and choices about their lives as they possibly can. With the coherence of our principles confirmed one last time, we can now return to the closely related principle of exclusivity. It is here where we will see the force of the Charter, as an instrument of social justice for the working class as a whole, and especially for the worst-off individuals in this group, work its most dramatic effects.

PART FOUR

Industrial Democracy and the Principle of Collective Representation

Everything that is really great and inspiring is created by individuals who can labour in freedom.
Albert Einstein

THIRTEEN

A Constitutional Conversation: The Challenge

A. EXCLUSIVE REPRESENTATION AND FREEDOM OF ASSOCIATION

The principle of exclusive representation, it will be recalled, stipulates that whenever a majority of a group of workers which is appropriate to associate together for collective bargaining purposes chooses a union to represent them, that union becomes the exclusive bargaining agent for all the workers in the group. By virtue of this principle, it is unlawful for an employer to negotiate with any other union, association, or individual unless the union so certified consents to such arrangements. All dealings between an employer and employee in all aspects of their relationship – in the bargaining for as well as in the administration of the collective agreement – must be conducted through the union which has been designated by the majority to be the exclusive representative of the group.

After the analysis we have just undertaken of union security rules, it should be clear how easily a challenge could be mounted to demonstrate that, prima facie, the exclusivity principle fundamentally impairs people's freedom to associate. The analysis in both cases is substantially, though not exactly, the same. If anything, because there can be no question that this principle is the product of the state action,[1] the argument is even more straightforward. In addition, whereas union security rules violate only the negative aspect of a person's freedom of association, exclusivity offends the freedom of those who do not want to join the certified union in two separate ways. In the first place, those workers who voted against the union chosen by the majority will not be able to limit their membership to associations to which they choose to belong.[2] Their "positive" freedom to form associations only with workers who share a particular skill or trade (for example, law or nursing), or a specific philosophy (for example, social democrat or Christian), or theory of dispute resolution (for example, strike or arbitration) will have been drastically curtailed. Physiotherapists (though, interestingly, not nurses,[3] to take a topical Canadian example) are not free to associate in unions with those of similar training to pursue common occupational objectives. Because the principle of exclusive representation requires the interest of every employee to be represented through the union which has been certified, the most important – indeed, the only – reason these employees would have to form associations with those who have a common skill or philosophy will have been lost. Every other association formed by these employees would be prohibited from performing the very legislative and adjudicative functions such organizations are intended to discharge. In these circumstances, to advance the claim that there was nothing in law which constrained the "freedom" of such persons to organize into such groups would be disingenuous in the extreme.

The European Court of Human Rights certainly recognized this point when it considered the legal status of the closed shop. In its view, "An individual does not enjoy the right of freedom of association if in reality the freedom of action or choice which remains available to him is either non-existent or so reduced as to be of no practical value."[4] Similarly, if the Ontario Divisional Court was correct in its decision in *Broadway Manor Nursing Home* that the Inflation Restraint Act was unconstitutional because it denied workers the freedom to choose a union that would be recognized by their employer, the principle of exclusive representation must fall as well.[5] Both pieces of legislation circumscribe the freedom of individuals to choose the particular organization they believe will most effectively promote their vocational goals in a process of collective decision-making. Indeed, because of its more enduring effect, the principle of exclusivity is a more serious restriction on workers' freedom to choose their own union than the temporary restriction imposed by the Inflation Restraint Act. Practically speaking, the exclusivity principle restrains the freedom of workers to form associations of their own choosing just as effectively as if it denied workers the opportunity to join any other union except that chosen by the majority.[6]

But it is not just the case that the freedom of workers to form their associations has been effectively compromised. As a practical matter, for Canadian workers to secure the "benefit" of and be "protected" by our system of collective industrial relations, they will be required to join the association which has been designated their exclusive representative. Their freedom to remain apart from associations which they do not want to join will also have been compromised. Exclusivity compromises the "negative" as well as the "positive" aspect of their freedom of association.[7]

If a worker wants to participate in the formulation and administration of the rules which will govern how she can realize her occupational objectives, the principle of exclusive representation requires her to join the association which has been granted this decision-making monopoly by the state. Because the principle makes the union chosen by the majority of workers the exclusive agent for all dealings between employers and their employees, a worker must join that particular union to be able to participate in the collective processes of industrial government. Practically speaking she has no other choice. To say that a person must give up the benefits of participation and personal self-government that the legislation is intended to promote, unless she joins an association which may be antagonistic to her beliefs, entails a degree of coercion which is no different to the imposition of a fine.[8] If the worker insists on her freedom to remain outside that organization she cannot, by definition, have any further involvement in the decision-making processes except in trivial and peripheral ways. If the parallel principle were applied to the rule-making processes of our society at large, it would mean all opposition members in Parliament would have to take out membership in the governing party if they wished to have any further involvement in the legislative and executive processes of government.[9]

How exclusivity interferes more with workers' freedom to organize associations of their own choosing than union security rules can be described in another way. In our analysis of the latter we commented on how a person's freedom of association is curtailed when an employer insists a worker sign a "yellow-dog" contract in which she agrees not to join any union at all.[10] Laws which validate principles of exclusive representation and yellow-dog contracts are similar in one respect. While the person doing the coercing obviously differs, each of these rules denies employees the freedom to control their own development by inhibiting their ability to form associations with other workers to pursue common occupational objectives. Both of these legal rules constrain workers' rights to determine for themselves the associations through which they will participate in the decision-making process in the places they work.

Exclusivity, however, interferes with a person's freedom of association in a separate and more coercive way. As we have just seen, not only does exclusivity deny the worker the right to form associations of her own making, it effectively constrains her to join an association to which she may not want to belong. With exclusivity, freedom of non-association is rendered illusory as well. In this negative sense, exclusivity is like the stronger forms of union security we considered at the end of the last part. It does even more violence to an individual's freedom of association than the traditional forms of employer interference, like the yellow-dog contract, which have long been accepted as being illegitimate invasions of workers' freedom of choice.

Even though it is clear that the principle of exclusive representation compromises the freedom of large numbers of employees, we know from our analysis in Part Three that this fact will not determine whether this feature of our labour code will pass constitutional scrutiny. Simply pointing out that a legal rule infringes the rights and freedoms of some members of the community does not bring a constitutional conversation to a close. As we have seen so often, rights collide and on such occasions, some aspects of those rights will have to give way.

It is to be expected that many of those who have a vested interest in the retention of the principle of exclusive representation will argue that this is one of those occasions. Their argument will be, as it was for all forms of union security,[11] that exclusivity is essential for the ethic of solidarity to have any effect. They will say it is needed to ensure workers are not hopelessly and helplessly divided. They will claim that exclusivity keeps workers sufficiently united so that each of them can have some meaningful opportunity to participate in the settlement of the rules which will control their working lives.

Defenders of the principle of exclusive representation will argue that, whatever the limitations imposed on the rights and freedoms of those who do not want to join the certified union, these are justified by the protection it affords to the freedom of those who do. In the language of the competing freedoms we used to consider the different conceptions of union security, defenders of the faith will claim that the positive freedom of the majority of employees to form associations of their own choosing justifies overriding the negative freedom of the minority to remain free of an association to which they do not want to belong.

This rejoinder should have the same effect here as it did in defending the different conceptions of union security. Certainly, for the reasons we canvassed at the end of Part Three, it is difficult to imagine a court holding that legislators cannot pursue such an objective through a system of collective labour relations. Canadian legislators have manifested a long-standing commitment to the ethic of solidarity on the ground that it furthers our constitutional commitment to equality. Solidarity promotes an equality in liberty and personal self-government in two quite separate ways. First, by protecting the equal right of employees to form associations with those with whom they work, it ensures that large numbers of individuals will be able to participate more equally with their employer in setting their terms and conditions of employment. Exclusivity will allow employees to have more control over the direction their lives will take. Secondly, drawing on the "exit-voice" analysis developed by Hirschman, and applied by Freeman and Medhoff, it can be said that solidarity also equalizes the extent to which each worker participates in the processes of industrial government by making the average, rather than the marginal, worker the effective criterion of decision.[12] To the extent exclusivity imposes limits on some workers' freedom to associate, it does so to further the same values and objectives which underlie freedom of association itself.

To support their claim that the exclusivity principle is a reasonable limitation on the freedom of association of dissident workers, advocates can be expected to turn to two independent and highly influential sources of authority. First, they will likely point to an international "jurisprudence" in which the compatibility between exclusivity and freedom of association is a conclusion of long standing. According to the International Labour Organization's Committee on Freedom of Association and its Committee of Experts, freedom of association in the workplace, which is protected by Convention 87, is "not necessarily" offended by the principle of exclusivity.[13] Secondly, defenders of the existing regime will likely point out that American constitutional law has considered this same question on several occasions and it has always come to the conclusion that the exclusivity principle is a constitutional rule of their labour law. Indeed, the Americans have endorsed this conclusion even though they recognize exclusivity necessarily compromises the freedom of association that is implicitly guaranteed by the First Amendment to the American Constitution.[14]

With supporting authority of that pedigree, the claim that the exclusivity principle is a reasonable limitation on the freedom of association of Canadian workers seems a strong and compelling one. If the major international agency charged with supervising the freedom of workers to associate in organizations for their own protection concludes that exclusivity is "not necessarily inconsistent" with its governing instrument on the subject, that strongly suggests that this principle can be demonstrably justified as reasonable constraint in our community as well. Similarly, if the country whose labour laws, liberal democratic heritage, and social and economic environment are so comparable to our own concludes that this principle can be reconciled with its constitutional commitment to freedom of association, that might be thought to be conclusive evidence of its integrity in Canada as well.

On closer analysis, however, it turns out that neither of these references provides any authority for Canadian courts to conclude that the principle of exclusivity is consistent with or can be justified as a reasonable limit on the freedom of workers to associate with whomever they chose. In the case of the determinations made by the relevant committees of the ILO, their rulings do not, as we shall see, even address the challenge of workers who claim exclusivity violates their constitutional rights to associate only with employees of their own choosing. For both historical and organizational reasons the ILO has never even considered the constitutional challenge that exclusivity violates a person's freedom of association in the sense we have described. In the case of the American authorities, while they ultimately recognized that the principle does infringe on the freedom of workers to associate with whomever they please, they justified that limitation in a way which will not satisfy Canadian courts if they adhere to the analysis we have been following. For the American Supreme Court to uphold the constitutionality of the exclusivity principle, it was sufficient to find that it protected legitimate congressional objectives such as eliminating free riders and securing the necessary degree of solidarity within the workforce. In none of the cases in which it considered the issue did it ever ask whether those objectives could be achieved in a way which derogated less from their constitutional guarantees.[15]

Neither of these conclusions will be self-evident and each requires some elaboration. It will, I think, facilitate our analysis to consider first the reasons why the experience and the decisions of the ILO are not relevant to the resolution of this question in the Canadian context. The explanation here is straightforward and easy to summarize. Quite simply, the commitment to freedom of association in Convention 87 and in our Charter of Rights refer to two entirely different conceptions of this state of human affairs.[16] The fact that exclusivity can be reconciled with the meaning it takes on in the former says nothing about whether it can meet the definition of the latter.

In the Canadian context, there is nothing to suggest that freedom of association has some special industrial relations meaning.[17] In addition to the very general character of the Charter itself, all the discussions leading up to its entrenchment indicate the federal government did not want to single out collective bargaining, and associations of individuals at the workplace, for fear of diminishing all other forms of association.[18] Freedom of association means the same thing regardless of whether the individual is engaged with others in a workplace or in other social spheres in which he or she interacts. It has the same triadic definition regardless of the nature and objects the association may have.

By contrast, even the most casual perusal of the relevant decisions and literature of the ILO makes it clear that the guarantee of freedom of association that is contained in Convention 87 has a very special, and especially narrow, meaning. Both the history leading up to the adoption of Convention 87,[19] and the detailed language of its text, make it plain that the freedom workers were guaranteed to form their own associations did not include protection against restraints that might be effected by their fellow employees. Rather, Convention 87 insulated workers' freedom to form their own associations only against interference by government and by employers/consumers of their labour.[20]

On this definition, exclusivity is not regarded as being inconsistent with the freedom of workers to form associations of their own choosing precisely because it does not "necessarily" imply excessive governmental or employer control. If certain safeguards concerning the selection and certification of the exclusive representative are maintained, the exclusivity principle will be consistent with the workers' right to form their own associations free from governmental control. Once those guarantees – pertaining to the independence of the certifying agency and the integrity of the employees' choice – are secured, exclusivity would not be regarded as a technique by which governments could dominate workers' associations. With those safeguards in place, the ILO is prepared to recognize organizations designated by state agencies as the exclusive representatives of workers as products of the employees' "own choosing," rather than of the government's imposition or of an employer's manipulation.

Now, it still might strike some as being foolhardy or even arrogant to dismiss the conclusions of an organization charged with establishing and administering international standards on the freedom of workers to organize in associations of their own choosing. If that definition was sufficient for the purposes of the world community, why should Canadian courts impose a different conception of their own? Why wouldn't it be reasonable for Canadian legislators to adopt the definition embraced by an international agency whose expertise and integrity are recognized by all?

There are several answers that might be given to respond to this concern. First, and as the history leading up to the adoption of Convention 87 clearly suggests, it could be explained that it was in large part owing to the political context and structural organization within which the ILO is constrained to operate that such a cramped definition of freedom of association was adopted. The conception of freedom of association recognized by the ILO has never been defended on its merits. Operating in a political context much more fractured and diverse than our own, and within a tripartite[21] organizational structure which had no constituency strongly committed to any other definition, it is hardly surprising that the ILO's commitment to freedom of association is as partial and shallow as it is. Indeed, the failure of the ILO to protect workers from all forms of coerced membership whatever their source provides yet another example of how, even in the international arena, imperfections in the structures and forums of politics can seriously compromise the integrity of the rules they adopt.

Secondly, it would hardly be unique if our courts held Canadian legislators to a more rigorous standard than one on which the international community, acting collectively, has agreed. This happens all the time. There are many countries in western Europe for whom the meaning of freedom of association in Convention 87 does not provide the relevant standard against which its principle of employee representation is defined. Some of these societies have acted in response to the dictates of their own constitutional criteria; others have simply followed the logic that is inherent in the concept itself. Regardless of the motivation, countries as diverse as Austria, Belgium, the Federal Republic of Germany, France, Ireland, Italy, the Netherlands, Norway, and Switzerland all have developed systems regulating relations between employers and employees that either guarantee completely an individual's freedom to belong only to those organizations he or she chooses, or provide for substantially more freedom than the principle of exclusivity allows.[22] All of these societies have developed processes by which employees may be involved in decision-making at their workplaces consistent with the more robust understanding of freedom of association which is part of our constitutional law. For these countries, the ILO convention establishes only minimal conditions of social justice. It does not provide the governing criteria against which their own legal institutions will be measured.

Unable to derive any assistance from the position of the ILO, those who argue the exclusivity principle fits within a constitutional labour code will naturally turn next to American constitutional law to support their claim. As a branch plant operation in so many other aspects of our social organization, it is not unreasonable to suppose that the major organizing principles governing how people will be involved in the decision-making processes at the workplace will also be substantially the same. Given the strong similarities in the liberal democratic theories which underlie both our systems of government, it would be expected that decisions of the United States Supreme Court would have a strong influence on our own constitutional development.

However pertinent this observation may turn out to be, in the particular case we are considering American jurisprudence will not provide much assistance to our courts. To understand why this is so, it should be recognized that, like the ILO decisions of today, initially American constitutional jurisprudence did not consider the question of whether the principle of exclusivity violated a person's freedom of association in the full meaning of that term. It did not consider whether it was legitimate for one group of workers to be able to constrain the freedom of a minority of their fellow employees. Rather, the earliest American cases only dealt with the statutory prohibitions against discriminatory and coercive acts by employers which interfered with the employees' selection of their bargaining representatives. They did not deal directly with the question of whether the selection of an exclusive bargaining agent by itself violated the freedom of association of those it bound. In fact, the first cases were primarily concerned with the limitations which the principle of exclusivity imposed on the employer's freedom of association and ability to manage its business by restricting its opportunity to deal with its employees directly. Indeed, when the Supreme Court first considered the constitutionality of the National Labor Relations Act in *Jones and Laughlin Steel*, it interpreted the concept of exclusive representation in a way that permitted individual employees to continue to negotiate directly with their employers, thus avoiding the issue of freedom of (contractual) association altogether.[23]

It is true that shortly thereafter the Supreme Court abandoned this view. Eventually, it held that exclusivity did preclude virtually all dealings between an employer and its employees except through one exclusive representative chosen by the majority of employees.[24] However, even when it explicitly acknowledged that exclusivity did limit the freedom of association of those who voted against membership in the union that was certified, it did so without considering its constitutional propriety. Rather, in *Steele* v. *Louisville*,[25] the Supreme Court relied on its recognition that a principle like exclusivity granted unions law-making powers over those who did not consent to their jurisdiction, as the basis for implying, out of whole cloth, an obligation on the unions to represent all of those bound by its statutory authority fairly and without discrimination.[26] Rather than considering whether the discriminatory exercise of the law-making powers which had been delegated to unions could offend a worker's constitutional right to equal protection of the laws, the court declared that unions must discharge their public function fairly and without discrimination. It imposed a "duty of fair representation" precisely to avoid the question of whether it was constitutional to give a union the exclusive authority to bargain with the employer and treat minorities in ways that could offend their right to equality and freedom of choice.[27] And that, at least with respect to labour relations legislation in the private sector, has been its position ever since.[28]

The closest the American Supreme Court has come to squarely confronting the constitutional integrity of the principle of exclusivity occurred within the last decade when it was faced with a challenge by a group of school teachers who wanted to remain apart from the union which had been designated as their exclusive representative. Although the Supreme Court was concerned primarily with the con-stitutionality of an agency shop clause which had been negotiated by the union, and with the extent to which compulsory dues interfered with their First Amendment rights of free speech, the court used the occasion to comment on the constitutional validity of the principle of exclusive representation.

In *Abood* v. *Detroit Board of Education*, the United States Supreme Court unequivocally characterized the exclusivity principle as a reasonable limitation on the freedom of association of the teachers who were bound by it. However, a review of that judgment indicates that the Court came to this conclusion for a set of reasons which, if our principles of interpretation are applied, will not be sufficient to resolve the issue in the Canadian context. The essence of its judgment was that considerations of industrial peace, stabilized labour-management relations, and the sharing of costs by those who enjoy the benefits secured by the exclusive representative, justified whatever limitation on workers' rights and freedoms the exclusivity principle entailed. In contrast with the ILO, the American Supreme Court has come to recognize that the principle of exclusivity does entail a serious infringement on the freedom of the minority to join only associations of their own making. However, it has fashioned the same solution as that adopted by the international community, by holding that the labour relations objectives which are furthered by this principle justify the infringements of constitutional freedoms it tolerates.[29]

Although such legislative objectives, especially when they are tempered by a duty of fair representation, may be sufficient to validate the exclusivity principle as a matter of American constitutional law,[30] they will not be sufficient in Canada. For the reasons we have elaborated at length in the last part, in constitutional conversations before Canadian courts it will not be enough for Canadian legislators to justify encroachments on the fundamental freedoms and rights enshrined by the Charter by pointing to the integrity of their objectives.[31] Canadian legislators must also establish that the method they have chosen to realize their objectives meets the principle of reasonable alternative means. As with every other rule in our labour code, our second principle of judicial review will stipulate that if there are other ways of accomplishing such objectives as worker solidarity, the elimination of free riders, equality of participation, and industrial peace and stability which compromise our rights and freedoms less, those alternatives have to be chosen by the legislature to accomplish those purposes.

B. PRINCIPLES OF EMPLOYEE REPRESENTATION IN OTHER FREE AND DEMOCRATIC SOCIETIES

Once one accepts that the means-oriented principle of the reasonable alternative will figure prominently in any analysis of the exclusivity principle, this cornerstone of Canadian industrial relations policy seems especially vulnerable to a constitutional challenge. Quite simply, alternate means abound. As just noted, a large number of very diverse systems of collective labour relations have been developed in such countries as Austria, Belgium, the Federal Republic of Germany, France, Ireland, Italy, the Netherlands, Norway, and Switzerland, using principles of employee representation which either respect an individual's freedom of association completely, or at least provide a good deal more freedom than the exclusivity principle allows. The viable operation of these models of industrial relations presents a decisive argument against the claim that the principle of exclusive representation, even when it is qualified by a duty of fair representation, can be accepted as a reasonable limitation on a worker's freedom of association. To paraphrase one commentator, if each of these free and democratic societies can design systems of collective labour relations without imposing any or much fewer limitations on the freedom of workers to join associations of their own making, it is difficult to argue that a principle like exclusivity is necessary in our own.[32]

For some, what will be most startling about the systems of collective labour relations which the European communities have developed is the diversity in the institutional structures and legal rules which they embrace. If you are not careful you can be dazzled by the detail. Each of the labour codes in operation in western Europe today is, after all, the end point of an evolution as idiosyncratic as the one we followed in Part One. The differences in details between these national systems confirm our earlier observation that a labour code, like any collection of legal norms, is the product of the social, economic, cultural, and technological forces which it is meant to control.

And yet, although in their particulars each of these national systems is unique, on closer examination it can be seen that the rule which governs how the employees' interests will be represented collectively is grounded in one of two broad principles of employee representation. Certainly, the diversity in the specific rules and processes which distinguish each of these labour codes will mean that the nature and extent of their commitment to freedom of association will vary in numerous ways. That said, the fact remains that all of these systems of collective labour relations are based on one of two principles which allow for the workers' interests to be represented collectively in ways which are more respectful of each person's freedom of association than any system which, like our own, relies on the exclusivity rule.

(a) Plural Representation

The industrial relations systems in Belgium, France, Ireland, Norway, and Switzerland all employ variations of a principle we might characterize as plural or multiple representation. According to these models, in order to be able to participate in the various decision-making processes of the workplace an employee must join a union, but she or he is given a choice among several competing unions. How much choice a worker has in selecting a representative through which her or his interests will be protected varies from country to country. Generally, only those unions formally designated by a governmental agency as being "most representative" are able to represent the workers' interests in the various processes of decision-making that may exist at the workplace.[33] So, to participate at all, a worker's freedom of association is limited to one of those unions so designated. In some instances, however, as for example in Switzerland, such governmental accreditation processes do not exist and workers are free to join any association they want and to pursue their interests with their employer through that association.

On this principle, which also has had a long history in European labour relations at the levels of national and industry-wide bargaining, freedom of association is not unfettered. Those who are opposed to joining any trade union as well as those who claim membership in smaller, independent, "less representative" unions, are not able to enjoy the same degree of freedom of association as those who are committed to the more mainstream trade unions. Still, to the extent it offers workers a choice of organizations to which they may belong, it clearly infringes a person's freedom of association less drastically than our own principle of exclusive representation and so would be constitutionally preferred.[34]

The industrial relations systems in operation at the level of the enterprise in these countries parallel closely and compare favourably with the institutions of representative parliamentary democracy we employ to govern our societies at large. By contrast, in major respects the principle of exclusivity mirrors more closely the one party state.[35] In the former, even if a worker is not a member of the governing association (whether a party or union) which commands the support of a majority of the community (whether social or industrial), she is able to remain a member of her own ("most representative") organization *and no other*, and continue to participate fully in the processes and institutions of decision-making. By contrast, in a community (be it political or economic) which vests exclusive and absolute control over the decision-making process in one association (whether party or union), membership in that organization becomes an essential condition for all further possibilities of self-government.

To some, the analogy between the principle of exclusive representation and participation in the wider political processes which govern our society at large may not seem apt. It might be argued that the impairment of a person's freedom of association by the principle of exclusive representation is more properly compared to that of the citizen in a general election who casts a losing vote. But a moment's reflection shows why this parallel is wide of the mark. In analysing how individual workers participate in a system of collective labour relations, our concern is with a person's involvement in the institutions of industrial self-government *after* and not simply *when* they cast their ballots. While it is obvious that in the democratic processes we use to control our social relations in the community at large not everyone casts a winning vote, individuals whose preferences and politics are different from the majority of their neighbours are not compelled to join the party of the successful candidate in order to continue their participation in the processes of government. The process itself retains its pluralistic character. By contrast, in the legislative and adjudicative institutions we currently use to govern social relations in the workplace, only one party is permitted to be involved. No one who voted against and who belongs to a union other than that which secured majority support will be allowed to participate in the decision-making processes unless and until she joins the union to which the state has granted a monopoly in the representation of everyone's interest in the enterprise.

(b) Voluntary Representation

As solicitous as the principle of plural representation may be of the freedom of workers to join only those associations of their own choosing, the second principle of employee representation the other European communities have included in their systems of collective labour relations is even more congenial to this political ideal. We might characterize this principle as purely voluntary or consensual representation. It ensures that every worker, regardless of her union affiliation, is equally entitled to vote for, be represented on and/or elected to, the institution through which the interests of workers must be expressed collectively. In the systems of collective labour relations in these countries, which include Austria, Italy, the Netherlands, and the Federal Republic of Germany, the freedom of association of those individuals who do not want to join any formal association (to remain and/or run as independents as it were), is guaranteed. So is the freedom of those whose religious, political, or nationalist views incline them to unions that would not attract sufficient support in the community to be designated "most representative" by the government. Every individual, whether he or she belongs to the association which commands the support of a majority of employees in the plant – or indeed to any association at all – is entitled to participate as an equal in the election and operation of the institutions through which employees are integrated into the collective decision-making processes of the firm.

In the Federal Republic of Germany, for example, non-union candidates, just as much as those who are affiliated with slates drawn up by unions,[36] can be elected as members of the works council, which acts as the exclusive agency through which the employees bargain[37] with their employers. Indeed, as we shall see, the West German model calls for a rough system of proportional representation between wage and salary personnel and between males and females, as well as for adequate representation of the various skills, occupations, and departments which exist in the plant.[38] A different system has been developed in Italy, where the principle of voluntary representation has been attached to a process of collective decision-making known as the delegates system.[39] In this model, which in some ways is more directly analogous to the collective bargaining process characteristic of the North American method of labour relations, those whose political, philosophical, religious, etc. views predispose them to remain outside the major, or indeed all, union organizations are still able to propose, run for, and be elected as "delegates" of workers in the different sections and units of the plant. The delegates in turn collectively present to management the workers' views about the terms and conditions on which they should be employed.

In both these systems it is no doubt true that, in practice, those candidates who represent the most important unions in the industry or region in which an enterprise operates will most often prevail. What figures are available in West Germany suggest over 80 per cent of the members of works councils and an even higher number of their chairpersons are union members.[40] Nevertheless, the fact remains that those who choose not to join any union can be and in fact are elected to these institutions. While the non-union group is a distinct minority, as independents generally are, the important point for our purposes is that they are a minority whose freedom of association has been respected and preserved. In all of these societies the right of the individual to belong to or remain apart from any and all religious groups or political parties is mirrored in her right to remain autonomous in the processes of industrial government as well. Indeed, so sensitive is the law to the individual's right to remain free of all economic associations that in some of these countries it is considered unlawful for a union to negotiate special benefits exclusively for its members.[41] Positive inducements of this kind are regarded as threatening to a worker's freedom of association as the more direct requirements like union security clauses, which compel membership in a particular union.

In drawing attention to the large number of European communities which have built one of these two distinct principles of representing employees' interests into their system of collective labour relations, it is not my intention to review any of them in detail. In the first place, I do not suggest that any of these models should be substituted in their entirety for the system we have in Canada. Against the historical chronology we traced in Part One, it would be foolish to think a whole system of collective labour relations would be able to survive a complete transplantation and remain unaffected by local environments. It would be very poor comparative law scholarship to suggest otherwise.[42] It is most likely that our policy-makers would endeavour to incorporate either of the principles of voluntary or plural representation into our established structures of collective bargaining, rather than bringing over one of the European systems as a whole. All the idiosyncrasies and subtleties of the different national systems which make use of either the plural or voluntary principle of employee representation show that those who have already faced this choice have made these principles conform to their social and institutional needs.

For the purposes of our analysis, it will be sufficient to focus on the principle of employee representation which is the most reasonable means of accomplishing the objectives legislators pursue when they develop a system of collective labour relations. Indeed, to be consistent with the approach we have followed so far, it would be inappropriate not to constrain our analysis in this way. At this stage of the analysis we will simply note the rich diversity of alternate legal institutions through which this principle can and has been expressed. If it should transpire that the principle which is most consistent with our constitution cannot be adapted to the Canadian environment, then all of these European models of collective labour relations will provide a wide selection of alternate institutional structures by which freedom of association in the workplace can be more fully protected. For the moment, we can take comfort that our legislatures will see that these two principles of representation can be expressed through institutional structures as diverse as works councils, bargaining coalitions, and delegate councils – all of which are constitutionally superior to our own.

To illustrate how a mature system incorporates one of these principles of employee representation I have chosen the West German model. The choice of the West German system is motivated as much by pragmatic and strategic factors as theoretical considerations. Certainly for those who do not want to join any union, the West German model will carry the logic of freedom of association further than any of the systems that adopt the principle of plural representation. Moreover, of all of the systems which incorporate the more liberal principle of voluntary representation, the German system seems the most developed. It is the one that has received the most extensive academic scrutiny by far, and will best illustrate how the principle of voluntary representation operates within a larger system of collective labour relations.

The basic structure of the West German system is fairly familiar to students of labour law. The institution through which the principle of voluntary representation has been expressed in West Germany is the works council. Like a union which has been certified as the exclusive bargaining agent for a group of employees, the sovereignty of a works council extends to all employees within the unit over which it is given jurisdiction. Unlike the system in North America, however, the scope of its jurisdiction within an enterprise is comprehensive and, at a minimum, will cover all employees in an organization, including both blue-collar and white-collar employees and a certain percentage of middle management as well.[43] Indeed, as we have noted, the works council envisages that proper representation of the different skills, occupations, sections, and even sexes within a plant will also be respected.

Paralleling the rules which govern the selection of an exclusive bargaining agent in Canada, essentially all persons who will be governed by the decisions of the works council are entitled to vote for its members. Specifically, everyone who is over the age of eighteen years who has been employed for six months is enfranchised.[44] However, in contrast with our own system, the guarantee of a worker's freedom of association goes well beyond the opportunity to cast a losing vote. All workers, regardless of their union affiliation, are able to propose or stand as candidates for the council and, if elected, participate directly in its affairs. In the German model, members are elected as representatives for a three-year term during which, except in extreme cases, they cannot be removed from office.[45]

The size of a works council varies according to the establishment in which it is constituted. The smallest enterprises in which a council can be established must have five or more employees. In those companies, the council consists of a single person. In the largest economic units, with integrated and multi-plant establishments of fifteen thousand or more employees, councils of over thirty-five members, with provision for smaller executive and composite committees and councils of the integrated operation, are contemplated. Unless otherwise provided, the statute requires the works council and the employer to meet at least once a month to deal with all matters related to the operation of the enterprise.

Even from such a cursory description of the institutional structures through which the principle of voluntary representation is expressed, it is quite apparent how much more the West German model respects the freedom of those who either do not want to join any union or, if they do, to join one different from that to which a majority of their colleagues want to belong, than our system of collective bargaining does. Were this structure to replace our system of local unions and form the basis of a new, constitutionally valid system of collective labour relations in Canada, it is easy to see how the freedom of Canadian workers would be greatly enhanced. Each worker would be able to participate through the organization or representative of his or her choice. The collective would look more like a parliament in which individuals would associate by belief and personal commitment than an assembly controlled by a single party whose membership was, for some, the consequence of coercion and the force of law.

More democratic processes and institutions of industrial government are an important, but not the only constitutional advantage that incorporation of the principle of voluntary representation into our labour relations laws would likely carry with it. As well, it turns out that models that make use of this principle are able to extend the benefit and protection of the whole system more evenly to *all* workers. When a state designs its system of collective labour relations to include this principle, it is able to create a legal environment which is available more equally to all individuals in the society. Indeed, it should be emphasized that a significantly larger percentage of the workforce is involved in all of the various European models of collective labour relations than in the Canadian system. If we focus again on the West German experience, it would appear that the percentage of workers who benefit directly from their system is almost double our own. Such a staggering discrepancy between these two competing systems of work regulation provides a second powerful reason why a system of labour relations like the West German model, which incorporates the principle of voluntary representation, should be constitutionally preferred.

The best evidence of our own circumstances suggests that our system of collective bargaining actually "benefits" and offers "protection" to between 35 and 40 per cent of our workforce. At the most optimistic, the figure is 45 per cent.[46] Whatever the source of one's statistics, the fact is that the majority of Canadians do not receive any direct benefit or protection from the policies we use to involve employees in the decision-making processes in the places they work. Indeed, if one excludes the public sector, the extent to which our model of collective bargaining can be said to enhance the opportunity of Canadian workers to participate in the decision-making processes of the workplace would be lower still. Moreover, even if the unorganized sectors of our work-force do enjoy some of the advantages of our system of collective bargaining indirectly through a process of "trickling down," they gain no direct experience in the practice of collective self-government, which is the central objective these systems are designed to promote.[47] Finally, and most tragically, within the private sector our model of collective labour relations characteristically fails to reach many of those workers whose opportunities are the most constrained.

Nor is it likely that the percentages will change. Although at one time the limited reach of our system of collective bargaining might have been explained by its novelty or by a natural aversion to collective processes of decision-making, that can no longer be said. The system is now forty years old (over fifty in the United States) and the extent of its reach has been stable, if not declining, for years. It must be accepted that the characteristics of the unorganized, "secondary" sectors of the economy present permanent barriers against the people who work in these environments ever being able to enjoy the fruits of a process of collective decision-making. The highly competitive nature of the product market, high employee turnover, the seemingly inexhaustible supply of alternate labour (all of which can be exploited and exacerbated by employer resistance to expressions of solidarity among its workers), are immutable elements of this sector of our labour market. Unless the basic principle of exclusivity, on which our system of collective bargaining it is predicated, is radically reformulated it is unlikely that those who are already among the most disadvantaged members of our labour force will ever be protected by a system of industrial government.

By contrast, in most of the countries that incorporate a principle of either voluntary or plural representation into their systems of collective labour relations, by far the largest percentage of their workforce directly benefit from and is protected by their terms. Although there are differences in the experiences of each of these countries, the figures in all of them are impressive. In Germany, to return to our primary example, over 80 per cent of the workforce benefits from being able to participate directly in the decision-making processes which organize the places they work.[48]

The substantial difference in how these alternate principles and institutions of collective labour relations are able to reach those workers who in our system now have the least meaningful involvement in making the decisions which order their working lives allows us to return to the theme which has motivated this study from the beginning. The very different coverage these two methods of representing employees' interests are able to achieve reveals most clearly how dramatically the process of judicial review can enhance the cause of social justice for the majority of workers in our country. Putting the Charter to work according to the principles we have been using, and requiring our system of collective labour relations to take into account one of the principles of employee representation which underlie the different European models, would mean democratic processes of government in the workplace could finally be made available to those workers our model has never been able to adequately serve.

In comparing the differences in coverage between the European models of collective labour relations and our own, it would be facile to suggest that the broader reach of their systems can largely be put down to the fact that they are much more attractive to workers because they offer them the choice to remain free of associations which they do not want to join. Obviously, systems based on a principle of purely voluntary representation will be more congenial to individuals for whom all unions are an anathema. However, we have already seen in the West German experience that the non-union group is very much in the minority. Moreover, in Germany, like Canada, the central trade union federation is so dominant that its constituent unions have a virtual monopoly on membership and the institutions of industrial government.

In fact, the better explanation seems to be that because institutions like the West German works council or the Italian delegates system do not compel a person to join a particular union against his or her will, the legislature can permit the system to be claimed as a matter of right at the initiative of a tiny fraction of the workforce. For example, in West Germany, the Works Constitution Act provides that on the petition of three or more workers in an enterprise, or of a union which represents that number of the staff, the electoral process by which a works council is established must be set in motion.[49]

Because this system of collective labour relations does not require individuals to join particular associations to which they may not want to belong, there is no need for the legislature to insist a majority of workers be in favour of its adoption. All of the debilitating and expensive efforts of organizing a majority of workers to choose a system of collective bargaining and resisting any unfair practices by the employer to undermine that objective can be avoided.[50] When a system of collective labour relations is based on a principle of voluntary representation, there is no more coercion imposed on the will of a worker than is caused by the democratic institutions we use to govern our society at large. The works council method is a system of industrial government in which the interests of each worker is weighed through processes which closely mirror parliamentary democracy in the community at large.[51] Institutions and processes of free and democratic government can be claimed as the legitimate right of every person in the place she or he works as much as in any of the other spheres of the community in which she or he lives. It is that parallel, which the West German model can draw with our political tradition of pluralism, rather than the existence of a large group of persons who are hostile to organized groups of workers, which best explains the much more even and equal participation of workers in the German model of collective decision-making than we have ever been able to realize in our own.

So far we have identified two ways in which the works council system of collective labour relations is able, by utilizing a principle of voluntary representation, to promote our constitutional values further than our system of collective bargaining. First, it secures a greater degree of freedom of association in the workplace.[52] In addition, works councils, at least in West Germany, are more in keeping with the commitment in our Charter to enact laws which protect and benefit people equally. In fact, there is still a third way in which the West German model has an advantage in better promoting our constitutional commitment to justice and equality. Specifically, the works council defines the group of employees that must act collectively in a way which also advances the ethic of solidarity and the concept of equality much more than the parallel rule in our own system allows.

Now in drawing attention to this third dimension of the West German model, it is important that its relationship to the principle of voluntary representation be kept clearly in mind. The aspect of the West German system we are now considering parallels the rules we use to define the units into which employees are placed to bargain. These rules, like the principles of employee representation, are integral to all systems in which the interests of workers will be represented collectively. Both are linked and give expression to the ethic of solidarity which is the central objective of all regimes of collective labour relations. Nevertheless, and their common moral roots notwithstanding, they are quite separate and distinct parts of their respective labour codes. Principles of employee representation, whether exclusive or voluntary, regulate the way workers' interests will be organized and presented collectively in the decision-making processes through which that community is governed.[53] So far our attention has focused exclusively on this dimension. What we are now concerned with involves defining the unit of employees whose interests can be represented collectively. The focus is on the breadth of the group of employees which the ethic of solidarity will join. Exclusivity is concerned with the way in which the interest of employees are represented collectively in the decision-making processes of the enterprise, while the rules that define which employees will be grouped in the same bargaining units govern how the boundaries of the industrial community will be drawn.

With that distinction in mind, it will be recalled that a works council generally applies to all of the employees in an enterprise. Blue-collar and white-collar, skilled and unskilled, and even some employees in middle management,[54] are all embraced in a single, sovereign, decision-making institution. By requiring that all of these workers be represented in a single unit of industrial government, the German model insists each worker within an enterprise deal with every other person as an equal. Unlike our own system, neither skill differentials nor the colour of one's collar can be the basis on which an employee's opportunity to participate can be made to depend.[55] By insisting that all workers within an enterprise participate as equals in a unified decision-making institution, the German works councils require that all differentials and inequalities existing in the terms and conditions on which individuals work be discussed and agreed upon by the workers as a group. In short, not only do the works councils protect the freedom of workers to associate more rigorously than our system of collective bargaining, they take the Charter's conception of equality more seriously as well.

On all three counts, then, the West German model seems a more reasonable means by which the objectives common to all systems of collective labour relations can be realized. A vote for a system based on a principle of exclusive representation, and especially one which defines the bargaining unit which the union has been empowered to represent on the basis of the colour of a person's shirt collar, is a needless restriction on freedom and compromise of equality. All the European systems entail more freedom (of association) and greater equality (in participation) than our existing system has ever achieved. The ideals of freedom and democracy are extended beyond the political institutions which govern their society at large to the economic enterprises in which most people spend the majority of their waking lives. On the principles we have said will figure prominently in the interpretation of the Charter, the conclusion follows naturally and unavoidably that such a method of industrial organization is constitutionally to be preferred. The systems of collective labour relations in West Germany in particular, and the communities of western Europe in general, offer powerful evidence of how, properly interpreted, the Charter can work as an instrument of social justice for those in the unorganized sectors of our labour markets. In a constitutional conversation about the validity of our principle of employee representation, those who have had the least involvement in settling the terms and conditions under which they work can insist that our lawmakers offer an adequate explanation to justify their failure to embrace one of these alternative models under which their opportunity for personal self-government would be enormously enhanced.

FOURTEEN

A Constitutional Conversation: The Defence

Faced with such a challenge to this cornerstone of our current system of collective bargaining, defenders of the principle of exclusivity have two independent though related strategies they can fall back on to try to salvage their position. Both question the assumption, which is implicit in the argument we have advanced so far, that the European models in general and the West German works council in particular are suitable alternatives for legislators in Canada in designing systems of collective labour relations.

According to the first argument, systems of industrial relations are the product of the unique social, economic, and cultural experience of each society and they simply cannot be transplanted to another community with different historical traditions and environmental conditions. Drawing on the evolution of our labour laws, labour relations principles and policies are depicted as foreign matter which do not easily lend themselves to being grafted onto the basic social institutions of different countries. On this view, neither of the two principles of employee representation which underlie the European systems are suitable to the Canadian environment and as such cannot be characterized as alternate means by which the labour relations objectives of our legislators could be accomplished.

A second line of defence would shift the focus from the premises underlying these different principles to their results. On this line of reasoning, even if it were conceded that the principles of voluntary and plural representation, and the institutions through which they are effected, could take root in the Canadian context, their application could be disputed on the basis of the results they could be expected to achieve. Even if an institution like the West German works council is accepted as being more egalitarian and more sensitive to workers' freedom of association, it may not be a reasonable alternative because it may not be able to match North American style collective bargaining in realizing other important objects that are promoted by our system of collective labour relations. On this highly utilitarian view, "all other things" may not, as I have so conveniently assumed, be equal as between these different principles of representation. Here the claim would be that legislators in Canada ought to be able to decide, without the interference of the courts, that the additional benefits which are uniquely secured by our own model outweigh whatever marginal limitations on our rights and freedoms it entails.

A. THE LIMITS OF COMPARATIVE LAW

In one sense the two responses are related. Each challenges whether the principles of employee representation in the European systems are "alternate means" which are realistically available to our legislators. However, the two positions challenge the substitutability of these competing principles in different ways. Therefore it is necessary to consider each in turn. The first, which underscores the unique historical, technological, economic, geographic, sociological, and cultural environment in which each national system develops, is for many analysts of labour relations the more serious and potentially more fatal challenge and so merits our immediate attention. If the most basic principles of industrial relations systems, like those which organize the representation of employee interests collectively, are culture-bound, there is little need to address the second question of how well each of them realizes the objectives which all systems of collective labour relations are expected to promote.

The first observation that springs to mind in considering the initial argument is that it is neither absolutely nor universally true. However powerful it may be when applied to the law we are considering, it is certainly not one which applies uniformly to all aspects of our labour code. Certainly when they are analysed at a sufficiently broad level of generality, the labour codes in all societies which, like Canada, are conventionally regarded as being more or less free and democratic, can be seen to be structured along similar principles. Standards fixing minimum terms and conditions of employment – wages, hours, security, opportunity, and so on – are common to all legal regimes in North America, western Europe, the Commonwealth, and Japan. So are processes and institutions of collective labour relations. Workers' compensation, unemployment insurance, and pension programs are other integral components of the labour codes which regulate employment relationships in all these countries.

These obvious counter examples illustrate how many of the most important parts of our labour code are able to spread easily across the boundaries of all free and democratic countries. Still, the argument is one which has an air of conventional wisdom about it. It certainly has a recognized academic pedigree. It is a view which has characterized many comparative studies carried out by policy-makers in Canada[1] and, as noted earlier, it is one that distinguishes some of the most important essays on comparative labour law.[2] From both of these sources one is fairly cautioned of the dangers of ignoring the contextual backdrop within which legal systems are developed when attempting to draw on foreign experience as the basis of radical national reform.

A classic formulation of this position is presented by Derek Bok in his "Reflections on the Distinctive Character of American Labor Law." To the extent that the principle of exclusive representation in the United States is identical with our own, his essay is also relevant to understanding the evolution of the model in Canada and the extent to which it is amenable to change. Bok's thesis is a simple one. Rejecting earlier historical, political, and cultural explanations for the unique character of American labour law, Bok argues that many of the most distinctive features of the legal rules we use to regulate labour relationships (including the principle of exclusivity), can best be explained as derivatives of special features or institutions which distinguish our system of industrial relations. Ultimately, he believes it is the attitudes the principal players in the system have to industrial organization that best explains the shape and substance of the legal rules of each labour relations system. Reduced to its essentials, Bok's thesis is that the virtues of individualism and competition, pragmatism and decentralization have dominated the attitudes of employers, employees, and unions alike, and consequently have had an immutable impact on the processes and rules of North American collective labour relations. Lack of any sense of class consciousness and solidarity on the part of the workers, matched by a zeal for individual initiative and competition on the part of their employers, has given rise to the highly decentralized, adversarial, and very partial system of collective bargaining which our labour relations acts have institutionalized.

It would, I think, be difficult for anyone to take issue with this characterization of the system of labour relations that has evolved in North America or with its derivation from the attitudes held by its principal actors. And yet, that said, there really is nothing in Bok's description or analysis to suggest that the more liberal and egalitarian principles of employee representation we have been considering would be unable to take root in North America. In fact, these principles and the institutions in which they are embedded seem to take the values and attitudes Bok ascribes to our employers and employees even more seriously than we do. The West German works council system, which has been adopted with variations to meet local needs in Austria and the Netherlands, seems to be the most developed expression of the attitudes Bok identifies as permeating our own social fabric. The principle of voluntary representation, at least when it is expressed in the German model, seems to support processes by which employee interests can be represented collectively in as decentralized, pragmatic, and non-ideological a way as could possibly be devised. In fact, sometimes works councils are criticized precisely because they seem to manifest these characteristics too strongly.

Listen to the reasons the German Trade Union Federation (DGB) gives for its support of this system of collective labour relations and the principle of representation on which it is grounded: "[Works Councils] represent an institutional measure by virtue of which the position of the worker in an enterprise or workshop is shaped in accordance with the basic values of a free and democratic society ... [E]very individual must be in a position, in free association with others of his own persuasion, to ensure adequate consideration of his own ideas within the play of forces in a pluralist society."[3]

But even if, in their commitment to principles of freedom and democracy, concepts like voluntary or plural representation of workers' collective interests could be regarded as superior to exclusivity, those who would resist their transplantation might be expected to refer to other, more specific, features of these systems to support their claim that they cannot be regarded as reasonable alternatives in the Canadian context. Even if these principles best express the attitudes and values held by the principal actors in our own system of collective bargaining, an argument might still be made that these systems have developed unique institutional features which, on Bok's analysis, would make their implantation in Canadian soil difficult, if not impossible, to effect.

The idea here is that the principle by which employees' interests are represented collectively is said to be inextricably linked to the institutional structures through which it is expressed. The strategy is to say you must take the whole (structure) to embrace any part (principle). Thus, at this point in our constitutional conversation the claim might be made that the principle involved in the works council model, for example, and the institution through which it is expressed, are integral parts of a much broader structure of cooperative labour relations. Such a system entails, among other rules, restrictions on strikes and industrial conflict which are utterly at odds with the adversarial, conflictual system of labour relations we have developed.[4] Furthermore, it might be pointed out that all these systems which accommodate more liberal principles of employee representation are interwoven in a much larger, multilevel system of employer/employee relations in which industry-wide bargaining, which is a relatively rare phenomenon in the North American system, figures prominently. Unless similar industry-wide or even broader-based institutions of decision-making were put in place simultaneously with redesigning the local institutions we have been considering, the experiment would, so the argument would go, be doomed to failure. In short, a change in the principle of employee representation would be said to carry with it such a radical restructuring of other equally fundamental features of our system that, however compatible the European principles may be at some ethical level of abstraction, their transplantation would entail a serious clash at the point of application and institutional design.

Now the claim that the principle of voluntary representation which underlies the West German system of works councils cannot be separated from the larger system of industrial relations of which it is a part is potentially a serious one. If valid, it would mean that to adopt either of the more liberal principles of employee representation Canadian legislatures would have to introduce other features of these systems which are regarded by many as so dissimilar to our own as to preclude their being regarded as reasonable alternatives. The thrust of this argument is that it would be reasonable for Canadian legislators to reject a principle of voluntary representation if, taken with the larger institutional structures through which it was expressed, it meant virtually completely transforming the major institutions and processes of our system of industrial relations. Building on Bok's analysis of the close connection that exists between the context and institutions of the industrial relations system and the substance of labour law rules, this claim, if sustained, would lead to the legitimation of the exclusivity principle by default. Exclusivity would prevail simply because there would be no "reasonable alternatives" which could be used in its place.

At this stage of the debate, in responding to what we might characterize as a polycentric theory of labour relations, there are two broad arguments those challenging the principle of exclusivity might advance. First, they might simply deny its validity. They could endeavour to show that the principle which governs employee representation in the decision-making processes in the workplace and the institutions which give expression to it are independent, self-sufficient, and viable in a wide variety of industrial relations systems. Alternatively, they might respond that, even if the principles of voluntary and/or plural representation are inextricably attached to other principles and structures of bargaining and dispute resolution, this would not be fatal in the case we are considering because the western European systems are not so different from our own as the defenders of exclusivity would suggest. They could argue that even when they are viewed in their entirety, the European systems of collective labour relations are reasonable alternatives to the one that we have put in place.

The most immediate and obvious reply is, of course, simply to deny that the adoption of the principle of voluntary employee representation entails buying into a whole cooperative theory of collective labour relations which renounces conflict in general and strikes in particular. Not that the description of the West German system is false. Certainly one cannot take issue with its being depicted as a system which emphasizes cooperation and trust rather than conflict and confrontation. This ethical orientation is, without question, the pre-eminent cornerstone of the West German method of involving employees collectively in the decision-making processes which govern the places in which they work.

Many of the most distinguishing institutional features and rules of the West German model of "co-determination" – for example, the renunciation of the right to strike to resolve disputes within the enterprise, as well as the representation of workers' interests on boards of directors – are predicated on this ethic. However, it simply is not true, either as a matter of fact or theory, that the principle of voluntary representation can only be established in non-conflictual systems of labour relations. There is no necessary connection between the two. The principle of voluntary representation, and the institutions through which it may be expressed, is concerned with the question of how employee interests can be reconciled and represented collectively to those who employ or consume their services. The principle that employees shall not engage in strikes is concerned with the quite separate issue of the method or criteria[5] by which disputes between the competing interests of labour and capital can be resolved. Conceptually, the two principles deal with entirely separate aspects of industrial relations policy and can be juxtaposed in whatever permutation or combination we choose. All the evidence confirms that each of the principles of representation we have considered can be adapted to and made to operate within any of the western systems of industrial relations regardless of the criteria of dispute resolution it employs.

Even the most casual perusal of our own industrial relations policies confirms that fact. A quick canvass of the different models of collective labour relations currently employed in Canada shows that the principle of exclusive representation has been incorporated into systems which invoke compulsory arbitration as the method of dispute resolution as well as those which rely on the strike. The fact the principle of exclusive representation is the operating rule in both our public sector and private industry demonstrates conclusively that there is no necessary connection between principles of employee representation and the rules governing dispute resolution.

If additional proof of the indepenence of these two principles of industrial relations policy were required, it could be secured from any of the countries that have adopted either the principle of plural or voluntary representation. Their experience confirms that both of these principles are equally adaptable to either adversarial or cooperative processes. With respect to the former, in countries such as Belgium and France plural representation is as much the operative rule in the processes of collective bargaining as it is in the various works councils and internal committees through which employee interests are also expressed. As well, there is parallel evidence that the principle of voluntary representation can easily be combined with either process of dispute resolution. Thus, the Italian system of collective bargaining through councils of delegates proves that this principle of employee representation can exist within the context of a conflictual model of industrial relations. The Italian experience makes it plain that there is nothing which would preclude Canadian legislators from preserving the method of the strike in our system of labour relations while simultaneously adopting the principle of voluntary representation.[6]

All this evidence argues against the claim that the principles of representation which the Europeans have adopted cannot be separated from the comprehensive systems of collective labour relations of which they are a part. But we still must consider whether the same holds true of the relationship between these principles and industry-wide bargaining structures which is the other institutional characteristic thought to distinguish the European systems. Before doing so, however, it is perhaps worth pausing to observe that even if those who argued that the principles of employee representation and conflict resolution were inseparable prevailed on this point of the debate, that would not necessarily lead to the constitutional validation of exclusivity. Even if, against all the evidence, it were accepted that the principle of voluntary representation was uniquely adapted to a cooperative model of collective labour relations, it still would not follow that, taken as a whole, the resulting system would be so foreign to our own environment as to preclude its transplantation. In fact, and while one would not want to deny the separate character of these two models of collective labour relations, neither in theory nor in practice are they so antagonistic and dissimilar as those who seem to suffer xenophobia might have us believe.

History teaches us that, regardless of the method of dispute resolution that is used, the interests of employers (consumers) and producers of labour compete and conflict. In all systems of collective labour relations, regardless of what happens when the parties reach the terminal point in their negotiations, ambitions collide and pressure is applied to persuade the other side of the reasonableness of one's views. According to one who has had extensive experience with the cooperative system of German works councils:

Experience has shown that participation [works councils, or co-determination] does not necessarily mean cooperation, nor does collective bargaining mean conflict. In a broad sense, it is natural for workers to bargain with their employers over differing interests to reach a workable compromise ...

The final outcome of a bargain in each case is dependent on the actual power relationship of labour and capital, irrespective of the legal form through which this influence is exercised.[7]

Systems of collective labour relations are all essentially similar in their objective of mediating the conflicting interests of employers and workers and even in the social behaviours they allow the parties to use to fashion rules to which all can "consent." In practice, it is only at the very end of the process, in the institutional devices and criteria which they invoke to resolve impasses the parties cannot otherwise overcome, that these systems differ. For those most familiar with the two different systems, the day-to-day methods and strategies works councils use to press their views parallel closely the way local unions carry on within our enterprises.[8]

Even when one contemplates the terminal principles and processes of dispute resolution, where the two systems are obviously unique in the criteria on which and the methods by which impasses are broken, there is a sense in which the contrast between arbitration and concerted activity is overdrawn. In fact, compulsory arbitration is not a stranger to Canadian industrial relations policy. Industrial relations in general and trade unions in particular have gained a good deal of experience with arbitration, especially in the public sector. On the basis of that experience, there is no reason to think this principle of dispute resolution would be the anathema to the principal participants that proponents of exclusivity would have us believe. Certainly for those unions which were given the choice in our own federal public sector, arbitration rather than confrontation was overwhelmingly the preferred alternative. If their experience held true, adjudication would be preferable to conflict as a means of resolving disputes with their employer for many of the groups with only modest bargaining power who have traditionally been ignored by our system of collective bargaining. The example of the public health nurses in Ontario who struck, without success, in order to have their employers agree to arbitration to resolve future disputes, makes the point as clearly as one can.

More generally, it seems certain that all workers who are disadvantaged because they are not well endowed in the resources which determine bargaining power in the market, would have a greater influence in decision-making processes which conclude in arbitration than those which may result in a strike. By comparison to the criteria applied in a process of compulsory arbitration, the standards the market invokes to resolve differences between workers with little bargaining power and those with whom they contract are not likely to be particularly sensitive to the interests of the former.[9] Indeed, recent governmental initiatives promoting the establishment of redundancy committees in private enterprises that are unorganized suggests policy-makers increasingly have come to see the relevance of arbitration as a principal instrument of dispute resolution in the private sector as well.[10] In short, for those who are most disadvantaged by our existing legislative policy on collective labour relations, the German model of works councils would likely be an attractive alternative not only because it incorporates the principle of voluntary representation but because its criteria of dispute resolution are likely to favour them as well. Certainly for them, and perhaps even for many workers in those sectors already organized,[11] the complete institutional apparatus of these systems and not just their principles of representation may be regarded as preferable alternatives to our existing collective bargaining process.

Whenever a court considers the second feature which is said to distinguish European systems of collective labour relations in general and the West German model of works councils in particular and to make them incompatible with the Canadian environment, it will find the analysis repeats itself. Again, the description of the larger decision-making structures in the European systems is accurate enough. Industry-wide and broader-based bargaining structures between employees, employers, and even governments have traditionally been one of the most distinctive characteristics of western European systems of industrial relations. All the local, enterprise-level decision-making structures we have identified have grown up within and sometimes directly as a result of these wider processes of industrial law making.[12] Industry-wide bargaining rather than local institutions such as works councils have traditionally dominated the process of settling the most important terms and conditions of employment.[13]

But again, the existence and even importance of these structures to the European models affords no basis for the conclusion that it is only within the protection of these broader-based institutions that the principles of voluntary and plural representation can be expressed. Moreover, even if industry-wide structures of decision-making were necessary for the more liberal principles of employee representation to survive, again our courts will discover their adoption in Canada would not be such a foreign event. Industry-wide and broader-based bargaining structures, like compulsory arbitration, are reasonably familiar phenomena on the Canadian industrial relations scene.

In considering the relationship between industry-wide bargaining structures and principles of employee representation, what attracts immediate attention is that whatever functions these structures were expected to perform in theory, and may have performed in the past, does not always accord with practice today. Commonly, these structures have been used to establish only minimum terms and conditions of employment for an industry or sector and on occasion for a country as a whole.[14] They often fix the most basic but not the actual terms and conditions according to which people work. Even in a system such as the West German model, where the legal validity of such extended local law-making is a matter of serious doubt, frequently the terms which actually govern the basis on which labour is bought and sold have been settled in the works councils themselves.[15] More generally, it can be said that in all the countries of western Europe, local decision-making structures such as works councils have taken on increasing importance over the past twenty-five years and now frequently settle matters which traditionally have been set in the wider bargaining structures.[16] The different responsibilities of the various levels of decision-making, so sharp in theory,[17] have become much more blurred in practice.[18]

The extent of this shift can be conveyed most dramatically by noting the "wage drift" which occurred during the economic expansion of the 1970s. Here again, even in West Germany, where by law works councils are not permitted to bargain about wages and hours of work except in very narrow circumstances, wage differentials as high as 20 per cent between enterprises in an industry were reported.[19] In other countries the differentials ranged even higher.[20] It is true that in the circumstances of the most recent economic recession, the industry-wide processes reasserted some of their authority in West Germany to establish the most basic rules of employment. However, overall the trend continues in the direction of emphasizing the local over the broader-based bargaining structures. In Italy, for example, local bargaining has on occasion generated solutions which eventually formed the basis of industry-wide norms.[21]

The latter example, while it could never be considered as commonplace in any European system of collective labour relations, is particularly pertinent to this aspect of the debate. It suggests an important reason why the relative lack of industry-wide and broader-based bargaining structures in Canada would not likely preclude the transplantation of the principle of voluntary representation to Canadian soil. While it may still be the exception in Europe, it is common in North American labour relations for the results of local bargaining to have an impact well beyond the unit to which they legally apply. In industrial relations jargon this phenomenon is described as the relationship between the election unit and the unit of direct impact.[22] The relevance of this feature of our system of collective labour relations is, of course, that the role that industry-wide bargaining serves in the European models has already been accommodated by our local decision-making processes.

At the inception of the North American system of collective labour relations, multi-party, broadly based bargaining structures were not common.[23] In this void, not surprisingly local bargaining processes frequently settled the most basic terms of employment in an industry or a sector by means of the pattern settlement or award. If one envisages labour law operating at three different levels of generality – across the economy as a whole, in an industry or region, and at a particular plant or enterprise – local bargaining in Canada often settles the terms at the latter two levels at one and the same time. While in both Canadian and European societies the minimum terms on which any work can be performed are set by the governments of the day, industry-wide and enterprise-specific rules are not set so separately and independently in Canada as they tend to be in Europe. In Canada a collective agreement negotiated by the Autoworkers with General Motors or Ford serves as the industry standard, while the pact negotiated at each plant parallels the terms a works council might typically settle.[24] The North American institution of pattern bargaining in effect renders industry-wide structures quite redundant.[25] This prevalence of pattern decision-making, together with the increasing reliance by policy-makers on legislation and regulations to establish minimum terms and conditions of employment for all workers, makes it highly doubtful that the general lack of industry-wide bargaining structures would jeopardize the viability of local decision-making processes which incorporated a principle of voluntary representation.

In response to all of this, however, it might be said those who challenge the constitutional integrity of the exclusivity principle have missed the most important function that industry-wide and broader-based decision-making structures perform. Even conceding the availability of other institutions and processes to set intermediate standards of employment, defenders of exclusivity might argue these wider structures are still necessary to protect and secure the independence and the power of the labour movement as a whole. Without a vehicle for a broader base of class solidarity, the concern would be that an independent and isolated works council would be vulnerable to employer influence and eventual control. The fear would be that if local decision-making institutions were denied the shelter of the wider rule-making processes through which unions can maintain their power, they would eventually collapse into little more than company-dominated organizations. The argument would be that the effectiveness of the bargaining experience in local institutions that has been emerging across Europe in recent years was crucially dependent upon these supporting structures at the level of industry and the economy as a whole.

In theory, the claim is a plausible one. Certainly it is true that labour movements in Europe and North America have been alive to the danger that independent local decision-making processes such as works councils could be used as an instrument to blunt rather than further the collective representation of workers' interests. European labour movements still harbour that concern and there is no doubt, as a matter of historical fact, that many of the works councils which came into being at the time collective bargaining was first beginning to develop in the United States ultimately met such a demise.[26] It is conventional wisdom that any system of collective labour relations, at whatever level it is practised, requires a strong independent labour movement if it is to enhance the opportunity of workers to participate effectively in settling the rules which govern the workplace. All the commentators who have addressed this question are one on that point. At worst, works councils which are separate from the unions tend to become instruments of management. At best, without the support of a strong union movement, works councils are less effective and seem incapable of guaranteeing meaningful standards of employment protection.[27] Even our own limited experience with how health and safety committees function in the organized and unorganized sectors of our labour market makes it plain that the integrity and efficiency of any collective processes of decision-making are directly dependent on the strength and independence of the trade union movement that supports them.[28]

But again, it does not follow that industry-wide bargaining is the only way a viable and independent labour movement can either come into being or survive. Certainly, Shirley Carr and the Canadian Labour Congress would be surprised to learn of that fact. However susceptible to cooptation and coercion the labour movement may have been when works councils underwent their aborted delivery in North America, it cannot be regarded as being so vulnerable today. The eighties are not the twenties and our labour movement must be considered to be as independent, both financially and politically, as any in the world. The participation of the Canadian Labour Congress in national forums and processes of policy-making; the powerful influence which the largest industrial and public sector unions have on the policies of the New Democratic Party; and the ability of Canadian unions such as the Canadian Autoworkers to negotiate benefits their American counterparts have been unable to achieve, all attest to the independence and authority of the Canadian trade union movement.

There is, of course, even more compelling evidence that the trade union movement in Canada is strong enough to supervise local decision-making institutions like works councils without the protection of broader-based bargaining structures. The fact is they operate such a system already, since our own system is one of the most localized and highly decentralized of any in the free and democratic world. If our unions are independent enough to preserve the integrity of our system of local bargaining, there should be no question of their capacity to do the same for a system which would differ only in the principle of representation on which it is based. Indeed, if the West German experience holds true, the same union officers who control our local bargaining at present would be expected to assume similar positions of authority in a restructured collective decision-making process. Because the Canadian trade union movement is so similar to the West German federation (DGB) in its homogeneous and monolithic structure, there is every reason to assume the control unions exercise over works councils in Germany would be replicated if that system were transplanted to Canadian soil.

So industry-wide bargaining, it turns out, should not be any more essential to the integrity and effectiveness of a system of employee participation based on a principle of voluntary or plural representation than was the adoption of any particular rule of conflict resolution. Once again, these two features, which are common to all conventional systems of collective labour relations, are conceptually and practically distinct. But again, it should be pointed out that even if one remained doubtful of the strength of the Canadian labour movement to make such a system effective in the absence of more formal industry-wide standards, there is simply no basis for the suggestion that such structures would flounder in the Canadian environment. Again, like compulsory arbitration, multi-party bargaining structures are, if not characteristic of the Canadian scene, certainly not uncommon.[29] Initially developed in industries like the garment trade, shipping, and fishing, where they were of mutual advantage to employers and employees alike, increasingly Canadian policy-makers have had occasion to make use of them where they promoted their labour relations objectives. Whether designed for particular sectors such as the construction industry[30] or made available for use in industry at large,[31] multi- or poly-party bargaining structures are becoming increasingly familiar features of Canadian industrial relations policy. Thus again, their proliferation would represent more of a logical evolution than a new beginning in the development of Canadian industrial relations policy.

When one reaches the end of this phase of the debate it seems there is nothing in either the ethical or the institutional character of those labour relations systems incoporating principles of voluntary or plural representation which would retard or inhibit their taking hold in Canadian soil. Either the rules and institutional aspects that some believe distinguish these systems are quite independent of the principle of employee representation, and/or alternative mechanisms already exist in Canada to effect their purpose.

Actually, in the course of his analysis, Bok was himself quite sensitive to just such a conclusion. He recognized that works councils might be considered as a reasonable alternative to our system of decentralized bargaining by associations which are granted monopolistic powers of representation by the state. For his purposes, however, it was sufficient to consider the historical and pragmatic reasons why works councils never took root in North America. Here again, when Bok describes and explains why local, enterprise bargaining, based on a principle of exclusive representation, came to dominate and distinguish our system of labour relations it is difficult to quarrel with him. At the time works councils were first being established in the Weimar Republic and discussed in the United States they could easily become, and were therefore regarded by many as, a means to divide the loyalties of workers and avoid union organization. At that time, European unions were stronger and more independent than their counterparts in North America. As a result, for both practical and ideological reasons, they lent their support to the development of these local institutions of decision-making at the places their members worked. By contrast, in North America where unions were primarily organized on a local basis, works councils were regarded as largely redundant, if not antagonistic, to the purposes and ambitions of the labour movement.

In identifying the opposition of a strong local trade union movement in the United States as one of the primary reasons why more liberal principles and institutions of employee representation failed to take hold, Bok's analysis ties in with a second powerful statement about the constraints which are said invariably to limit the extent to which "foreign" laws of labour relations can ever be transplanted to different soil. This second thesis has been articulated most powerfully by Professor Otto Kahn-Freund. According to him, it is much more "the role which is played by organized interests in the making and in the maintenance of legal institutions," which explains the development of labour (or indeed any) law in a particular country and the degree to which it can be used as a model or flourish in other national communities.[32] As Professor Kahn Freund persuasively illustrates, the way in which an organized interest group – be it a church, professional association, or a union – will be affected by a change in a particular law or legal institution will determine whether developments in matrimonial law, jury systems, and labour relations in one part of the world can successfully thrive in another.

The behaviour of powerful interest groups in the processes of politics certainly takes us some distance in explaining why principles of voluntary and plural representation never took root in North America. However, such groups' continued opposition can no longer justify the rejection of these models if they are more consistent with the constitutional criteria against which our labour code must now be measured. That is, of course, precisely what constitutional conversations are all about. As we saw in the last part, that is what differentiates the circumstances of the least advantaged workers in our own community from those who preceded them. Following the entrenchment of their rights and freedoms in our constitution, workers now have the legal authority to insist they receive equal protection and benefit of the law and that their rights and freedoms receive the respect which is their constitutional due. No longer must they pursue their rights in the legislative process in which they are so materially disadvantaged. As the earlier examples of agricultural workers, domestics, younger and female workers were intended to illustrate, judicial review offers a process through which the less powerful groups in our society can neutralize imperfections in the political processes. Today the relevant criterion for determining the continued validity of a legal rule such as exclusivity is not the power that a group of individuals can collectively wield in the political processes to support it. On the contrary, the test is whether the constitutional objectives which our system of collective labour relations endeavours to promote are being accomplished in a way that infringes least on the most fundamental rights and freedoms everyone is now entitled to enjoy.

B. QUESTIONING THE CONSEQUENCES: COMPARATIVE ADVANTAGES OF ALTERNATIVE LEGAL SYSTEMS

Even though the political opposition of organized interest groups can no longer act as an automatic veto over the constitutional entitlements of others, their continued hostility to alternate principles of employee representation might still be a reason why legislators would resist opting for such systems in favour of the model we currently employ. If the most important participants in our current system of collective labour relations felt they would be prejudiced by its alteration, if they remained unconvinced of its integrity and worth, no innovation could be expected to flourish. Decision-making structures predicated on a principle of voluntary representation could not be considered reasonable alternate methods of representing employees collectively if the parties responsible for their implementation and operation were not committed to their success. We have already acknowledged the conventional wisdom that any model of collective labour relations, no matter which principle of representation it uses, relies on a strong and independent labour movement to effectively represent the interests of workers. Faced with the opposition of organized business or labour, it would be more difficult for a court to say our legislators were acting unreasonably if they decided to continue with what we have. However imperfect and unjust it is, the existing system at least has the virtue of being able to secure the allegiance of the parties who have been delegated the function to make it work.

In this final rejoinder we can see how those who question the substitutability of the two European principles join forces with those who deny that the European decision-making structures would be able to accomplish all of the objectives we expect our own model of collective bargaining to achieve. Unless those charged with making the system work have faith in its viability and integrity, there would be no reasonable basis to expect that these models of collective labour relations would be able to foster labour peace, secure a more just share of the fruits of progress for all and, ultimately, promote a strong and responsible labour movement capable of effectively representing the interests of employees.

Born of such desperate motives, it will not be surprising that this final attempt to save the principle of exclusive representation should fare no better than those which preceded it. In this phase of the debate the burden of proof, both logically and legally, is on those who would argue that incorporating the principle of voluntary representation would interfere with the accomplishments that our present model of collective bargaining has achieved.[33] It will be incumbent on them to establish that both of the European principles are not reasonable alternatives. All of the evidence suggests they will have considerable difficulty doing so. On the merits of the debate, there is little, if anything, to support the claim that either of these different principles of employee representation, and the processes of participation to which they give rise, will encounter any special difficulty in accomplishing the objectives common to all systems of collective labour relations.

Given the way the debate has unfolded, this particular challenge would be expected to be mounted primarily from those trade union associations which would stand to lose their monopoly on the law-making authority if the constitutional challenge to the existing system were to succeed. I will focus, therefore, on how their interests would be affected if our system of collective bargaining were to incorporate a more liberal principle of employee representation. If it can be established that their primary interests would be enhanced rather than prejudiced by such an amendment, any other opposition would be expected to give way. If the experience in Europe holds true, a legislative initiative which incorporated either of the European principles of employee representation would be expected to have the support of the business community.

That has certainly been the attitude of employers in West Germany. There, all of the evidence suggests that works councils have been accepted by employers as part of the enterprise in a way unionized procedures of local bargaining never were. West German employers seem prepared to share their decision-making authority with their employees, who have a loyalty to the enterprise, in a way they will not with outside agencies.[34] This support of the West German business community for their method of collective labour relations contrasts sharply with the aversion North American employers continue to have for our own system. While such attitudes are obviously the product of a variety of factors, self-interest plays no small part. All the conventional economic indicators give credence to the idea that more liberal systems of employee participation are at least consonant with, if they do not actually promote, the interests of employers.[35] While obviously one cannot attribute all of the credit to the principle of employee representation around which their institutions of industrial organization are structured, the fact remains the German and Austrian economies are among the strongest, most stable, and robust in the world.[36] Certainly the general support of employers in West Germany for their system of collective labour relations shows how difficult it will be for defenders of exclusivity to claim that the liberalization of our structures of employee participation would compromise the allocative and economic objectives of the system as a whole.

But enthusiasm for this method of reconciling relations between employees and employers should not be limited to the latter. At least not if the West German experience holds true. As we have seen, whatever their initial concerns for the integrity of the institution, the German trade union movement has also become increasingly supportive of the works council system. It has not transpired that this method of organizing collective labour relations at the enterprise has undermined the vitality or power of the labour movement or has been captured as a pawn of managerial control.

Quite the contrary. As a matter of coverage, we have already seen the superiority of the European systems in general and the West German model in particular. Whereas North American collective bargaining has never been able to reach a majority of workers, the European systems directly benefit and protect between two-thirds and four-fifths of the workforce. In a direct comparison between the West German and Canadian systems, we saw the difference in coverage is almost two to one. If the European experiences held true, adoption of either of these principles of employee representation would provide the vehicle through which unions could finally reach the "unskilled, unlucky and unorganized" who, under our existing institutional arrangements, have been left largely to fend for themselves. Reorganization of our system of collective labour relations around a principle of voluntary representation would offer our trade union movement the vehicle through which they could finally serve the constituencies most in need of their services.

Nor would the unions need to worry that the extension of this system of collective labour relations throughout the labour market might be achieved by a dilution or diminution in the influence of the unions themselves. In the first place, in any reformulation of our system of collective labour relations we could recognize a set of entitlements by which unions could integrate themselves into the restructured institutions and processes to ensure that their involvement is preserved.[37] In West Germany, for example, within specified guidelines, unions can call for the initiation of elections and the convening of meetings of the council, attend its sessions, commence proceedings for the expulsion of members and, most obviously, propose lists of candidates for election. In all the countries which have adopted the works council model, the experience has been that the unions have used these powers to dominate its membership. Over 80 per cent of the membership and 90 per cent of the chairpersons in works councils in Germany are drawn from the ranks of union supporters and adherents.

Another conventional measurement of the strength of the union movement is the percentage of rank and file employees who have actually joined unions. This indicator also suggests organized labour does not suffer when the system of collective labour relations is organized around a principle of voluntary or plural representation. In fact, even protected by the state monopoly that our system bestows, North American unionism continues to recruit one of the lowest percentages of workers in the free and democratic world.[38] By contrast, European labour movements routinely attract the support of at least half the working population even though they are commonly prevented by law from dealing with the problem of free riders.[39] In some countries, such as Belgium, unions enlist the support of three-quarters of the workers qualified to join their ranks. The correct correlation, it seems, is that when a state respects the freedom of its people to associate as they please, that enhances rather than detracts from the support unions will enjoy.

That kind of evidence confirms our earlier observation that if the principle of voluntary representation were grafted onto an existing collective bargaining relationship, nothing would look very different. On those statistics, those who would occupy the positions of authority in representing the collective interests of employees would, for the most part, remain the same. A works council at General Motors, if that structure was chosen to give expression to the principle of voluntary representation, would look pretty much the same as the executive and subordinate committees of Local 222 of the Canadian Autoworkers in the union affiliation of its members. There is no reason to think their strength in numbers or authority would shrink in any significant way.

Nor should the bargaining power of any group of employees be adversely affected by such a change. Assuming the definition of the bargaining unit remained the same, its power would, by definition, remain unaffected. Indeed if, to refer to the West German model one last time, we considered the rules they use to regulate the bargaining processes, it is likely the opportunity to participate in the decision-making structures of the enterprise would actually increase. Even for the groups that have traditionally opted for collective bargaining in North America, decision-making institutions like the works councils in West Germany[40] or the delegates councils in Italy[41] offer an opportunity to participate in a more meaningful way and on a wider range of issues than even the most successful experiments in collective bargaining have been able to realize. Works councils should enhance employee participation in the decision-making processes qualitatively as well as quantitatively. Not only would more workers be involved in a process in which, for the first time, they could participate in formulating the rules which govern their lives, many others would be involved in a more comprehensive way than ever before.

The cooperative character of the West German model is as apparent in this part of their labour law as it is in the rules governing employee representation, industrial conflict, and defining the boundaries of the collective. We have already witnessed how these latter rules reflect a commitment to the ethic of solidarity and to effective participation by employees, so it should not be surprising to see the parallel principles of bargaining promote these values as well. The West German model is characterized as a system of co-determination precisely because it involves workers in the resolution of the rules which govern their lives in ways which are unavailable even to those Canadian workers who at present are represented in a bargaining process by a certified representative.

On social matters, which encompass working conditions in the broadest sense, the power of co-decision-making is comprehensive. Only the most powerful trade unions in Canada would be able to claim, as all workers in West Germany can, that they have a veto over almost every aspect of their schedule of work, vacations, leaves, principles of remuneration (including bonuses, piece rates, and other methods of payment by result), welfare plans, dress, and the ways in which management can monitor their performance.[42] Equally, on "staff matters," where Canadian collective bargaining typically exhausts itself in the negotiation of a clause stipulating such decisions must be made on the dual criteria of the seniority and qualifications of the individuals involved, the West German model involves workers much earlier and much more extensively in the decision-making process. Rather than simply reacting to decisions already made, works councils are intimately involved in the formulation of principles governing staff evaluation, of guidelines for the selection, recruitment, transfer, regrading and dismissal of employees, as well as of corporate policy pertaining to all aspects of manpower planning and training.[43] To appreciate how much more extensive the power of the works council is in matters of staff policy one need only observe that it not only has the authority to challenge the termination of an employee on the ground of social hardship; but it can call for the discharge of persons whose conduct it feels warrants it.[44]

However, it is with respect to the economic and financial matters of the enterprise, and especially those decisions affecting a person's work and livelihood, where the difference in the two systems may be the greatest. In Canada, apart from those covered by the recent federal initiatives on redundancy committees, most employees are only entitled to minimal notice of impending lay-offs.[45] In West Germany, by contrast, workers are able to insist that an employer formulate a social plan to ameliorate the impact of termination on those who are redundant. Indeed, in the event it is not satisfied with the reasonableness of the employer's plan, the council can insist the matter be resolved by arbitration.[46]

Even with respect to corporate decisions dealing with the constriction, alteration, or extension of the operation which do not impose special burdens on the workforce, the rights of works councils to be given information and to be consulted is simply beyond anything most Canadian workers, organized or not, yet know. Works councils are required to receive information concerning the most basic aspects of a company's financial and operational existence at a time and in a manner which ensures that a meaningful opportunity to consider and explore alternative solutions is still available.[47] Typically, Canadian and American workers are entitled to almost no information on a company's financial standing, investment, and marketing strategies, and they have only the most limited access to information concerning corporate reorganization. Only when such decisions have already been taken – and then only if they ask[48] – do Canadian workers get the information necessary to participate meaningfully in these decisions which are so central to their lives.

It is here, in fact, in what are regarded as the weakest powers of the works councils (in that they do not have a power of co-decision) that the distinction between the two systems is seen by many students of comparative labour relations to be the sharpest.[49] Whereas it is expected that employees in West Germany will participate in the earliest stages of policy formulation, those in charge of the administration of our system of collective bargaining have said that it was not intended to take employees into the boardrooms where the most fundamental issues of corporate planning are resolved.

In these examples one can appreciate why the difference between the Canadian and West German models of industrial relations that has attracted most academic comment is the *extent* to which – rather than the *means* by which – employees participate in the decision-making processes of the enterprise. What has drawn most of the attention to the West German model has been the fact that generally employee participation is both broader and deeper, not that it is freer and more democratic, than our own. Regardless of which emphasis it properly deserves, these features of the West German model should effectively rebut any counterclaim that a similar shift in our own system of collective bargaining could in any way prejudice the control employees would be able to maintain over their lives.

In the final analysis, then, there is no evidence which would justify the Canadian trade union movement resisting what seems to be the next logical step in the ongoing liberalization of our labour code. Only a propensity of peevishness, a proclivity to perversity, which can carry no weight in a constitutional conversation committed to the principles we have been applying, could explain unions reacting antagonistically to a legislative initiative of this kind.[50] For unions, as well as those whose interest they are committed to serve, reformulating our system of collective labour relations to incorporate principles more sensitive to our political traditions of freedom and democracy would represent an enhancement in their interests in every way.

Here, then, is the kind of conversation we have been looking for. Here is a case where, even restricting themselves to the two principles of constitutional review we have been using, courts can strike a blow for social justice in a spectacular way. Fighting with principles rather than with resources they don't really have, the most disadvantaged and under-represented workers in our community can participate in the formulation of the most fundamental rules which control their lives in a way the democratic processes of politics have never allowed.[51] This example makes clear that for such groups, interest-group advocacy rather than grass-roots politicization may be the most effective means by which social justice can be claimed.[52]

In this example we can see just how much more attentive Canadian legislators would have to be to principles of freedom and democracy, of self-development and equality, in their design of systems of collective labour relations. This example involves a large group of people who have laboured a long time without effective representation of their interests, and who have been inadequately represented in the formulation of labour policy in the past. Overnight they should be able to invoke the Charter to secure a substantial measure of social justice in the rules which govern the activity which is so central to their lives. In terms of the judicial function, it is unlikely there will be a greater opportunity for the courts to participate in the creation of a legal environment in which institutions of responsible self-government can be promoted in our economic affairs. It is hard to imagine another issue in which the representation-reinforcing function many think best integrates judicial review with our other institutions of democratic government can be carried out on such a massive scale.

In terms of the historical chronology with which we began this inquiry, the example of the exclusivity principle confirms our observation that major changes in our system of politics and government, like entrenching a Charter of Rights and Freedoms, will have a correspondingly profound effect on the substantive rules we adopt to govern our relations at work. In one sense, entrenchment of our most basic political ideals in a Charter of Rights confirms that, at least on the question of how workers are to associate together, our legislators have, as some have claimed, gone too far. In their enthusiasm to correct injustices of the past, our legislators have allowed themselves to get off the track. No doubt their objectives have, for the most part, been laudable. Undoubtedly the principle of exclusivity was an improvement on the policies which preceded it. Still, the entrenchment of the Charter now requires us to develop even more sophisticated and sensitive rules of employee association. Though not nearly as draconian as the earlier prohibitions on employee associations, compared to the principles used by other free and democratic societies, our current rule of exclusive representation tolerates an unnecessary degree of compulsion and coercion. By adhering to the interpretation we have been following, our courts can substantially enhance the prospect that the gradual liberalization and democratization of the law of work relations that we traced in Part One will be taken its next logical and natural step.

For some, I suspect, one of the most problematic parts of everything that has been said so far is contained in that last sentence. Even if, as a matter of constitutional theory, every conclusion we have derived were logically sound, a gnawing disquiet would remain as to precisely what the next step would turn out to be. Certainly, if the analysis is sound, there would have to be another legislative step. If the principle of exclusive representation is inconsistent with s.2 and s.15 of the Charter in the ways our conversation revealed, then s.52 of the Charter admits of no other conclusion. This cornerstone of our current model of collective bargaining would be null and void and of no further legal force or effect. In these circumstances, once again our legislatures would be obliged to "act."

Such concern is, evidently, a legitimate one, but it is one which we need not rush too quickly to allay. If the invalidation of the principle of exclusive representation means that to remain faithful to our constitutional ideals a legislature must take a new initiative, it is important that we take the time to develop a new set of rules and institutions that will allow us to liberalize our labour code as sensitively as we can. The issue of the collective representation of employee interests is so vital to the shape and structure of the system as a whole, that we ought to think through as carefully as we can all of the principles on which, and the institutions through which, our constitutional guarantees can be realized.

Although I have focused my attention on the German model of works councils, I have been at pains to emphasize that it is not my purpose to recommend that specific system in all of its detail. At the level of principle and historical experience the German model is unquestionably one of the most developed systems of its kind. But so are the other European systems we have identified. They are also a good deal more compatible with our constitutional values and they may be integrated more easily in other ways with the other aspects of our labour code. Which of these models and what other features of these systems of collective labour relations are most adaptable to our larger code of labour relations are matters that warrant close study before any final decision is made.

The fact that our own analysis must stop here, at the level of principle, should not be considered a failing or even cause for concern. Principle, after all, is precisely what the process of constitutional review and the method of our third branch of government is all about. The legislative process, with its systems of committees and powers of investigation, enjoys a comparative advantage on matters of detail and institutional design. Once again, the rich diversity in the various institutions which have given effect to the principles of employee representation are testimonials to the legislature's expertise in this respect.

Finally, there is no question that we can have the time if we care to take it. Any legislature committed to extending our values of freedom and democracy to the rules and processes through which we govern the places people work could easily declare its intention to bring such a policy into effect by a stipulated date in the future. Either a court could rule that our existing model and the principle of exclusivity was temporarily valid,[53] or the legislature could invoke its override power to continue in force the existing rule until the new policy was fully formulated and ready to take effect.[54] For any legislature so inclined we have available all the legal tools, institutional structures, and demonstrated experience that is necessary to fashion a reformulation of our labour code which would be as significant as any in the past six hundred years.

Postscript

All of us who are concerned for peace and the
triumph of justice must be keenly aware how small
an influence reason and honest good will exert upon
events in the political field.
Albert Einstein

We have followed this conversation concerning the constitutional validity
of our system of collective labour relations in general and its principle
of employee representation in particular about as far as we can. Even
though we have not particularized the institutional design which a
revitalized system of collective bargaining would take, we have come
far enough to allow us to bring our inquiry to a close. With our
assessment of the exclusivity rule, we have reached a stage where it
can, I think, be said that we have realized the objectives we set for
ourselves at the beginning of this project.

Certainly at the most practical level of policy formulation, the basic
shape and substance of a constitutional labour code is now clearly visible.
We have in hand a fairly clear idea of the most basic principles and
institutional features of a labour code which can be certified as being
constitutional. Both as a matter of procedural fairness and substantive
justice we can say that a constitutional labour code will show considerably more concern and respect for the interests of those who are
less advantaged in our society than does our existing legal regime.

By "constitutionalizing" our labour code, judicial review should silence
those who argue that we should dismantle our existing collective model
of work relations. A constitutional labour code will have no part of
that. The invalidity of that kind of a system would be plain for all
to see. The Charter will recommend something quite different: a blend

of the old with some new. It will authorize the retention of many existing rules such as minimum wages, maximum hours and years of employment, fair treatment, affirmative action, and the like. All these laws enhance the opportunity of each person to have access to and be treated as an equal in this human activity which is so vital to our well-being. Properly confined, these central parts of our labour code can meet our two principles of judicial review. But not all aspects of it can. Entrenchment of the Charter will not mean the validation of every feature of our existing legal regime. It will also result in an amended set of legal rules which will show more concern and respect for those who, like agricultural and domestic workers, women, our youth, and the less skilled, have too frequently been denied the equal benefit and protection of our labour code.

Beyond having a fairly clear idea of the broad parameters of a labour code which is constitutional all the way through, we have also come some distance in satisfying a second objective we had set for this project. With our conclusions on the validity of the principle of exclusivity, we have accumulated enough evidence to take Mill's hypothesis as proven. Our analysis offers strong support for his claim that the sensitivity any set of legal rules shows for the interests of those who are governed by them will depend directly on the effectiveness with which those interests can be advanced in the decision-making process which enacts them. Recognizing and exploiting the institution of judicial review as a new opportunity for participating in the processes of government can lead directly to an amelioration of the worst excesses of the existing legal regime. Even when it is kept within its most narrow and conservative confines, judicial review can mean that those who traditionally have had very little influence in the formulation of labour policy will be able to participate more effectively than they generally have in the other two branches of government. Compared to the kinds of debates which take place in our legislatures, judicial review offers a much fairer and more neutral forum for citizen participation. In the courts the merits of the debate are not judged by those who are directly involved in the defence of the law under scrutiny. Equally, all participation is more equitable and effective when reason and not rhetoric, principle and not material resources, determine the outcome. The quality of the dialogue and the resolutions it generates can only be enhanced when they are the product of closely argued affidavits prepared by the experts in the field rather than the result of pleas of passion and panderings to prejudice by those whose understanding of the issues may be marginal at best.

And finally, our analysis has come far enough to be able to see the outline of a theory concerning the relation between law and politics, which offers the beginnings of a description of and justification for the practice of judicial review.[1] It is now possible to conceptualize the relationship between the judiciary and the other two branches of government as a cooperative venture rather than an adversarial and antagonistic confrontation. To secure a constitutional labour code requires that all three branches of government articulate, apply, amend, and adjudicate our labour law in an equally principled way. On the analysis we have followed, both Commons and courts must be committed to the same constitutional exercise. Judges and legislators are cast in roles which oblige them to fashion together a labour code which meets our constitutional commitments. Only by their joint efforts can all our labour laws, both legislated and adjudicated, become supportive of the possibility of each individual in our society being able to exercise a meaningful degree of control over the direction and development of his or her life.

In such a joint endeavour, judicial review is necessarily the catalyst. In a sense it represents the most basic opportunity for individual participation in the process of democratic government. From the perspective of the participants, judicial review initiates a conversation of justification in which the majority benefiting from a particular rule is obliged to offer an adequate explanation to those who feel their constitutional entitlements have been unreasonably compromised. Judicial review offers a more structured and a more equal debate as to what laws can be legitimately included in our labour code than that which can take place in our political arenas. In all the examples we have worked through, the court takes over the role of umpire supervising a debate which, as we saw in the first part, has been going on for centuries. Indeed, as the example of differential regulations governing exposure to certain toxic substances made plain, even when an adequate justification is forthcoming, the fact of the debate itself will have enhanced the opportunity for individual involvement in the formulation of social policy.

Obviously, judicial review will have an even more dramatic impact on the democratic quality of our system of government when, as in the conversation about the constitutional integrity of the principle of exclusive representation, the dialogue reveals there is no reasonable justification for the burdens some disadvantaged group is made to bear. A ruling by our courts that the legislative branch must incorporate a principle of voluntary or plural representation into its system of collective labour relations would provide an immediate opportunity for more than half of our workforce to participate more meaningfully than ever before in framing the rules under which they will work.

I recognize that the characterization I have been developing of the relation between law and politics is open to another, quite different, challenge. For those who are sceptical of the integrity of the legislative and executive branches of government, the thread holding my analysis together may seem far too slender to make credible the connection it establishes between politics and law. Such a cooperative characterization will appear far too romantic and remote from the reality of how the different branches of government have traditionally related to each other. In the central case we have considered, the political sceptic will challenge the assumption that, properly chastened, our legislative assemblies will respect and respond to the logic of law. Instead they will likely point to the popular assault labour is currently weathering to support a prediction that the more likely legislative response to the judicial invalidation of their principle of exclusivity will be the enactment of some other rule even more prejudicial to the interest of the workers.

There are two ways of responding to this final appeal that the status quo may be the best we should expect because our processes of law and especially politics are so vulnerable to the forces of wealth and power. First, as a matter of law it makes little sense. When a court strikes down a rule in our labour code, such as exclusivity, it is for the purpose of requiring that a different law, more sensitive and less abusive of workers' interests, be put in its place. If the existing principle of exclusive representation, or any other part of our labour code was found to be unconstitutional, by definition so would every other law which offended our constitutional commitment to equality of liberty.

Knowing that any law it enacts is subject to judicial review is likely to enhance the quality of participation in the legislature itself. To avoid the prospect of having its decisions reviewed in the courts, a legislature would be expected to anticipate and accommodate possible challenges to the policies it proposes, and to tailor its legislation accordingly. In a symbiotic way, the opportunity for increased citizen participation that judicial review provides should in the end make our legislatures and their executives more democratic as well.

Secondly, as a matter of politics, such scepticism that our labour code can be developed cooperatively by the three branches of government does not seem well grounded. To suggest that our legislators would resist the liberalization of our rules of employee representation would be quite at odds with the historical evolution we followed in Part One. Our labour laws, and especially those rules promulgated by our parliaments, have been moving in the opposite direction for a very long time. Our chronology would predict liberalization, not deregulation, to be the path our legislators are likely to follow.

Moreover, legislators themselves would be direct beneficiaries if they responded positively to such prompting by the courts. Both theory and experience strongly support the expectation that enhanced participation in local law-making institutions encourages more active, grass roots, popular involvement in the larger and more centralized processes of our legislative and executive branches of government.[2] Practical experience with democratic institutions in the workplace promotes more effective participation in the larger rule-making processes which organize the society at large. More democratic decision-making processes in the workplace should make it more likely that all of our institutions and processes of government will respect our equal entitlement to self-determination and personal self-rule.

In predicting legislatures will respond negatively to the judicial invalidation of their declared choice of policy, the sceptic misses this most basic point. By adhering to the principle that the equal status of each individual as an autonomous agent must be respected in all of the rules and law-making processes which govern our lives, legislators will have done everything in their power to make our society as free and democratic as possible. They will have dedicated their law-making authority to the values of fraternity and reciprocity on which all communities of principle are ultimately grounded.[3] They will have set an example, so far as law-makers can, of how each of us, even when we control the coercive authority of the state, must "act" if we are to live by the ethical principles that distinguish societies whose constitutions depict them to be both democratic and free.

Notes

1 This definition is not meant to deny or diminish the importance of other institutional forms (cooperatives, partnerships, families, etc.) in which work is performed. While work is frequently organized within these alternate legal forms, employment is unquestionably the legal institution in which the majority of people pursue their work activities and it will be the sole focus of my inquiry. Vocations as varied as garagemen and grocers, teachers and lawyers have all evolved from stages where services once provided almost exclusively by independent workers are now increasingly performed in an employment relationship. For an introduction to the debate about the nature of the rules appropriate for governing work performed in the family relation, see Carol Lopate, "Pay for Housework," *Social Policy* 5 (1974): 27–31.

2 For an initial review of the range of issues raised by the Charter in the area of employment law, see Joel Fichaud, "Analysis of the Charter and its Application to Labour Law," *Dalhousie Law Journal* 8, no. 2 (1984): 402–34. See also the cases cited in n.22 infra.

3 When I refer to our own and/or earlier societies' labour codes, I mean to include all the major legislative rules, such as standards governing wages and hours, human rights, collective bargaining, occupational health and safety, as well as those adjudicated by courts, labour boards, arbitrators, and parallel administrative agencies.

4 I have already indicated that the analysis is not intended as a comprehensive statement of the constitutional validity of every rule in our labour code. Nor is it exhaustive in terms of the constitutional principles against which the validity of the labour code will be assessed. With respect to the latter, I realize that for some restricting my analysis to "liberal" criteria of constitutionality will be fatal to everything that follows. For those who employ

a neo-realist or critical method of analysis, proceeding within such a constrained theoretical framework begs the very question of the legitimacy of judges performing the task of validating social policy enacted by the peoples' representatives. See Andrew Altman, "Legal Realism, Critical Legal Studies and Dworkin," in *Philosophy and Public Affairs* 15 (1986): 205–35. For others, who accept the integrity and coherence of the institution of judicial review, different principles of interpretation may be thought to provide more accurate descriptions and justifications of the constitutional order that is seen to be embraced by the text.

It would take me well beyond my particular project to organize adequate responses to either of these challenges to my method of constitutional theorizing. To those who question the legitimacy of the enterprise itself, I would only say that for me the compelling point is that the entrenchment of our Charter of Rights and Freedoms is a constitutional fact. It is now part of our legal practice and its interpretation cannot be avoided. Whatever the theoretical force of this challenge, as a practical matter the courts cannot avoid the task of formulating a set of principles, and ultimately a larger political theory, to organize their analysis of the constitutional validity of the social policy they will be required to assess.

To those who would employ other principles and alternate theories of judicial review, the text must speak for itself. There is nothing in the thesis I embrace to preclude alternate principles or theories of the constitution being put forward. My analysis is not intended as a full theory of judicial review and I explicitly acknowledge that additional principles will and indeed have been developed by the courts. My only claim is that the two principles I read as being immanent in the text and practice of our constitutional law provide a very strong explanation of and justification for both the rights and freedoms set out in the Charter as well as most of the important features of the legal order we have created to govern the places in which people work. If others believe alternate principles provide as good a fit of and justification for the constitutional order the courts have been asked to interpret, they should be offered in essays parallel to this. Writing of this kind can only inform and enhance the development of our constitutional jurisprudence. As I suggest in Part Two, ours is a unique moment in Canada's constitutional history when essays of this kind, as much as the "black letter" authority of past cases, can make an important contribution to the integrity of the legal order according to which our society will come to be governed.

5 It is generally recognized that any coherent account of constitutional law must integrate the practice of adjudication and interpretation into a larger legal theory which addresses and endeavours to justify and reconcile the coercive powers exercised by all three branches of government. See, e.g., Ronald Dworkin, *Law's Empire* (Cambridge, Mass.: Belknap Press 1986),

90. See also W.E. Conklin, "Interpreting and Applying the Limitations Clause: An Analysis of s.1," and R.A. Macdonald, "Postscript and Prelude – the Jurisprudence of the Charter: Eight Theses," in *The New Constitution and the Charter of Rights*, ed. E.P. Belobaba and Eric Gertner (Toronto: Butterworths 1982), 75–99 and 321–50.

6 Friedrich A. Hayek, *The Constitution of Liberty* (Chicago: Regnery 1972), 267.

7 It would be unfair and inaccurate to suggest that the legislative record in any of our communities has succumbed completely to the pressure of those advocating such policy initiatives. At the same time that they have considered the policy options noted in the text, almost all of the relevant governmental authorities have, with varying degrees of commitment, simultaneously pursued policies promoting (i) pay and wider employment equity plans; (ii) improved occupational health and safety programs; and (iii) laws imposing collective agreements on employers who unlawfully interfere with their employees' attempts to institute a system of collective labour relations.

8 Some of the leading essays discussing the purposes and programs of bills of rights are collected in Peter W. Hogg, *Constitutional Law of Canada*, 2nd ed. (Toronto: Carswell 1985), 651.

9 See, e.g., *Brown* v. *Board of Education*, 349 U.S. 294 (1955).

10 See, e.g., *Roe* v. *Wade*, 410 U.S. 113 (1973).

11 See, e.g., *Miranda* v. *Arizona*, 384 U.S. 436 (1966).

12 See, e.g., *Goldberg* v. *Kelly*, 397 U.S. 254 (1970).

13 That the Charter will result in some individuals and groups in society having greater influence in policy formulation seems beyond doubt. See Peter Russell, "The Effect of the Charter of Rights on the Policy-Making Role of Canadian Courts," in *Law, Politics and the Judicial Process in Canada*, ed. F.L. Morton (Calgary: University of Calgary Press 1984), 291–305. The particular focus of this study is to determine whether workers who are not particularly well off will be among those for whom the Charter will enhance their participation and involvement in the processes of government.

14 John Stuart Mill, "Considerations on Representative Government," in *Utilitarianism, Liberty and Representative Government* (New York: Dutton 1951), 280. It goes without saying that the ultimate effect of any change in our labour code which results from the exercise of judicial review will be significantly influenced by and mediated through the customary and contextual processes that surround the places in which people actually perform their work. Recognizing that there are a plurality of sources for the rules which organize all social relationships, including those in the workplace, does not alter the conclusion that changes in the formal, legal context itself may also have a profound impact on the control that the different

constituencies in the workplace will enjoy in pursuing their particular interests and ambitions. For a discussion of the impact of such informal processes of rule-making in the workplace, see H.W. Arthurs, "Understanding Labour Law: The Debate over Industrial Pluralism," in *Current Legal Problems* (1985): 83–116.

15 Part Four, which focuses on different models of collective decision-making in the workplace, forms the basis of an article to be published in the *American Journal of Comparative Law* (forthcoming 1987).

16 This metaphor has been developed by Ronald Dworkin in many of his writings. A summary of the idea is presented in *Law's Empire*, 228. A more extensive treatment can be found in his "Law and Interpretation," in *The Politics of Interpretation*, ed. W.J.T. Mitchell (Chicago: University of Chicago Press 1983), 249–70. See also, the symposium "Law and Literature," *Texas Law Review* 60, no. 3 (1982): 373–586.

17 The characterization of workers as industrial citizens is borrowed from H.W. Arthurs, "Developing Industrial Citizenship: A Challenge for Canada's Second Century," *Canadian Bar Review* 45 (1967): 786–830, who describes and analyses the various attributes of citizenship workers in industry now enjoy.

18 The standard texts describing the extent to which different segments of our society participate in the political process include Robert A. Dahl, *Who Governs: Democracy and Power in an American City* (New Haven, Conn.: Yale University Press 1961), and William Mishler, *Political Participation in Canada* (Toronto: Macmillan 1979). The idea that the most disadvantaged workers, who are frequently the least skilled, will not participate effectively in the political process is developed in Harold D. Lasswell, *Politics: Who Gets What, When and How* (New York: World Publishing 1958). For a more theoretical analysis, see Anthony Downs, *An Economic Theory of Democracy* (New York: Harper & Row 1965). See also, C.B. Macpherson, "Pluralism, Individualism and Participation," *Economic and Industrial Democracy* 1, no. 1 (1980): 21–30.

19 The standard text on the secondary or dual labour market is Peter B. Doeringer and Michael J. Piore, *Internal Labor Markets and Manpower Analysis* (Lexington, Mass.: D.C. Heath 1971). For a brief summary of the theory and empirical evidence pertaining to this sector of our labour market, see Morley Gunderson, *Labour Market Economics* (Toronto: McGraw-Hill Ryerson 1980).

20 On the basis of the historical record it cannot be assumed that unions will automatically promote the interests of working people who toil in the secondary and unorganized sectors of our economy. Historically, organized labour's attitude towards labour laws which establish, for example, minimum wages or protection against unjust dismissal for all workers has ranged from indifference to outright hostility. See, e.g., David M. Beatty, "Ideology,

Politics and Unionism," in *Studies in Labour Law*, ed. Kenneth P. Swan and Katherine E. Swinton (Toronto: Butterworths 1983), 299–340, and Paul Malles, *Canadian Labour Standards in Law, Agreement and Practice* (Toronto: Economic Council of Canada 1976), 7.

21 So far only the government of Saskatchewan has invoked the power, conferred by s.33 of the Charter, to declare one of its enactments (in this case legislation ordering public servants to return to work), to be operative notwithstanding any potential conflict with the fundamental rights and freedoms set out in s.2 and ss.7–15. See the SGEU Dispute Settlement Act, Bill 144, 1986 (29th Leg. Sask., 4th sess.).

22 At the time of writing four cases concerning the constitutional validity of limitations on the right to strike and picket have worked their way through the appellate process to the Supreme Court of Canada. See *Retail, Wholesale and Department Store Union* v. *Dolphin Delivery Ltd.* (1984), 10 DLR (4th) 198 (BCCA), appeal dismissed by Supreme Court of Canada, 18 Dec. 1986; *Public Service Alliance of Canada* v. *The Queen in Right of Canada* (1984), 11 DLR (4th) 387 (Fed. CA); *Re Retail, Wholesale, and Department Store Union et al. and Government of Saskatchewan et al.* (1985), 19 DLR (4th) 609 (Sask. CA); and *Re Public Service Employees Act, Labour Relations Act and Police Officers Collective Bargaining Act* (1984), 16 DLR (4th) 359 (Alta. CA). Although the method of analysis I have employed would be relevant to each of these cases, and especially to the law of secondary picketing, because they have already been argued before the court I have refrained from addressing these parts of our labour code here. For my evaluation of the Supreme Court's analysis of the law of secondary picketing, see "Constitutional Conceits: The Coercive Authority of the Courts," *University of Toronto Law Journal* 37, no. 2 (1987), forthcoming.

Challenges have been initiated against other rules in our labour code. Most of these relate to various aspects of our collective bargaining regime and have been made to the relevant administrative tribunals. See, e.g., *Retail, Wholesale and Department Store Union* v. *Simpsons Ltd.* [1984], OLRB Reports 1255 (September) – (requirement to join or pay dues to union); *Municipal Technicians Association of the City of Thunder Bay* v. *The Corporation of the City of Thunder Bay* [1984], OLRB Reports 1032 (July), and *International Brotherhood of Electrical Workers Local Union 1687* v. *Kidd Creek Mines* [1986], OLRB Reports 736 (June) – (group of employees not allowed to carve out own unit); *Union of Bank Employees* v. *Canadian Imperial Bank of Commerce*, 85 CLLC para. 16,021 (CLRB) – (restriction on union contact with employees during working hours); *Union of Bank Employees and Bank of Montreal* (1985), 10 CLRBR (NS) 129 – (prohibition of employer communications to employees concerning union activity which constituted unfair labour practice). See also, *Prime et al.* v. *Manitoba Labour Relations Board et al.* (1983), 3 DLR (4th) 74; rev'd. 8 DLR (4th) 461; *United*

Headgear, Optical and Allied Workers Union of Canada, Local 3 v. *Biltmore Stetson (Canada) Inc.* (1983), 43 OR (2d) 243.

23 There is a large literature canvassing the decisions of the courts which gave rise to the suspicion and scepticism of organized labour towards the judiciary. See, e.g., Arthurs, "Developing Industrial Citizenship"; Karl E. Klare, "Judicial Deradicalization of the Wagner Act and the Origins of Modern Legal Consciousness, 1937-41," *Minnesota Law Review* 62 (1978): 265–339, Otto Kahn-Freund, *Labour Law: Old Traditions and New Developments* (Toronto: Clarke, Irwin 1968).

24 This characterization of the distinguishing feature of rule-making by courts as opposed to legislatures features prominently in recent U.S. constitutional law scholarship. See, e.g., Ronald Dworkin, *A Matter of Principle* (Cambridge, Mass.: Harvard University Press 1985), and Alexander M. Bickel, "Foreword: The Passive Virtues," *Harvard Law Review* 75 (1961): 40–79.

25 The most frequently cited instances of terms implied by the courts for the benefit of employees include the employer's duty to provide a safe working environment, to pay wages for the duration of the contract even if there may not be sufficient work to do or if the employee is too sick to work as well as to exercise its managerial prerogatives fairly. For a description of the various terms implied by courts into the common law contract of employment, see Innis Christie, *Employment Law in Canada* (Toronto: Butterworths 1980), 235–48; Mark R. Freedland, *The Contract of Employment* (Oxford: Clarendon Press 1976), 142–59; Labour Casebook Group, *Labour Law: Cases Materials and Commentary*, 4th ed. (Kingston, Ontario: Queen's University Industrial Relations Centre 1984), 52–84.

26 The connection between the judicial function in constitutional and common law adjudication is developed by Dworkin in *Law's Empire*, 310ff. See also, Harry Wellington, "Common Law Rules and Constitutional Double Standards: Some Notes on Adjudication," *Yale Law Journal* 83, no. 2 (1983): 221–311.

27 One of the areas of employment law in which the courts' confusion of means and ends was most pronounced was with respect to civil and criminal conspiracy. For an introduction to the judicial development of this law in Canada, see Innis Christie, *The Liability of Strikers in the Law of Tort* (Kingston, Ont.: Queen's University Industrial Relations Centre 1967); and A.W.R. Carrothers, *Collective Bargaining Law in Canada* (Toronto: Butterworths 1965), chap. 2. For more general discussions of the commitment of Anglo-American courts to the institution of the market and the ethic of free trade, see Patrick S. Atiyah, *The Rise and Fall of Freedom of Contract* (Oxford: Clarendon Press 1979), 398–405; and Roscoe Pound, "Liberty of Contract," *Yale Law Journal* 18 (1909): 454–87.

28 Otto Kahn-Freund, *Labour and the Law* (London: Stevens 1972), chaps. 1 and 2.

ONE

1 The idea of understanding law as integrity is a central theme developed by Ronald Dworkin in his *Law's Empire* (Cambridge, Mass.: Belknap Press 1986).

2 See L. Fuller and W. Perdue, Jr., "The Reliance Interest in Contract Damages," *Yale Law Journal* 46 (1936): 52, who made the point this way: "The proposition that legal rules can be understood only with reference to the purposes they serve would today scarcely be regarded as an exciting truth. The notion that law exists as a means to an end has been commonplace for at least half a century. There is, however, no justification for assuming, because this attitude has now achieved respectability, and even triteness, that it enjoys a pervasive application in practice. Certainly there are even today few legal treatises of which it may be said that the author has throughout clearly defined the purposes which his definitions and distinctions serve. We are still all too willing to embrace the conceit that it is possible to manipulate legal concepts without the orientation which comes from the simple inquiry: toward what end is this activity directed? Nietzsche's observation, that the most common stupidity consists in forgetting what one is trying to do, retains a discomforting relevance to legal science."

3 S. Jevons, *The State in Relation to Labour* (London: Macmillan 1894), 101.

4 Recognition of the commonality of interests between labour and non-labour producer groups, and the potential detriment to consumers' interests that can be caused by collusion between the two, lies behind the limitations our competition laws place on the extent to which the monopolization of labour (which is promoted by our collective bargaining legislation) can be effected with the aid of non-labour (capitalist) producers. See Combines Investigation Act, RSC 1970, c. C–23, ss.4 and 32. See also *Allen-Bradely v. Local Union No. 3 IBEW*, U.S. 797 (1945).

5 The interdependence of each of our lives on the productive ambitions and efforts of others is a central theme in Emile Durkheim, *On the Division of Labour in Society* (London: Macmillan 1933). See also R. Heilbroner, *The Making of Economic Society* (Englewood Cliffs, NJ: Prentice Hall 1962).

6 D.M. Beatty, "Labour is not a Commodity," in *Studies in Canadian Contract Law*, ed. John Swan and Barry J. Reiter (Toronto: Butterworths 1980), 313–55.

7 Karl Renner, *The Institutions of Private Law and their Social Functions* (London: Routlege and Kegan Paul 1949), 115.

8 It is presumably this aspect of our general understanding of working, of making or doing something for others in the community, which distinguishes this behaviour from an activity like play, which is undertaken primarily to divert or amuse the person who engages in it. See the Special Task Force

to the Secretary of Health, Education and Welfare, *Work in America* (Cambridge, Mass.: MIT Press 1973), 3.

9 Leo XIII, *Rerum Novarum* 1891; Pius XI, *Quadragesimo Anno* 1931; John Paul II, *Laborem Exercens* 1981.

10 The most famous philosopher who concerned himself with the meaning of work was, of course, Karl Marx. For a contemporary appreciation of Marx's analysis, see Adina Schwartz, "Toward a Jurisprudence of Labour Law: Methodological Preliminaries," *Valparaiso University Law Review* 19 (1984): 71–94. See also her "Meaningful Work," *Ethics* 92 (1982): 634–46, and Michael Walzer, *Spheres of Justice* (New York: Basic Books 1983), chap. 6.

11 Abraham Maslow, "A Theory of Human Motivation: The Goals of Work," in *The Future of Work*, ed. Fred Best (Englewood Cliffs, NJ: Prentice Hall 1973); Sigmund Freud, *Civilization and Its Discontents* (New York: Norton 1962).

12 Studs Terkel, *Working* (New York: Pantheon Books 1974); and Special Task Force, *Work in America*.

13 Maslow, "Theory of Human Motivation."

14 Terkel, *Working*, xxiv, 589.

15 Special Task Force, *Work in America*, 173. See also *Langston v. Amalgamated Union of Engineering Workers* [1974] AII ER 980 at 987.

16 The psychological scars borne by people who, for whatever reason, are induced to undertake the most brutal and boring sorts of work is poignantly presented in Studs Terkel's anthology of autobiographical sketches of those who perform such tasks in our own communities. Earlier studies reflecting similar experiences are collected in *Work in America*. More philosophical treatments of alternate methods available to societies to organize the performance of such dirty work are presented by Walzer in *Spheres of Justice*, and Bertrand Russell, "In Praise of Idleness," in *Why Work*, ed. Vernon Richards (London: Freedom Press 1983), 25–34.

17 It should be clear that I am concerned only with the role work plays in our own communities. In other societies and at different times, work has served entirely different purposes. Classical Greek societies, for example, are commonly described as communities in which work was regarded primarily as a negative and odious experience. For a somewhat different interpretation of the classical Greek attitude towards work, see H.D. Kitto, *The Greeks* (Harmondsworth: Pelican 1970), 239ff.

18 Special Task Force, *Work in America*, 3.

19 One of the earliest functions of trade unions was to encourage and support social relations between workers with common interests beyond the hours and places of work. See Henry Pelling, *A History of British Trade Unionism*, 2nd ed. (London: Macmillan 1971), and Durkheim, *Division of Labour*.

20 John A. Brittain, *The Inheritance of Economic Status* (Washington, DC: Brookings Institution 1977).

TWO

1 For a description of the extent to which enslavement was used as part of our own earliest efforts in the social regulation of the labour relationship and the reasons why its use and impact was as limited as it was, see H.C. Pentland, *Labour and Capital in Canada* (Toronto: Lorimer 1981).

2 For an argument to this effect, see Robert W. Fogel and Stanley Engerman, *Time on the Cross* (Boston: Little Brown and Co. 1974).

3 Pentland, *Labour and Capital*, fixes 1797 as the date at which slavery ceased to be a legal method of regulating labour relationships.

4 Which is not to say slaves could not be persons for other purposes, for example, for purchasing their freedom *from* enslavement.

5 Sir William Blackstone, *Commentaries on the Laws of England*, 4th ed. Book 1 (Dublin: J. Exshaw 1771), 423, cf Gerald Dworkin, "Paternalism," in *Morality and the Law*, ed. Richard A. Wasserstrom (Belmont, California: Wadsworth Publishing Co. 1971), 107–26, who discusses the apparent paradox of denying an individual the liberty to enter such relationships voluntarily.

6 E.P. Thompson, *The Making of the English Working Class* (Harmondsworth: Pelican 1968), 594.

7 The outlines of the codes of labour of pre-industrial English society are set out in W.S. Holdsworth, *A History of English Law*, 3rd ed., 16 vols. (London: Methuen 1923), 2:459–64, 4:340–54, and 379–87. A brief summary of the major features of the legal regime can be found in E. Merrick Dodd, "From Maximum Wages to Minimum Wages: Six Centuries of Regulation of Employment Contracts," *Columbia Law Review* 43, no. 5 (1943): 643–87. For additional analysis of various features of this legal regime, see Jevons, *The State in Relation to Labour*, and Karl Polanyi, *The Great Transformation* (Boston: Beacon Press 1957).

8 Blackstone, *Commentaries*, Book 1, 425.

9 For a description of the parallel legal rule in pre-industrial Canadian society, see Pentland, *Labour and Capitalism*.

10 See, e.g. *Colgate* v. *Bacheler* (1601), Cro. Eliz. 872, 78 ER 1097; *Mitchell* v. *Reynolds* (1711), 1 P. Wms. 181, 24 ER 347; and, generally, see Michael Trebilcock, *The Common Law of Restraint of Trade: A Legal and Economic Analysis* (Toronto: Carswell 1986), chap. 1.

11 S. Atiyah, *The Rise and Fall of Freedom of Contract* (Oxford: Clarendon Press 1979), 126ff.

12 It is more than coincidental that the workers who consistently show the

highest self-esteem in their work and standing in our communities are those such as doctors and lawyers who continue to exercise extensive powers of self-regulation and self-government.

13 Much of the same concern motivates recent academic and public interest inquiries into the modern derivations of the guild societies – the professional organizations. See Michael Trebilcock *et al.*, *Professional Regulation* (Toronto: Ontario Ministry of the Attorney General 1979).

14 A.H. Ruegg, *The Laws Regulating the Relation of Employer and Workman in England* (London: W. Clowes & Sons 1905).

15 Ibid., 95.

16 This is still the premise which underlies the "anti-parasite" laws characteristic of the labour codes in Eastern Europe. See Laurence C. Becker, "The Obligation to Work," *Ethics* 91 (1980): 35–49.

17 Jevons, *The State in Relation to Labour*, 35.

18 Because, as we have noted, they created the potential of workers actively pursuing their own interests by monopolizing the provision of the service or trade.

19 Blackstone, *Commentaries*, Book I, 415.

20 Poor Law, 13 and 14 Charles II, c.12 (1662).

21 *R. v. Journeyman Tailors of Cambridge* (1721), 8 Mod. 10, 88 ER 9.

22 Statute of Artificers, 5 Elizabeth I, c.4 (1563). For an analysis of the parallel legal rule in Canada, see P. Craven "The Law of Master and Servant in Mid-Nineteenth Century Ontario," in *Essays in The History of Canadian Law*, ed. D. Flaherty (Toronto: University of Toronto Press 1981), 175–211.

23 Thompson, *Making of the English Working Class*, 219. See, generally, R.H. Tawney, *Religion and the Rise of Capitalism* (Harmondsworth: Penguin 1975).

THREE

1 Atiyah, *Freedom of Contract*, 219.

2 Carlo M. Copolla, *The Industrial Revolution* (Glasgow: Fontana/Collins 1977), introduction.

3 For a description of the parallel phenomena that accompanied the emergence of an industrialized society in Canada, see Pentland, *Labour and Capital in Canada*.

4 C.B. Macpherson, *The Real World of Democracy* (Toronto: CBC 1966), and *The Life and Times of Liberal Democracy* (Toronto: Oxford University Press 1972).

5 Tawney, *Religion and the Rise of Capitalism*. See also, Atiyah, *Freedom of Contract*, Part I.

6 Ibid., chap. 10.

7 Ruegg, in *Employer and Workman*, claims that as a practical matter the feudal code of state control of the work relationship had largely given way to individual bargaining by the close of the eighteenth century. For a description of the Canadian law of the same period, see Craven, "The Law of Master and Servant."

8 Ruegg, *Employer and Workman*, 25.

9 The settlement laws were repealed in 1795, by An Act Relating to the Laws Relating to the Settlement, Employment and Relief of the Poor, 36 George III, c. 23; see Polanyi, *Great Transformation*, 78.

10 The Poor Laws were repealed in 1834, by the Poor Laws Amendment Act, 4 and 5 William IV, c. 76.

11 As already noted, the courts frequently failed to follow this logic of liberty and found combinations of workers to be criminal and civil wrongs. A partial explanation for this apparent inconsistency seems to lie in the fact that often the courts thought they were faced with situations in which it appeared that some workers were being coerced to accept rather than voluntarily subscribing to the objectives of the organization. See Atiyah, *Freedom of Contract*, 528, 532. As well, frequently, the courts posited free markets and free trade rather than individual autonomy as the basic objective of laws governing labour relationships. As Roscoe Pound observed, freedom of contract was adopted initially as a means to avoid antiquated legal institutions which stood in the way of human progress, but eventually it was treated as an end in itself. On that assumption of course, combinations and conspiracies would be seen as an anathema and as tending toward the creation of (anti-competitive) monopolies. For a discussion of the early caselaw in Canada, see A.W.R. Carrothers, *Collective Bargaining Law in Canada* (Toronto: Butterworths 1965), chap. 2; M. Chartrand, "The First Canadian Trade Union Legislation: A Historical Perspective," *Ottawa Law review* 16 (1984): 267–96.

12 Charles Lindblom, *Politics and Markets* (New York: Basic Books 1977), 48; and see, generally, C.B. Macpherson, *Democratic Theory: Essays in Retrieval* (Oxford: Clarendon Press 1973), 143–56.

13 Roscoe Pound, "Liberty of Contract," *Yale Law Journal* 18 (1909): 454–87; Friedrich A. Hayek, *The Constitution of Liberty* (Chicago: Regnery 1972), chap. 9, Anthony Kronman and Richard A. Posner, *The Economics of Contract Law* (Boston: Little, Brown 1979), chap. 7; Robert Nozick, *Anarchy State and Utopia* (New York: Basic Books 1974); Anthony Kronman, "Contract Law and Distributive Justice," *Yale Law Journal* 89 (1980): 472–511.

14 See, e.g., *Mallan* v. *May* (1843), 11 M and W. 653, 152 ER 967. See, generally, Trebilcock, *The Common Law of Restraint of Trade, A Legal and Economic Analysis*, 22–3, 47.

15 The seminal case is *Priestly* v. *Fowler* (1837), 3 M. and W. 1, 150 ER 1030.

See, generally, R.C.B. Risk, "This Nuisance of Litigation: The Origins of Workmen's Compensation Legislation in Ontario," in Flaherty, ed., *Essays in the History of Canadian Law*, vol. 2, and Eric Tucker, "The Law of Employer's Liability in Ontario 1861–1900: The Search for a Theory," *Osgoode Hall Law Journal* 22 (1984): 213–80.

16 See, generally, Carrothers, *Collective Bargaining Law*; Innis Christie, *The Liability of Strikers in the Law of Tort* (Kingston, Ont.: Queen's University Industrial Relations Centre 1967); Chartrand, "The First Canadian Trade Union Legislation."

17 See Atiyah, *Freedom of Contract*, 523ff; Dodd, in "From Maximum Wages to Minimum Wages," estimated the era of "free" bargaining in England to be twenty-two years.

18 Otto Kahn-Freund, "A Note on Status and Contract in British Labour Law," *Modern Law Review* 30 (1967): 635–44, and "Blackstone's Neglected Child: The Contract of Employment," *Law Quarterly Review* 93 (1977): 508–28.

19 A point recognized by Mill as early as 1848 and still argued for today. See J.S. Mill, *Principles of Political Economy*, Book v, chap. 11, para. 2; see also, Lawrence Tribe, *American Constitutional Law* (Mineola, NY: Foundation Press 1978), 447–8.

20 It is especially important, in the context of our new constitutional order, where precisely the same idea will come into play in determining when it can be said the government has acted and law has been made within the meaning of ss. 32 and 52 of the Charter.

21 Thompson, *Making of English Working Class* 279, 565, 575; and see Atiyah, *Freedom of Contract*, 263ff; Ruegg, *Employer and Workman*, 23.

22 Arnold Toynbee, "The Classical Definition of the Industrial Revolution," in *The Industrial Revolution in Britain: Triumph or Disaster*, ed. Philip A.M. Taylor (Boston: D.C. Heath and Co. 1958), 1–6.

23 B.L. Hutchins and A. Harrison, *A History of Factory Legislation*, 3rd ed. (New York: A.M. Kelley 1966), 27 and 62ff; see also Atiyah, *Freedom of Contract*, 541.

24 Polanyi, *The Great Transformation*, 83.

25 F.A. Hayek, ed., *Capitalism and the Historians* (Chicago: University of Chicago Press 1954); Taylor, *The Industrial Revolution in Britain*.

26 John L. and Barbara Hammond, *The Town Labourer 1760–1832*, *The New Civilization* (London: Longmans 1917), and *The Skilled Labourer 1760–1832* (New York: A.M. Kelley 1967); Friedrich Engels, *The Condition of the Working Class in England in 1844* (Oxford: Basil Blackwell 1971); Sidney and Beatrice Webb, *History of Trade Unionism*, rev. ed. (Clifton, NJ: A.M. Kelley 1973), and *Industrial Democracy* (London: Longmans 1920); Thompson, *Making of the English Working Class*; and T.S. Ashton, "The Treatment of Capitalism by Historians," in *Capitalism and the Historians*, ed. Hayek, 31–61.

27 Adam Smith, *The Wealth of Nations* (New York: Random House 1937), 625.

28 Atiyah, *Freedom of Contract*, 314.

29 This was particularly true after 1834 when, with the repeal of the Poor Laws, the workhouse was the only other social institution, besides contract, in which a worker's physiological needs could be met. For a modern treatment of this issue, see Harry J. Glasbeek, "Voluntarism, Liberalism and Grievance Arbitration – Holy Grail, Romance and Real Life," in *Essays in Labour Relations Law* ed. Geoffrey England (Don Mills, Ont.: CCH Canadian Ltd. 1986), 57–102.

30 The early common law rules that the courts developed to allocate responsibilities for the spate of industrial accidents that accompanied the industrial revolution was, on all counts, highly prejudiced against workers' interests. It is true that the courts did develop rules which imposed on employers a duty to take reasonable care to hire competent employees and to provide proper appliances and maintain them in a proper condition. See, e.g., *Smith* v. *Baker and Sons* [1891], AC 325; *Wilson and Clyde Coal* v. *English* [1938], AC 57; and *Marshment* v. *Borgstrom* [1942], SCR 374. In practice, however, these legal duties were drained of much of their significance by the development of parallel rules concerning the voluntary assumption of risk, contributory negligence, and fellow servants. See Tucker, "The Law of Employer's Liability in Ontario." However, as Tucker describes, both the American courts in their development of common law rules of employer liability and their Canadian colleagues in their application and development of legislative reforms initiated at the close of the nineteenth century, showed a good deal of sensitivity to workers' claims for compensation for injuries suffered as a result of employers' failure to provide a safe and healthy working environment.

31 *Whittle* v. *Frankland* (1862), 31 LJ (MC) 81; *Devonald* v. *Rosser & Sons* [1906], 2 KB 728. See M.R. Freedland, *The Contract of Employment* (Oxford: Clarendon Press 1976), 86–92. But see Craven, "The Law of Master and Servant," who describes why this legal principle did not always work to the advantage of the worker.

32 *Cuckson* v. *Stonee* (1858), 120 ER 902; *Dartmouth Ferry Commission* v. *Marks* (1904), 34 SCR 366.

33 Atiyah, *Freedom of Contract*, 510–11.

34 All the standard accounts of the development of the Factory Acts underscore this characteristic nature of their development; see Hutchins and Harrison, *History of Factory Legislation*; and M.W. Thomas, *The Early Factory Legislation* (Westport, Conn.: Greenwood Press 1970). Kahn-Freund describes the evolution of this body of law as one of "trial and error" in his *Labour and the Law*. See also Ruegg, *Employers and Workmen*, 117ff.

FOUR

1 Otto Kahn-Freund, *Labour Law: Old Traditions and New Developments* (Toronto: Clarke, Irwin 1968). Although there is an extensive radical critique which challenges whether our new legislative regime has been as protective of the interests of workers as it might have been, the fact remains that a shift in the legislative agenda developed dramatically with the enhanced opportunity workers had to bring their influence to bear on the political and legislative processes of government. Even if the shift was more one of form than substance and was, by and large, intended to buy off the claims of workers by making the least possible changes to the existing legal regime, the fact remains this transformation came when workers were able to exert the kind of pressure on the processes of politics that comes with enfranchisement. Among the better-known and more widely cited pieces of this new critical literature, see Karl E. Klare, "Judicial De-radicalization of the Wagner Act and The Origins of Modern Legal Consciousness 1237–1941," *Minnesota Law Review* 62 (1978): 265–339; Katherine Van Wezel Stone, "The Post-War Paradigmin in American Labor Law," *Yale Law Journal* 90 (1981): 1509–81; Karl E. Klare, "Labor Law as Ideology: Toward a New Historiography of Collective Bargaining Law"; Staughton Lynd, "Government Without Rights: The Labor Law Vision of Archibald Cox"; Melvyn Dubofsky, "Legal Theory and Workers' Rights: A Historian's Critique"; and Duncan Kennedy, "Critical Labour Law Theory: A Comment," *Industrial Relations Law Journal* 4, no. 3 (1981): 450–506.

2 Most of the major treatises explaining and justifying the major legislative initiatives of our own era, and in particular our system of collective bargaining, point to the enhanced opportunity for workers to participate in the settlement of the rules which organize their working lives. See Paul C. Weiler, *Reconcilable Differences* (Toronto: Carswell, 1980); Archibald Cox, *Law and the National Labour Policy* (Westport, Conn.: Greenwood Press 1960); Theodore J. St.Antoine, "National Labour Policy: Reflections and Distortions of Social Justice," *Catholic University Law Review* 29 (1980): 535–56; Clyde Summers, "Industrial Democracy, America's Unfulfilled Promise," *Cleveland State Law Review* 28 (1979): 29–49.

3 Brian Langille, "Labour Law is a Subset of Employment Law," *University of Toronto Law Journal* 31 (1981): 200–30.

4 E. West and M. McKee, *Minimum Wages* (Toronto: Economic Council of Canada 1980); Jacob J. Kaufman and Terry G. Foran, "The Minimum Wage and Poverty," in *Towards Freedom From Want*, ed. Sar A. Levitan, Wilbur J. Cohen, and Robert J. Campman (Madison, Wis.: Industrial Relations Research Association 1968).

5 *Coppage* v. *Kansas*, 236 U.S. 1 (1914).

6 See Weiler, *Reconcilable Differences*, 31.

7 For a description and analysis on the different schemes of "accredited employer associations" adopted in Canada, see Richard M. Brown, "The Reform of Bargaining Structure in the Canadian Construction Industry," *Industrial Relations Law Journal* 3 (1979): 539–65.

8 See A.W.R. Carrothers, *Collective Bargaining Law in Canada* (Toronto: Butterworths 1965), Chap. 2; M. Chartrand, "The First Canadian Trade Union Legislation," *Ottawa Law Review* 16 (1984): 267–96.

9 Roy J. Adams, "The Unorganized; A Rising Force," in *Jobs and Labour Peace and Agenda for Action*, ed. Lisa R. Cohen (Montreal: McGill University, Industrial Relations Centre 1983), 40–58.

10 James S. Fishkin, *Tyranny and Legitimacy* (New Haven: Yale University Press 1979).

11 For a description of organized labour's earliest involvement in the political areana in Ontario, see Greg Kealey, *Toronto Workers Respond to Capitalism* (Toronto: University of Toronto Press 1980).

12 See Atiyah, *Freedom of Contract*, 590.

13 Kahn-Freund, "A Note on Status and Contract in British Labour Law."

14 This interpretive technique, which looks beyond the motivations of those who enacted or declared a particular rule or policy to the underlying moral values of the legal practice as a whole, is what Ronald Dworkin has recently described and defended as the method of constructive interpretation. See Dworkin, *Law's Empire*.

15 H.W. Arthurs, "Developing Industrial Citizenship," *Canadian Bar Review* 45 (1967): 786–830.

16 Weiler, *Reconcilable Differences*, 32. Summers, "Industrial Democracy"; Karl E. Klare, "The Quest for Industrial Democracy and the Struggle Against Racism: Perspectives from Labor Law and Civil Rights Law," *Oregon Law Review* 61 (1982): 157–200.

FIVE

1 John Crispo, *The Canadian Industrial Relations System* (Toronto: McGraw Hill-Ryerson 1978).

2 See page 197, note 34. The same incremental character also seems to distinguish our human rights and income support legislation. See Donald Macdonald, *Report of the Royal Commission on the Economic Union and Development Prospects for Canada* (Toronto: University of Toronto Press 1985), vol. 2, 547.

3 Clyde Summers, "American and European Labor Law: The Use and Usefulness of Foreign Experience," *Buffalo Law Review* 16 (1967): 210–28. Paralleling Summers's characterization is Arthur Lenhoff's description

of the evolution of American law on the question of union security, which he calls "confused and entangled." See Arthur Lenhoff, "The Problem of Compulsory Unionism in Europe," *American Journal of Comparative Law* 5 (1956): 18–43.

4 See page 197, note 30.

5 The phrase, descriptive of the coercive character of the legislature's will, is taken from Bruce Ackerman, *Social Justice in a Liberal State* (New Haven: Yale University Press 1980). In a characteristically Canadian compromise, the framers of our Charter of Rights provided, in s.33, that a legislature could maintain its ultimate law-making authority by declaring any of its enactments or parts thereof exempted from judicial review. The origins and justification for s.33 are described by Paul Weiler in *Rights and Judges in a Democracy: A New Canadian Version*, Thomas M. Cooley Lectures (University of Michigan Law School 1982).

6 See Brian Dickson, "The Democratic Character of the Charter of Rights," in *Law, Politics and the Judicial Process in Canada*, ed. F.L. Morton (Calgary: Calgary University Press 1984), 325–27. In somewhat stronger language, Mr Justice Smith of the Ontario Supreme Court has written: "[The] sovereignty of Parliament as we have known it, is a thing of history." *Re Service Employees International Union, Local 204 and Broadway Manor Nursing Home* (1983), 4 DLR (4th) 231 at 300. The idea that judicial review necessarily entails some limitation on the sovereignty of Parliament is a matter of conventional wisdom for Canadian legal scholars. The live question, of course, is the extent of the limitation that our Charter should properly imply. For discussions of this issue see Morton, *Law, Politics and the Judicial Process*, chap. 13; Weiler, *Rights and Judges in a Democracy*; and Peter H. Russell, "The Effect of a Charter of Rights on the Policy-Making Role of Canadian Courts," *Canadian Public Administration* 25, no. 1 (1982): 1–33.

7 Ronald Dworkin, "The Forum of Principle," *New York University Law Review* 56 (1981): 469–518. The different role principle plays in legislation and adjudication has been the subject of extensive legal analysis. See, for example, Kent Greenawalt, "The Enduring Significance of Neutral Principles," *Columbia Law Review* 78, no. 5 (1978): 982–1021; Harry H. Wellington, "Common Law Rules and Constitutional Double Standards: Some Notes on Adjudication," *Yale Law Journal* 83; (1973): 221–311. See also, J. Rawls's discussion of the meaning of the rule of law in *A Theory of Justice* (Cambridge, Mass: Belknap Press 1971), 237.

8 Walter S. Tarnopolsky, "The Constitution and Human Rights," in *And No One Cheered*, ed. Keith Banting and Richard Simeon (Toronto: Methuen 1983), 261–77.

9 Ronald Dworkin, *Law's Empire* (Cambridge, Mass.: Harvard University Press 1986).

SIX

1 The flavour of this debate can be sensed from reading Katherine E. Swinton, "Application of the Canadian Charter of Rights and Freedoms," in *The Canadian Charter of Rights and Freedoms: Commentary*, ed. Walter S. Tarnopolsky and G.A. Beaudoin (Toronto: Carswell 1982), 41–59, with Dale Gibson, "Distinguishing the Governors from the Governed: The Meaning of 'Government' under s.32(1) of the Charter," *Manitoba Law Journal* 13 (1983): 505–22. See also Brian Slattery, "Charter of Rights and Freedoms: Does It Bind Private Persons?" *Canadian Bar Review* 63 (1985): 148–61; and John D. Whyte, "Is the Private Sector Affected by the Charter?" in *Righting the Balance: Canada's New Equality Rights*, ed. R. Elliott and L. Smith (1986). Early on, the courts have been generally quite cautious in extending the reach of the Charter. See *Bhindi et al.* v. *British Columbia Projectionists* (1986), 29 DLR (4th) 47 (BCCA); *Blainey* v. *Ontario Hockey Association* (1986), 26 DLR (4th) 728 (Ont. CA); *Kohn* v. *Globerman* (1987), 27 DLR (4th) 583 (Man. CA): *Peg-Win Real Estate Ltd.* v. *Winnipeg Real Estate Board* (1986), 27 DLR (4th) 767 (Man. CA). Cf. *Re Edmonton Journal and Attorney General for Alberta* (1983), 146 DLR (3d) 673 (Alta. QB); *R* v. *Lerke* (1986), 25 DLR (4th) 403 (Alta. CA).

2 See *Hunter et al.* v. *Southam Inc.* (1984), 11 DLR (4th) 641 (SCC) and *Law Society of Upper Canada* v. *Skapinker* (1984) 9 DLR (4th) 161 (SCC) per Estey J. at 168: "The Charter is designed and adopted to guide and serve the Canadian community for a long time. Narrow and technical interpretation ... can stunt the growth of the law and hence the community it serves." See also, Tarnopolsky, "The Constitution and Human Rights," Dale Gibson, "Interpretation of the Canadian Charter of Rights and Freedoms: Some General Considerations," in *Canadian Charter of Rights and Freedoms, Commentary*, ed. Tarnopolsky and Beaudoin, 25–39.

3 See, e.g., Tarnopolsky, "Constitution and Human Rights." After the manuscript had been typeset, the Supreme Court of Canada embraced this view in *Retail, Wholesale and Department Store Union, Local 580* v. *Dolphin Delivery Ltd*; see p. 189, note 22.

4 This exclusion would not apply in Quebec, of course, where the substantive rules of social regulation that parallel those in our common law have been codified in the Code Civile. The gross inconsistency that would result in the protection and benefit the Charter extended to the citizens of Quebec (if and when they ratify it) and those in the rest of Canada has already been commented on by others. See Gibson, "Distinguishing the Governors from the Governed"; Marc Gold, "The Constitutional Dimensions of Promoting Equality in Employment," in *Research Studies of the Commission on Equality in Employment*, Rosalie S. Abella, Commissioner (Ottawa: Canadian Government Publishing Centre 1985), 249–72. In a passage

expressed in obiter in his judgment in *Operation Dismantle* v. *The Queen* (1985), 18 DLR (4th) 481, 494, Chief Justice Dickson seems to suggest that the reference to "laws" in s.52 must include the common law as well. But now see *Retail, Wholesale and Department Store Union* v. *Dolphin Delivery Ltd.*, SCC 18 Dec. 1986.

5 In most provincial jurisdictions, the legislature has provided by statute that boards of arbitration, rather than courts or other institutions, are to enforce and interpret the terms of the collective agreement and accordingly, like labour boards, are regarded as agents of this branch of the state. See Peter Hogg, *Canada Act 1982 Annotated* (Toronto: Carswell 1982). See also, Donald J.M. Brown and David M. Beatty, *Canadian Labour Arbitration*, 2nd ed. (Aurora, Ontario: Canada Law Book 1984), paras. 1:2000 and 1:5100.

6 For a description and analysis of the concept of equality on which liberal theory is grounded and on the different conceptions to which it has given rise, see Amy Gutmann, *Liberal Equality* (Cambridge: Cambridge University Press 1980), especially 1–12. For the classic judicial formulation of this ultimate objective of the liberal state, see Mr Justice Brandeis in *Whitney* v. *California*, 274 US 356 (1927), cited with approval in *Re Lavigne and Ontario Public Employees' Service Union* (1986), 29 DLR (4th) 321, 381.

7 Courts and commentators have already made the connection between individual human rights and freedoms and the larger purposes of personal autonomy and self-realization which documents such as our Charter pursue. This is particularly true with respect to rights of speech, conscience, and religion. See, in this regard, Frederick Schauer, *Free Speech: A Philosophical Inquiry* (Cambridge: Cambridge University Press 1982); Joel Feinberg, *Social Philosophy* (Englewood Cliffs, NJ: Prentice Hall 1973), chaps. 2 and 3; and *R.* v. *Big M Drug Mart* (1985), 18 DLR (4th) 321. For more general treatments of this link, see Ronald Dworkin, "Hard Cases," in *Taking Rights Seriously* (Cambridge, Mass.: Harvard University Press 1977), 81–130; Roger Smith, "The Constitution and Autonomy," *Texas Law Review* 60 no. 2 (1982): 175–205; and W.E. Conklin, "Interpreting and Applying the Limitations Clause: An Analysis of s.1," in *The New Constitution and the Charter of Rights*, ed. E.P. Belobaba and E. Gertner (Toronto: Butterworths 1983), 75–87.

8 The phrase has received widespread recognition in American constitutional jurisprudence, see, for example, *Roe* v. *Wade*, 410 U.S. 113 (1973), per Blackmun J.; *Rochin* v. *California*, 342 U.S. 165 (1952), 169 per Frankfurter J.; *Palko* v. *Connecticut*, 302 U.S. 319 (1937), 325.

9 Ronald Dworkin, "Natural Law Revisited," *University of Florida Law Review* 34, no. 2 (1982): 185.

10 See E.C.S. Wade, "Introduction," A.V. Dicey, *Introduction to The Law of the Constitution*, 10th ed. (London: Macmillan 1960); see also Friedrich Hayek, *The Constitution of Liberty* (Chicago: Regnery 1972), chap. 14; Joseph Raz, "The Rule of Law and Its Virtue," *Law Quarterly Review*

93 (1977): 195–211. See also Bob Fine, *Democracy and the Rule of Law* (London: Pluto Press 1984), for a discussion of how a wide range of theorists including Hobbes, Rousseau, Smith, Hegel, and even Marx understood the rule of law as an attempt to reconcile the subjective and objective, the selfish and the rational, the particular and the universal character of law and collective authority.

11 Dicey, *Law of Constitution*, cviii.

12 Ronald Dworkin has described the rule of law in its most generalized conception, as insisting that the coercive authority of government not be used except as "licensed . . . by individual rights . . . flowing from past political decisions about when collective force is justified" (*Law's Empire*, 93). The same ideas also appear in his *A Matter of Principle* (Cambridge, Mass.: Harvard University Press 1985). For a similar understanding and depiction of the rule of law, see Fine, *Democracy and the Rule of Law*, Raz, "The Rule of Law and Its Virtue," and Hayek, *The Constitution of Liberty*.

13 Rawls, *A Theory of Justice*, 235.

14 Dicey, *Law of the Constitution*.

15 Arthur L. Goodhart, "The Rule of Law and Absolute Sovereignty," *University of Pennsylvania Law Review* 106, no. 7 (1958): 945.

16 Alan Gewirth, "Political Justice," in *Social Justice*, ed. Richard B. Brant (Englewood Cliffs, NJ: Prentice-Hall 1962), 154. See also Rawls, *Theory of Justice*, 235.

17 Dicey, *Law of the Constitution*, 197, 203, 207.

18 See *R. v. Oakes* (1986), 26 DLR (4th) 200, 225 (SCC), *Reference Re s.94(2) of the Motor Vehicle Act* (BC) (1985), 36 MVR 240 (SCC); see also, *R. v. Big M Drug Mart*, per Dickson at 353: "A free society is one which aims at equality with respect to the enjoyment of fundamental freedoms." *Blainey v. Ontario Hockey Association*, per Dubin J.A. at 529: "It is fundamental in a free and democratic society that all persons should be treated by the law on a footing of equality with equal concern and equal respect, to ensure each individual the greatest opportunity for his or her enhancement."

19 The various competing theories which have been advanced in American academic writing to reconcile judicial review with our commitment to democratic government are conveniently summarized in Paul Brest, "The Fundamental Rights Controversy: The Essential Contradictions of Normative Constitutional Scholarship," *Yale Law Journal* 90 (1981): 1063–109.

20 One of the most well-known exponents of this theory of judicial review in the American context is Raoul Berger, *Government by Judiciary* (Cambridge, Mass.: Harvard University Press 1977). The Supreme Court of Canada has already given some notice that in the appropriate case, as, for example, on the question of language rights, this is the perspective it may adopt. See *A. G. of Quebec v. Association of Protestant School Boards* (1984), 10 DLR (4th) 321 (SCC).

21 See, e.g., Pierre E. Trudeau, "A Constitutional Declaration of Rights," in *Federalism and the French Canadians* (Toronto: Macmillan 1968), 52; *A Canadian Charter of Human Rights* (Ottawa: Queen's Printer 1982). See also *Minutes* of Proceedings and Evidence of the Special Joint Committee of the Senate and of the House of Commons on the Constitution of Canada (1981).

22 H.L.A. Hart, "Are There Any Natural Rights?" *Philosophical Review*, no. 2 (1955): 175-91; see also David A.J. Richards, "Rights and Autonomy," *Ethics* 92 (1981): 3-20; Gewirth, "Political Justice," 145; *Human Rights* (Chicago: University of Chicago Press 1982).

23 The idea that the Charter protects rights and freedoms essential for the individual to participate in the political process in the way democratic theory contemplates, is one which has already received a good deal of academic and judicial support. See *R. v. Big M Drug Mart*, 321, 346; Dickson, "The Democratic Character of the Charter of Rights"; Fichaud, "Analysis of the Charter and Its Application to Labour Law," *Dalhousie Law Journal* 8, no. 2 (1984): 402-34; Russell, "The Effect of a Charter of Rights on the Policy-Making Role of Canadian Courts." A parallel line of analysis has long distinguished one strand of American constitutional law. Among the better-known works of this genre are: Robert Dahl, *A Preface to Economic Democracy* (Berkeley: University of California Press 1985), and John Hart Ely, *Democracy and Distrust* (Cambridge, Mass.: Harvard University Press 1981). The latter has been applied directly to the Canadian context by Patrick Monaghan in "Judicial Review and Democracy: A Theory of Judicial Review," *UBC Law Review* (1987), forthcoming.

24 Dickson, "The Democratic Character of the Charter of Rights." In the United States John Hart Ely has developed his "representing reinforcing" theory of constitutional review from essentially the same premise. See Ely, *Democracy and Distrust*.

25 Harry H. Wellington, "Common Law Rules and Constitutional Double Standards: Some Notes on Adjudication"; "The Nature of Judicial Review," *Yale Law Journal* 91 (1982): 486-520; Michael J. Perry, "Modern Equal Protection: A Conceptualization and Appraisal," *Columbia Law Review* 79 (1979): 1023-84, and *The Constitution, the Courts and Human Rights* (New Haven: Yale University Press 1982); see also Dworkin, *Law's Empire*, chap. 6.

26 David M. Beatty, "Industrial Democracy: A Liberal Law of Labour Relations," *Valparaiso Law Review* 19 (1984): 37-69. And generally, see Gutmann, *Liberal Equality*.

27 Charles Fried, "Artificial Reason of the Law or: What Lawyers Know," *Texas Law Review* 60 (1981): 57.

28 In several judgments the Supreme Court has already made it clear that

the rights and freedoms enumerated in the text are to be interpreted within and to be understood as furthering the purposes of the Charter itself. See *R. v. Big M Drug Mart*, 344, 359–60, cited with approval in *Reference Re s.94(2) of the Motor Vehicle Act*.

29 Though utilitarian considerations, such as the well-being of the community, may in certain situations provide a legitimate basis on which to restrict rights and freedoms, it is generally accepted that such justifications are much more controversial than if a legislature acts to protect the rights and freedoms of individuals who are less advantaged. See Katherine Swinton, "Restraints on Government Efforts to Promote Equality in Employment"; Marc Gold, "The Constitutional Dimensions of Promoting Equality in Employment," in *Research Studies of the Commission on Equality in Employment*, Rosalie S. Abella, Commissioner (Ottawa: Canadian Government Publishing Centre 1985), 275–96 and 249–72; and Alan Brudner, "What Are Reasonable Limits to Equality Rights," *Canadian Bar Review* 64 (1986): 469–506. This view seems to have been embraced by Madame Justice Wilson in *Singh v. Minister of Employment and Immigration* (1985), 17 DLR (4th) 442.

30 The integrity of this method of interpretation is defended by Ronald Dworkin in *Law's Empire*, chap. 2.

31 All liberal democratic theories of judicial review in American constitutional law recognize that constitutional review, like the development of the common law, entails some element of law-making by the court. What differentiates how courts discharge this function from the other two branches of government is the procedure through which and the criteria on which law is decreed by each. For a discussion of how the contemporary American theories of constitutional review characterize and organize this creative function, see Dworkin, *Law's Empire*. For a summary of various critiques of Dworkin's theory, see Andrew Altman, "Legal Realism, Critical Legal Studies and Dworkin," in *Philosophy and Public Affairs* 15 (1986): 205–35.

32 A review of the different formulations that have been used in contemporary human rights declarations to specify the grounds on which legislators can compromise rights and freedoms is contained in John Claydon, "International Human Rights Law and the Interpretation of the Canadian Charter of Rights and Freedoms," in *The New Constitution*, ed. Belobaba and Gertner, 287–302.

33 De Tocqueville was of the view that freedom of association "was the most natural right of man, after acting on his own." He wrote it was "a necessary guarantee against the tyranny of the majority" and was "almost as inalienable as individual liberty": *Democracy in America* (Garden City, NJ: Doubleday and Co. 1969), 192–3. See also Harold Laski, "Freedom of Association," *Encyclopædia of the Social Sciences* (1931): 6, 447–50. One judge in Canada

has already highlighted the importance of freedom of association in a free and democratic society; see Smith J. in *SEIU, Local 204 and Broadway Manor Nursing Home*, 301.

34 The Supreme Court has made it clear it will review both the objectives pursued by a legislature when it infringes rights and freedoms, as well as the means chosen to pursue those goals, in determining whether they are reasonable limits in a free and democratic society. See *R.* v. *Big M* and *R.* v. *Oakes*.

35 This characterization has already been suggested in American constitutional law scholarship. See Francis D. Wormuth and Harris G. Mirkin, "The Doctrine of the Reasonable Alternative," *Utah Law Review* 9 (1964): 254–307.

36 This characterization has been developed by Gregory Vlastos in "Justice and Equality," in *Social Justice*, 31–72. The same idea is developed by Alexander Bickel in *The Least Dangerous Branch* (Indianapolis: Bobbs-Merrill 1962), 59.

37 Whether all other things are equal between alternate social policies in any given case may be a difficult task for a court to determine. A particular social policy may be less restrictive of the rights of freedoms of one group but more restrictive of the same entitlements of another; or one alternate can accomplish a variety of objectives which cannot be secured by others. In either of these circumstances the condition which constrains this principle of constitutional review could not be met and so would render it inapplicable to that case. For a discussion of this aspect of the principle of reasonable alternate means, see Guy Miller Struve, "The Less-Restrictive-Alternative Principle and Economic Due Process," *Harvard Law Review* 80 (1967): 1463–88. See also *Re Soenen and Thomas et al.* (1983), 3 DLR (4th) 658 (Alta. QB).

38 A practical question the courts will have to address is who bears the burden of proving that the means which are being held up as an alternative way to realize the legislative objectives are reasonable or not. As a general matter, the courts have been clear that the party endeavouring to uphold a policy which constrains or limits the rights and freedoms set out in the Charter bears the burden of showing that they are demonstrably justified. See *Big M Drug Mart* and *Oakes* cases. This general burden should carry with it the correlative obligation to produce evidence that an obvious alternative is not satisfactory. Considerations of cost, expertise, and commitment to the values the Charter seeks to realize, all call for the defenders of challenged legal principles to explain why such an alternative was not chosen. For a different conclusion, see Struve, "The Less-Restrictive-Alternative Principle."

39 See, e.g., *R.* v. *Oakes* and *R.* v. *Big M Drug Mart, Quebec Association of Protestant School Boards* v. *A. G. of Quebec* (1982), 140 DLR (3d) 33,

71-7; and June M. Ross, "Limitations on Human Rights in International Law: Their Relevance to the Canadian Charter of Rights and Freedoms," *Human Rights Quarterly* 6, no. 2 (1984): 180–223.

40 Conklin, "Interpreting and Applying the Limitations Clause": Marc Gold, "A Principled Approach to Equality Rights: A Preliminary Inquiry"; and Claydon, "International Human Rights Law and the Interpretation of the Canadian Charter of Rights and Freedoms," in *The New Constitution*, ed. Belobaba and Gertner, 75–87, 131–61, and 287–302. See also, Monaghan, "Judicial Review and Democracy."

41 See *Quebec North Shore Paper Co.* v. *Canadian Pacific* [1977], 2 SCR 1054, *McKay* v. *The Queen* [1965], SCR 798. See, generally, Hogg, *Constitutional Law of Canada*, 327–9.

42 See *Clark* v. *C.N.R. Co.* (1985), 17 DLR (4th) 58 (NBCA); *MacKay* v. *The Queen* (1980), 114 DLR (3d) 393 (SCC); *Fowler* v. *The Queen* (1980), 113 DLR (3d) 513 (SCC).

43 Carole Rogerson, "Overbreadth, Vagueness and Reading Down," a paper presented in the Charter Litigation Symposium, Faculty of Law, University of Toronto, 28 February 1986.

44 See, e.g., *MacKay* v. *The Queen*, 423 per McIntyre J. Even before the adoption of our earlier statutory Bill of Rights, legal scholars and political scientists had identified what they characterized as a method of "interpretive avoidance" by which courts would choose from among a number of possible interpretations of a legislative enactment that which most respected our traditional rights and freedoms recognized at common law. So described, "interpretive avoidance" is simply the principle I have called reasonable alternatives or less drastic means, by another name. See *Law, Politics and the Judicial Process in Canada*, ed. F.L. Morton (Calgary: Calgary University Press 1984).

45 See, e.g., *R.* v. *Big M Drug Mart*, *R.* v. *Oakes*, *SEIU Local 204 and Broadway Manor*, and *Quebec Association of Protestant School Boards* cases already cited; also *Re Mitchell and the Queen* (1983), 150 DLR (3d) 449 (Ont. HC), and *Re Canadian Newspapers and the Queen* (1983), 1 DLR (4th) 133 (BCSC).

46 *Re Southam and the Queen* (1983), 146 DLR (3d) 408 (Ont. CA).

47 See, generally, Lawrence Tribe, *American Constitutional Law* (Mineola, N.Y.: Foundation Press 1978), 700–10, and in particular, *U.S.* v. *Robel*, 389 US 258 (1967) and *NAACP* v. *Button*, 371 US 415 (1963).

48 *Shelton* v. *Tucker*, 364 US 479 (1960).

49 See *Craig* v. *Boren*, 429 US 190 (1976) and, generally, Perry, "Modern Equal Protection."

50 For a general review of the jurisprudence of the European Court and Commission of Human Rights, see Ross, "Limitations on Human Rights in International Law." Of the cases cited by Ross, the most pertinent for

our purposes is the "British Closed Shop" case: see *Young, James and Webster* v. *The United Kingdom* (1981), 2 HRLJ 185 (Eur. Ct. HR).

51 See Vlastos, "Justice and Equality," 62.

52 Jeremy Bentham, *The Principles of Morals and Legislation* (New York: Columbia University Pres 1945), chaps. 13 and 14.

53 This formulation of the rule of law was attributed to Coke by Theodore Plucknett in "Bonham's Case and Judicial Review," *Harvard Law Review* 40 (1926): 30–70. See also his *Concise History of the Common Law* (London: Butterworths 1936), 51.

54 In its judgment in *R. v. Oakes*, the Supreme Court made it clear that it would engage in the kind of balancing that is contemplated by the third proportionality principle it identified only after it had measured the challenged rule against the standard of reasonable alternative means. For an argument encouraging American courts to follow the same sequence in applying these two independent principles of constitutional review, see Struve, "The Less-Restrictive-Alternative Principle," 1486.

55 Just how intrusive the stronger principle of proportionality will turn out to be depends on the standard of proof courts will require the legislative and executive branches to meet in establishing that the benefits secured by the rule or policy under review are sufficient to offset the costs they entail.

56 See Rawls, *A Theory of Justice*, where the method of "reflective equilibrium" is developed.

57 I should acknowledge that this last question is different from the others in not specially affecting a particularly disadvantaged class of workers in the way the other issues do. However, this feature of our labour code so closely parallels the question which I believe most convincingly demonstrates the force of the Charter as an instrument of social justice for those traditionally ignored by the political process that it merits special consideration here. How our principles fare in the debate about the validity of laws which require or authorize some people to compel others to associate with particular unions against their will should give us the most relevant test of their integrity and the results they are able to achieve. The issue of union security will, in fact, be a dress rehearsal for what follows in Part Four. If we have confidence in the conclusions to which our two principles lead on this question, perhaps more than on any other, it will strengthen our resolve not to abandon their logic when, in the fourth part, we use them to scrutinize one of the most fundamental principles of our system of collective bargaining. Like each of the other examples which will have preceded it, the results to which our two principles will lead us on this question should make us more certain of the integrity of our analysis of the principle of exclusive representation even though, in that case, the results are very dramatic and demanding indeed.

SEVEN

1 For an introduction to human rights legislation, see Judith Keene, *Human Rights in Ontario* (Toronto: Carswell 1983).

2 For a summary of the evolution of our thinking on what social policies are required to satisfy the most basic conception of liberal equality, see Thomas Nagel, "Equal Treatment and Compensatory Discrimination," in *Equality and Preferential Treatment*, ed. Marshall Cohen, Thomas Nagel, and Thomas Scanlon (Princeton: Princeton University Press 1977), 3–18; Alfred W. Blumrosen, "Quotas, Common Sense, and Law in Labour Relations: Three Dimensions of Equal Opportunity," *Rutgers Law Review* 27 (1974): 675–703.

3 For an argument that this is the essence of the equality guarantee provided in s.15, see A. Brudner, "What Are Reasonable Limits to Equality Rights," *Canadian Law Review* 64 (1986): 469–506; see also Owen M. Fiss, "A Theory of Fair Employment Laws," *University of Chicago Law Review* 38 (1971): 235–314.

4 For an argument that the courts should show some respect for this right to discriminate "privately," see Katherine E. Swinton, "Application of the Canadian Charter of Rights and Freedoms," in *The Canadian Charter of Rights and Freedoms: Commentary*, ed. Walter S. Tarnopolsky and G.A. Beaudouin (Toronto: Carswell 1982), 41–59.

5 Where such characteristics do affect the employer's legitimate interests, such as the productivity of the enterprise, to a sufficient degree, these laws generally do allow distinctions to be drawn on what otherwise would be prohibited grounds. See Ontario Human Rights Code, so 1981, c.53, c.53, s.23(b), (c).

6 In fact the argument has already been made by Dale Gibson in "The Charter of Rights and the Private Sector," *Manitoba Law Journal* 12 (1982): 213–19; and "Distinguishing the Governors from the Governed: The Meaning of Government under s.32(1) of the Charter," *Manitoba Law Journal* 13 (1983): 505–22; cf. Brian Slattery, "The Charter of Rights and Freedoms – Does it Bind Private Persons?" *Canadian Bar Review* 63 (1985): 148–61. See also, Marc Gold, "The Constitutional Dimensions of Promoting Equality in Employment," in *Research Studies of the Commission on Equality in Employment*, Rosalie S. Abella, Commissioner (Ottawa: Canadian Government Publishing Centre 1985). But see *Retail, Wholesale and Department Store Union, Local 580* v. *Dolphin Delivery Ltd.*, supra p. 189, note 22.

7 *Board of Governors of Seneca College of Applied Arts and Technology* v. *Bhadauria* (1981), 124 DLR (3d) 193. See generally, E.J. Weinrib, "The Case for a Duty to Rescue," *Yale Law Journal* 90 (1980): 247–93.

8 A parallel argument, challenging the state's failure to re-enact a regulation under a different statutory regime, was rejected without reasons by Mr Justice

White in *Re Lavigne and Ontario Public Service Employees' Union* (1986), 29 DLR (4th) 321, 355.

9 For a discussion of the extent to which the Charter will support a claim for the legislative provision of legal aid, see Mary Jane Mossman, "The Charter and the Right to Legal Aid," *Journal of Law and Social Policy* 1 (1985): 21–41. For a review of the American jurisprudence, see Lawrence Tribe, *American Constitutional Law* (Mineola, NY: Foundation Press 1978), 1008, 1101–16.

10 Laws commonly found in labour relations acts prohibiting discrimination because a person belongs to a union, by outlawing what are known in labour jargon as "yellow dog" contracts, are another illustration of the anti-discrimination principle at work. See, e.g., Ontario Labour Relations Act, RSO 1980, c. 228, s.66.

EIGHT

1 Richard Posner, *Economic Analysis of Law*, 2nd ed. (Boston: Little, Brown 1977), 308–12; E.G. West and M. McKee, *Minimum Wages* (Toronto: Economic Council of Canada 1980). See also Bernard H. Siegan, *Economic Liberties and the Constitution* (Chicago: University of Chicago Press 1980), chaps. 11, 15.

2 Robert Nozick, *Anarchy, State and Utopia* (New York: Basic Books 1974), 163.

3 *Adkins* v. *Children's Hospital of the District of Columbia*, 261 U.S. 525 (1923), 554, 558. For a summary of the long list of parallel state and federal legislation which the U.S. Supreme Court struck down in this period, see Tribe, *American Constitutional Law* chap. 8.

4 It might be noted that while the U.S. Supreme Court never struck down legislation like our human rights codes, it did invalidate legislation which prohibited employers from discriminating against persons on the basis of their union affiliation. The leading cases in which the court ruled this particular application of the anti-discrimination principle invalid are *Coppage* v. *Kansas*, 236 U.S. 1 (1915) and *Adair* v. *U.S.*, 208 U.S. 161 (1908).

5 The idea that the court's role is to decide whether laws of this kind are constitutional, and not whether they are fair or efficient, is developed in Ronald Dworkin, *A Matter of Principle* (Cambridge, Mass.: Harvard University Press 1985), 33ff.

6 For some, the connection between a measure of material well-being and the status of self-governing agent can support a more general claim to certain welfare rights. See N.E. Simmons, "Welfare Rights and Freedom," *Journal of Social Welfare* (1979): 324. For a more extended analysis of the relationship between our basic liberties and the distribution of wealth, see Charles Lindblom, *Politics and Markets* (New York: Basic Books 1977); Norman

Daniels, "Equal Liberty and Unequal Worth of Liberty," in *Reading Rawls*, ed. Norman Daniels (New York: Basic Books 1975), 253-81; Amy Gutmann, *Liberal Equality* (Cambridge: Cambridge University Press 1980), 16; R.H. Tawney, *Equality* (London: Allen and Unwin 1964). See also Frank I. Michaelman, "Welfare Rights in a Constitutional Democracy," *Washington University Law Quarterly* 57, no. 3 (1979): 659-93; cf. A.I. Melden, "Are There Welfare Rights," in *Income Support*, ed. Peter G. Brown *et al.* (Totowa, NJ: Rowman and Littlefield 1981), 259-78.

7 The quote is attributed to Franklin Roosevelt by Siegan in *Economic Liberties and the Constitution*.

8 Harry H. Wellington, "Common Law Rules and Constitutional Double Standards: Some Notes on Adjudication," *Yale Law Journal* 83 (1973): 221-311.

9 *West Coast Hotel* v. *Parrish*, 300 U.S. 379 (1937), 393, 398-9; see also Tribe, *American Constitutional Law*, 447ff.

10 G.C. Cheshire and C.H.S. Fifoot, *The Law of Contracts*, 6th ed. (London: Butterworths 1964), 67ff; S.M. Waddams, *The Law of Contracts*, 2nd ed. (Toronto: Canada Law Book 1984), 88-9.

11 K. Polanyi, *The Great Transformation* (Boston: Beacon Press 1957).

12 For a discussion of the increasing unwillingness of the American Supreme Court to interfere with the choice of individuals not to associate with those whose interests seem antagonistic and antithetical to their own, see Robert A. Burt, "Constitutional Law and the Teaching of Parables," *Yale Law Journal* 93, no. 3 (1984): 455-502.

13 Holmes J. in *Adkins* v. *Children's Hospital*, 570.

14 It will be instructive, I think, for us to sketch the outline of the argument that such a challenge would have to take. First, it would seem that individuals who were willing to work for a living at less than the minimum wage but who were prevented from doing so by the terms of these laws and who were rendered redundant as a result, would be able to mount the strongest case. If conventional wisdom is accepted on this point, there will be a number of persons who, though intended as beneficiaries of these laws, may be put out of work instead. For these individuals, unlike their employers, a claim can be made that their *equal* entitlement to the legal conditions on which their autonomy depends has been sacrificed for the benefit of those who will maintain their employment at the higher wage. In contrast to their employers, the restriction on the freedom of association of these individuals is as fundamental as the liberty of the persons whom the law actually protects.

Even these individuals, however, would not be able to succeed if they mounted their challenge exclusively on the two principles we are employing. A legislature could respond to them in exactly the same way it silenced their employers. However prejudicial such legal rules are to the liberty of those who may lose their jobs because of them, our legislators can respond that its objectives are constitutionally valid and the means it chose to promote those ends were the most reasonable alternatives available.

For these persons to successfully challenge this part of our labour code, they must persuade the courts that these rules do not meet the more stringent proportionality principle of constitutional interpretation the Supreme Court has already recognized in the *Oakes* case, (129–30). They would have to show that the limitation on their freedom, by being put out of work, could not be justified by the benefits to those who retained their employment at the higher wage. For example, if the state did not provide an adequate standard of public income support, persons in these circumstances could plausibly argue that the benefits secured by minimum wage laws could not offset the more serious restrictions on the autonomy of those they put out of work.

While such a judgment is entirely conceivable, given the principles of interpretation now recognized by our courts, it is evident how much more activist it requires the judicial branch of government to be. Just contemplating the nature of the balancing process such a standard of review entails underscores how much more controversial such a judgment would be in terms of the institutional comity it establishes between the three branches of government.

For a discussion of whether there is a constitutional right to the basic material provisions necessary to sustain life in a liberal democratic community such as ours, see Frank I. Michaelman, "Welfare Rights in a Constitutional Democracy"; cf. A.I. Melden, "Are there Welfare Rights."

15 The literature condemning both the reasoning and the result in the landmark case of *Lochner* v. *New York* 198 U.S. 45 (1904) is immense. For a standard critique and a reference to others, see Tribe, *American Constitutional Law*, 427–55; see also Brest, "The Fundamental Rights Controversy: The Essential Contradictions of Normative Constitution Scholarship." For two quite different attempts to defend the decision, see Bruce A. Ackerman, "Discovering The Constitution," *Yale Law Journal* (1984): 1013–72, and Bernard H. Siegan, "Rehabilitating Lochner," *San Diego Law Review* 22 (1985): 453–97.

16 Tribe, *American Constitutional Law*, 447–8.

17 Morley Gunderson, *Economics of Poverty and Income Distribution* (Toronto: Butterworths 1983).

18 Derek Bok, "Reflections on the Distinctive Character of American Labor Law," *Harvard Law Review* 84 (1971): 1459–63.

NINE

1 For an analysis of the distinctions drawn between occupations in our labour

relations acts, see James E. Dorsey, "Freedom of Association in Employment: Excluded Employees and the Canadian Charter of Rights and Freedoms," in *Collective Bargaining and Industrial Democracy*, ed. Geoffrey England and George Lermer (Don Mills, Ont.: CCH Canadian 1983): 5–20.

2 For a general discussion of status of farm workers, see Kathryn Neilson and Innis Christie, "The Agricultural Labourer in Canada, A Legal Point of View," *Dalhousie Law Journal* 2 (1975): 330–68; see also Occupational Health and Safety Act, RSO 1980, c.321, s.3(2); Ontario Labour Relations Act, RSO 1980, c.228, s.2(b); Workers Compensation Act, schedule I, RRO 1980, Reg. 951.

3 The potential criminal and civil liability of unions who engage in normal collective bargaining activities like strikes, pickets, and boycotts outside of the protection of the statute is summarized in Innis M. Christie, *The Liability of Strikers in the Law of Tort* (Kingston, Ontario: Queen's University, Industrial Relations Centre 1967). See also A.W.R. Carrothers, *Collective Bargaining Law in Canada* (Toronto: Butterworths 1968).

4 See Labour Law Casebook Group, *Labour Law: Cases, Materials and Commentary*, 4th ed. (Kingston, Ontario: Queen's University 1984, Industrial Relations Centre), 130.

5 In a very real sense, collective bargaining legislation is like a minimum wage statute. Both are concerned with enhancing the economic liberty of the least advantaged. While collective bargaining legislation is more broadly concerned with the opportunity of employees to participate in the decision-making processes which govern their lives, it has always been expected that this enhanced opportunity would lead directly to wage increases. Implicitly in its inception and explicitly in its retention, collective bargaining legislation has been included in our labour code for the purpose of "ensuring a just share of the fruits of progress for all." See Preamble, Part V, Canada Labour Code, RSC 1970, c.L–1.

6 It may be observed that the same argument might justify excluding domestic workers whose relationship with the person who hires him/her is as intimate and personal as those which prevail on a family farm. See e.g. Labour Relations Act, RSO 1980 c.228, s.2(a). More broadly still, it might be said that such an argument justifies excluding all very small enterprises. As we shall see in Part Four, in West Germany the legislation regulating collective labour relations excludes firms which employ fewer than five other persons.

7 See section 8 supra, note 14.

8 See New Brunswick Industrial Relations Act, RSNB 1973, c.1–4, s.1(5)(a).

9 What protection is afforded to domestic workers commonly excludes those who work twenty-four hours a week or less (see, e.g., Ontario Employment Standards Act, RRO 1980, Reg. 283, s.3(f)).

10 See, e.g., ibid., s.6. Domestics are excluded from the Workers Compensation Act (RSO 1980, c.539, s.131) and the Occupational Health and Safety Act

(RSO 1980, c.321, s.3(1)). See also, *Re Domestic Workers Union and A.G. British Columbia* (1983), 1 DLR (4th) 560 (BCSC) for an early unsuccessful attempt by domestic workers to challenge the validity of these provisions under s.7 of the Charter.

A similar group of workers, who clean and do related service jobs in the industrial and commercial sectors, have been effectively denied the benefits of the Labour Relations Act because of the provision in the legislation which permits employers to evade collective bargaining by contracting out their work to unorganized firms. Although I have not dealt with this area of law in the text, it does seem vulnerable to a successful constitutional challenge by those workers who are prejudiced by it. For a description of this body of law, see G.W. Adams, *Canadian Labour Law* (Aurora: Canada Law Book 1985), 415–19.

11 It is interesting to note that these groups of workers have been discriminated against in other liberal democratic societies such as the Federal Republic of Germany. It is distressing to report such injustices were brought to end there over fifty years ago. See Otto Kahn-Freund, "The Impact of Constitutions on Labour Law," *Cambridge Law Journal* 35, no. 2 (1976): 240–71.

TEN

1 See *Massachusetts Board of Retirement* v. *Murgia*, 427 U.S. 307 (1976).
2 See Morley Gunderson and James Pesando, "Eliminating Mandatory Retirement: Economics and Human Rights," *Canadian Public Policy* 6, no. 2 (1980): 352–60.
3 In at least three judgments, courts in Ontario and British Columbia have held that the term of a collective agreement between a private employer and a union are not sufficiently infused by state action or governmental functions to be brought within the scope of s.32 of the Charter; see *Bhindi et al.* v. *British Columbia Projectionists* (1986), 29 DLR (4th) 47 (BCCA), *Baldwin* v. *B.C. Government Employee's Union* (1986) 28 DLR (4th) 301 (BCSC) and *Re Lavigne and Ontario Public Service Employees' Union*.
4 The classic American statements include Louis Henkin, "*Shelley* v. *Kraemer*: Notes for a Revised Opinion," *University of Pennsylvania Law Review* 110 (1962): 473–505; Charles L. Black Jr., "Foreword: State Action, Equal Protection and California's Proposition 14," *Harvard Law Review* 81 (1967): 69–109; Lawrence Tribe, *American Constitutional Law* (Mineola New York: Foundation Press, 1978), 1167–70. For a more provocative rendition on this subject of long-standing academic controversy, see Duncan Kennedy, "The Stage of the Decline of the Public/Private Distinction," *University of Pennsylvania Law Review* 130 (1982): 1349–57.
5 See, e.g., Public Service Act, RSO 1980, c.418, s.17, and Public Service

Superannuation Act, RSC 1970, c.P-36, s.32(1)(y). In some cases a question may arise as to whether a group can properly be characterized as public servants or governmental employees. The status of university and community college teachers is somewhat ambiguous in this respect, although White J. of the Ontario Supreme Court came to the conclusion that community college teachers were employees of the crown; see *Re Lavigne and OPSEU*. Cf. *McKinney et al.* v. *Board of Governors of the University of Guelph et al.* unreported judgment of Mr Justice Gray, 15 Oct. 1986, Ont. SC; *Harrison* v. *University of British Columbia* [1986] 6 WWR 7 (BCSC).

6 *Re Lavigne and OPSEU, Baldwin* v. *BCGEU*, and *Bhindi* v. *B.C. Projectionists*.

7 *Teamsters* v. *Therien* (1960), 22 DLR (2d) 1 (SCC).

8 Grounding governmental activity in the state policy which encourages and supports the practice of collective bargaining and the agreements to which it gives rise has already received some support in the literature. See, e.g., Harry Wellington, "The Constitution, the Labour Union and Governmental Action," *Yale Law Journal* 70 (1961): 345-75; Peter W. Hogg, *Constitutional Law of Canada*, 2nd ed. (Toronto: Carswell 1985), 455.

9 For a description of the various legal forms used by American courts to uphold the enforceability of collective agreements see: William Gorham Rice, Jr., "Collective Labor Agreeements in American Law," *Harvard Law Review* 44 (1930-1): 572-608; and T. Richard Witmer, "Collective Labour Agreements in the Courts," *Yale Law Journal* 48 (1938): 195-239.

10 *Young* v. *Canadian Northern Railway* [1931], 1 DLR 645 (PC). See also, T.S. Kuttner, "Is the Collective Agreement a Contract," in *Issues in Contract Law* ed. Mary Hatherly and T.S. Kuttner (Frederiction: University of New Brunswick Press 1987).

11 *Steele* v. *Louisville and Nashville Railroad*, 323 U.S. 192 (1944), 198 and 202. See also, *Emporium Capwell Co.* v. *Western Addition Community Organization*, 420 U.S. 50 (1975). For a description of a parallel characterization of the system of collective labour relations in West Germany, see Thilo Ramm, "Labour Courts and Grievance Settlement in West Germany," in *Labour Courts and Grievance Settlement in Western Europe*, ed. Benjamin Aaron (Berkeley: University of California Press 1971), 83-157. See also, Reinhard Richardi, "Worker Participation within Undertakings in the Federal Republic of Germany," *Comparative Labor Law* 5 (1982): 23-50; and Otto Kahn-Freund, "The Impact of Constitutions on Labour Law," *Cambridge Law Journal* 35, no. 2 (1976): 240-71. The Supreme Court of Canada has itself shown some sensitivity to the legal authority unions have been given in *Oil, Chemical and Atomic Workers International Union* v. *Imperial Oil Ltd. et al.* (1963), 41 DLR (2d) 1, 11-12.

12 *Young, James and Webster* v. *U.K.* [1982] EHRR 38, 54. The U.S. Supreme Court has reached essentially the same conclusion in *Railway Employees*

Department v. *Hanson*, 351 U.S. 225 (1956); *Abood* v. *Detroit Board of Education*, 431 U.S. 209 (1976); and see generally, T. Haggard, *Compulsory Unions, the NLRB and the Courts* (Philadelphia: Industrial Research Unit, University of Pennsylvania 1977).

13 See *Bhindi* v. *British Columbia Projectionists*. See also *Re Lavigne and OPSEU*.

14 See, e.g., Human Rights Code, s.o. 1981, c.53, s.9(a).

15 *Board of Governors of Seneca College of Applied Arts and Technology* v. *Bhaduria* (1981), 124 DLR (3d) 193 (SCC).

16 See Donald J.M. Brown and David M. Beatty, *Canadian Labour Arbitration*, 2nd ed. (Aurora: Canada Law Book 1984), topics 3:1200 and 2:3120.

17 For academics, see Dale Gibson, "Distinguishing the Governors from the Governed," *Manitoba Law Journal* 3 (1983): 520; and Karl Klare, "The Quest for Judicial Democracy and the Struggle Against Racism: Perspectives from Labour Law and Civil Rights Law," *Oregon Law Review* 61 (1982): 157–200. See also Michael J. Perry, "The Principle of Equal Protection," *Hastings Law Journal* 32 (1981): 1133–56. For legislatures, see, e.g., *Equality for All: Report of the Parliamentary Committee on Equality Rights* (Ottawa: Canadian Government Publishing Centre 1985), 21; Human Rights Act, SM 1974, c.65, s.6(1). For courts, see *McKinney et al.* v. *University of Guelph*. But see *Harrison* v. *University of British Columbia*. See also *Craton* v. *Winnipeg School Division* (1985), 61 NR 241, where the Supreme Court held the mandatory retirement rule in the public schools of Manitoba was inconsistent with the human rights code. Given the common purpose and parallel language of our human rights laws and the Charter, it would be expected that a similar ruling will eventually prevail in our constitutional law as well.

18 The literature evaluating mandatory retirement from an economic analysis is by far the most pervasive. Among the most recent publications are: Gunderson and Pesando, "Eliminating Mandatory Retirement: Economics and Human Rights"; Morley Gunderson, "Mandatory Retirement and Personnel Policies," *Columbia Journal of World Business* (1983): 8–15; Donald P. Dunlop, *Mandatory Retirement Policy: A Human Rights Dilemma* (Toronto: Conference Board of Canada 1980); *Mandatory Retirement Study* (Washington, D.C.: The Urban Institute 1981).

19 See *Ontario Human Rights Commission* v. *Borough of Etobicoke* (1982), 132 DLR (3d) 14 (SCC) for a discussion of the quality of evidence the court is likely to require in order to discharge the burden of proving that age is a relevant and reasonable occupational qualification.

20 Perry, "The Principle of Equal Protection," 1155.

21 See, generally, the Urban Institute of Washington's *Mandatory Retirement Study*. This uncertainty is illustrated in the present dispute about the impact of retiring workers at a specified age on the job opportunities at Canadian

universities. Economists were solicited to swear affidavits affirming and denying the relevance of the lump of labour theory to the university environment.

22 See, e.g., M.E. Atcheson and Lynne Sullivan, "Passage to Retirement: Age Discrimination and the Charter," in *Equality Rights and the Canadian Charter of Rights and Freedoms*, ed. Anne F. Bayefsky and Mary Eberts (Toronto: Carswell 1985), 231–92.

23 Consistent with our constitutional commitment to pluralism, each workplace could decide for itself the circumstances in which any person could be said to have had his or her fair share of relevant work experience.

24 The Constitutional Court in Spain basically came to the same conclusion when it considered a mandatory retirement rule in the Spanish Workers' Code. The decision is reported in Boletin Oficial Del Estado Gaceta De Madrid, 20 July 1981, suplement al Num 172, 16,237. For a summary of this decision, see "Judicial Decisions in the Field of Labour Law," *International Labour Review* 123, no. 2 (1984): 183–201, esp. 193.

25 Other conditions might also be deemed essential to the constitutional validation of mandatory retirement rules. Thus the integrity of mandatory retirement schemes might well be conditioned on the provision of financial security (most likely the provision of public and private pension programs) for those whose employment is being terminated. Again, this was a factor considered by the Spanish Constitutional Court in its consideration of the mandatory retirement scheme included in the Workers' Charter governing employment relations in Spain.

26 The parallel between the constitutionality of compulsory retirement and employment standards respecting overtime work is matched at the policy level by the preoccupation of economists with whether either of these programs can be counted on to effectively generate additional work. It is as much a question for overtime standards as for compulsory retirement rules whether the lump of labour theory renders these policies of worksharing problematic from a policy point of view.

ELEVEN

1 As soon as the Charter was entrenched, women's groups began to organize their resources to optimize the benefits they could claim from judicial review. Among other initiatives, they formed the Women's Legal Education and Action Fund (LEAF), a public interest advocacy institution, to initiate and coordinate challenges to social policies which are regarded as offensive to the constitutional rights of women.

2 Part of the complexity of analysing the claims women can advance under the Charter derives from the special reference in s.28 to equality between the sexes. For a review of the various interpretations that have so far been

advanced to integrate this section with the rest of the Charter, see Swinton, "Restraints on Government Efforts to Promote Equality in Employment," Marc Gold, "The Constitutional Dimensions of Promoting Equality in Employment," in *Research Studies of the Commission on Equality in Employment*. See also Tarnopolsky, "The Equality Rights," in *The Canadian Charter of Rights and Freedoms, Commentary* (Toronto: Carswell 1982), 395–442, Mary Eberts, "Sex and Equality Rights," in *Equality Rights and the Canadian Charter of Rights and Freedoms* (Toronto: Carswell 1985), 183–229; and N. Colleen Sheppard, "Equality, Ideology and Oppression: Women and the Canadian Charter of Rights," *Dalhousie Law Journal* 10 (1986): 195–224.

3 Katherine Swinton, "Regulating Reproductive Hazards in the Workplace: Balancing Equality and Health," *University of Toronto Law Journal* 33 (1983): 45–73.

4 But see the Canadian Human Rights Act, SC 1976–77, c.33, s.3, as amended by SC 1980–83 c.143, s.2.

5 Swinton, "Regulating Reproductive Hazards in the Workplace," 65–7.

6 Although it might also be argued that radioactive substances are particularly damaging to the female reproductive organs and therefore that differential standards are warranted on that ground as well, there is some evidence to suggest the male reproductive capacity may also be adversely affected by exposure to such chemicals, although obviously in different ways. See ibid., 47.

7 Determining the legal and moral status of the fetus is unquestionably one of the most controversial questions our courts must face. For two particularly stimulating discussions, see Bruce A. Ackerman, *Social Justice in the Liberal State* (New Haven: Yale University Press 1980), and L.W. Sumner, *Abortion and Moral Theory* (Princeton, NJ: Princeton University Press 1981).

8 The cases are uniform that those defending laws which interfere with our constitutional guarantees bear the burden of proof on this point see e.g. *R.* v. *Oakes*, (1986) 26 DLR (4th) 200, *Operation Dismantle Inc.* v. *The Queen* (1985), 18 DLR (4th) 481; *R.* v. *Big M Drug Mart*; and see, generally, Peter W. Hogg, *Constitutional Law of Canada*, 2nd ed. (Toronto, Carswell 1985), 681.

9 See Swinton, "Regulating Reproductive Hazards in the Workplace," 54.

10 For a similar conclusion, see Swinton, "Restraints on Government Efforts to Promote Equality in Employment," in *Commission on Equality in Employment*, ed. Gold.

11 Uniform standards set at levels to protect the most vulnerable members of the workforce may not be possible because the technology does not exist to meet that standard. Alternatively, meeting it may prove so costly that it jeopardizes the life of the enterprise and the employment opportunities

of the other individuals who work there. See Swinton, "Regulating Reproductive Hazards in the Workplace," 48.

12 Ibid., 54, 59.

13 Ibid., 72.

14 In similar situations American constitutional law imposes a parallel obligation of explanation. See Lawrence Tribe, *American Constitutional Law*, (Mineola, NY: Foundation Press 1978), 1085-6.

15 For a discussion of the political factors which may constrain the choice of policy alternatives available to achieve the objectives these regulations seek to accomplish, see C.J. Tuohy and Michael Trebilcock, *Policy Options in the Regulation of Asbestos Related Health Hazards*, Study 3 (Toronto: Ontario Royal Commission on Matters of Health and Safety Arising from the Use of Asbestos in Ontario 1982).

16 See Ontario Human Rights Code, SO 1981, c.53, s.13.

17 Nagel, "Equal Discrimination and Compensatory Discrimination."

18 G. Vlastos, "Justice and Equality" in *Social Justice*, ed. R. Brant (Englewood Cliffs, NJ: Prentice Hall 1962), 31–72, 41.

19 For additional references to this distinction in liberal theory between what has been called equality of persons and equality of lot, see Ronald Dworkin, "What is Equality? Part I: Equality of Welfare," and "Part II: Equality of Resources," *Philosophy and Public Affairs* 10, no. 3 (1981): 185-246; and no. 4 (1981): 283-345. See also, Robert Dahl, *A Preface to Economic Democracy* (Berkeley: University of California Press 1985).

20 This certainly seems to have been the intention of the federal government when it explained the role it expected s.15(2) to play. See *Proceedings* of the Special Joint Committee of the Senate and the House of Commons on the Constitution, vol. 36:15 (12 Jan. 1981).

21 See Owen M. Fiss, "A Theory of Fair Employment Laws," Alfred Blumrosen, "Quotas, Common Sense, and Law in Labour Relations: Three Dimensions of Equal Opportunity."

22 For a description of a variety of legislative programs conferring special benefits in women which have been upheld by the U.S. Supreme Court, see Tribe, *American Constitution Law*, 1066-70.

23 Richard K. Walker, "The Exorbitant Cost of Redistributing Injustice: A Critical View of *United Steelworkers of America* v. *Weber* and the Misguided Policy of Numerical Employment," *Boston College Law Review* 21, no. 1 (1979): 1–83; M. Schiff, "Reverse Discrimination Redefined as Equal Protection: The Orwellian Nightmare in the Enforcement of Equal Protection Laws," *Harvard Journal of Law and Public Policy* 8 (1985): 627-86; Nathan Glazer, *Affirmative Discrimination* (New York: Basic Books 1975).

24 See, e.g., Richard A. Wasserstrom, "Preferential Treatment," in *Philosophical and Social Issues*, ed. R. Wasserstrom (Notre Dame, Ind.: University of Notre Dame Press 1980), 51–82.

25 For a catalogue of the various justifications which can be put forward in support of these policies, see ibid; also Kent R. Greenawalt, *Discrimination and Reverse Discrimination* (New York: Knopf 1982); and Robert K. Fullinwider, *The Reverse Discrimination Controversy* (Totowa, NJ: Rowman and Littlefield 1980).

26 The distinction between equal treatment and treatment as an equal is developed by Ronald Dworkin in his essay "Reverse Discrimination," in *Taking Rights Seriously* (Cambridge, Mass.: Harvard University Press 1977), 227.

27 *Regents of University of California* v. *Bakke*, 533 P. (2d) 1152 (1976).

28 *Regents of University of California* v. *Bakke*, 438 U.S. 265 (1977), per Powell J., 315–18; *DeFunis* v. *Odegaard*, 416 U.S. 312 (1974) at 321, per Douglas J. dissenting.

29 Fiss, "A Theory of Fair Employment Laws"; Blumrosen, "Quotas, Common Sense, and the Law in Labour Relations"; Alfred Blumrosen, "Affirmative Action in Employment after Weber," *Rutgers Law Review* 34, no. 1 (1981): 1–49; and Fullinwider, *Reverse Discrimination Controversy*.

30 This was the basis on which the four members of the Supreme Court who considered the question were prepared to uphold an affirmative action program to promote the hiring of native people who were, on the relevant criteria, less qualified than the whites against whom they competed. See *Re Athabasca Tribal Council and Amoco Canada Petroleum Ltd.* (1981), 124 DLR (3d), 1 (SCC). It also seems to have been the basis on which four of the five judges who considered the constitutional validity of the program that was in issue in the Bakke case grounded their analysis. See also *Califano* v. *Webster*, 430 U.S. 313 (1977), where the U.S. Supreme Court relied on the idea of compensation for past injustice to uphold employment-related social security laws which discriminated affirmatively in favour of women. For an academic justification of affirmative action as compensatory, remedial programs, see George Sher, "Justifying Reverse Discrimination in Employment," in *Equality and Preferential Treatment*.

31 See Thomas Nagel, "Equal Treatment and Compensatory Discrimination," Blumrosen, "Quotas, Common Sense, and Law in Labour Relations." As we have just seen in the example of differential regulations of occupational health, the corollory of this is that, until less drastic alternatives have been tried and found wanting, these stronger programs could not be used. For an example of a case in which the United States Supreme Court turned to this doctrine to cut down a law which a state legislature had enacted to the advantage of women outside of the employment area, see *Orr* v. *Orr*, 440 U.S. 268 (1979).

32 Fullinwider, *The Reverse Discrimination Controversy*, 53–5, and 244–7.

33 In American constitutional law, the validity of affirmative action programs which confer a benefit on those who themselves suffered no disadvantage

or discrimination in the past was raised, but not finally resolved in the various judgments written by the individual justices in the Supreme Court's decision in *Regents of the University of California* v. *Bakke*; see especially the judgments of Justices Powell, Brennan, and Marshall. For a critique of the last two judgments, which seek to defend such affirmative action programs from an argument of compensation and equality of liberty, see Fullinwider, *The Reverse Discrimination Controversy*.

34 *R.* v. *Oakes*.

35 There is some controversy as to what rights have been compromised of those who have not been offered one of the preferred positions because it was filled by a quota. See, e.g., George Sher, "Justifying Reverse Discrimination in Employment," *Philosophy and Public Affairs* 4 (1975): 159–70; Dworkin, *A Matter of Principle*, 298–303; and Wasserstrom, "Preferential Treatment." Cf the decision of Mr Justice Powell in *Regents of the University of California* v. *Bakke*, 315–18.

36 The immediate and derivative costs and benefits that are expected to follow in the wake of laws which authorize or impose quotas in the distribution of work opportunities are discussed in: Fullinwider, *The Reverse Discrimination Controversy*, especially chaps. 9 and 14, and Wasserstrom, "Preferential Treatment." See also Swinton, "Restraints on Government Efforts to Promote Equality in Employment," 287–92; Michael Perry, "Modern Equal Protection: A Conceptualization and Appraisal," *Columbia Law Review* 79 (1979): 1023–84, 1043–5, 1048–9.

TWELVE

1 In some vocations, such as teaching, the legislation prescribes membership in specific unions outside of the collective bargaining system. See Teaching Professions Act, RSO 1980, c.495. In most sectors of the economy, the law authorizes the parties to a collective agreement to negotiate compulsory membership rules. For a discussion of the legislature's responsibility for rules of this latter type, see note 9 below.

2 A more complete catalogue of the various definitions of union security are summarized in Thomas R. Haggard, *Compulsory Unionism, the NLRB and the Courts* (Philadelphia: Industrial Research Unit, University of Pennsylvania 1977).

3 See, e.g., Ontario Labour Relations Act, RSO 1980, c.228, s.43.

4 Compulsory membership in an association having monopoly powers over the exercise of a set of skills is a characteristic which medieval guilds, closed shops, and self-governing professions all have in common.

5 Paul C. Weiler, *Reconcilable Differences* (Toronto: Carswell 1980); Otto Kahn-Freund, *Labour and the Law* (London: Stevens 1972); John R. Commons and John B. Andrews, *Principles of Labour Legislation* (New

York: Harper 1936); *NLRB* v. *Allis Chalmers Manufacturing Co.*, 388 U.S. 175 (1967).

6 In certain sectors of the labour market – e.g., construction, entertainment, teaching and the professions – union security rules may double as devices to provide job security. In these vocations such rules control entry into the labour market and serve the same purposes as seniority in an industrial plant. As a distributive, job-sharing device the closed shop could be justified in the same way as a mandatory retirement law.

7 Weiler, *Reconcilable Differences*, 142.

8 In the United States, the U.S. Supreme Court has upheld the validity of such disciplinary powers over those who have voluntarily become members of the union. However, the relevant statutory provisions have been interpreted as denying unions this power over those who have not become members of their own free will. Of the different sorts of union security arrangements we have identified, only the agency shop clause has been found to be constitutional in the United States. See *NLRB* v. *Allis Chalmers Manufacturing Co.* and, generally, Haggard, *Compulsory Unionism, the NLRB and the Courts*, esp. chap. 2.

9 The question whether union security clauses, negotiated in collective agreements, can be attributed to state action ought to be answered in the same way our analysis characterized the status of mandatory retirement rules. See supra, pp. 94–100. One of the leading cases in American constitutional law, which deals explicitly with the question of union security clauses, is *Railway Employees Dept* v. *Hanson*, 351 U.S. 225 (1956), 231–2 where the court wrote that the relevant federal statute was "the source of the power and authority by which any private rights are lost or authorized." See also, *Abood* v. *Detroit Board of Education*, 431 U.S. 209 (1976), 226. For a general discussion of whether union security clauses have been infused with sufficient state action to qualify for constitutional review, see Haggard, *Compulsory Unions, the NLRB and the Courts*, chap. 11, and see Harry H. Wellington, "The Constitution, the Labor Union and Governmental Action," *Yale Law Journal* 70 (1961): 345–75.

10 One of the most common justifications for union security rules is their facilitation of reduced labour conflict. On this view, industrial peace is a derivative benefit of the legal rule which provides the glue binding individuals to the group. Union security rules insist on varying degrees of commitment to the group in order to increase the bargaining power and participation of the employees. Peace is a by-product of a legal regime which endeavours to secure compliance with the legal order by increased personal commitment and consent. See *Vegelahn* v. *Guntner* 44 N.E. 1077, 1081 (1896). And see generally, Weiler, *Reconcilable Differences*, 142–50; Haggard, *Compulsory Unionism*; Norman Cantor, "Forced Payments to Service Institutions and

Constitutional Interests in Ideological Non-Association," *Rutgers Law Review* 36, no. 1 (1984): 3–52.

We can again leave to one side the question of whether and/or the extent to which such utilitarian considerations can be reconciled with our principles of judicial review. For our purposes, what is important is that labour peace and the community's well-being is achieved by a policy which enhances the individual's ability to maximize his participation in the rule-making processes which govern the workplace.

11 The connection between respect for the personal autonomy of others and the ethic of fraternity and community is highlighted in Ronald Dworkin, *Law's Empire* (Cambridge, Mass.: Harvard University Press 1986). For a reply to the standard critique of liberal theories of justice, that they do not pay sufficient attention to communitarian values, see Amy Gutmann, "Communitarian Critics of Liberalism," *Philosophy and Public Affairs* 14, no. 2 (1985): 308–22. Recognition of this link is already part of our constitutional jurisprudence. See *Re Lavigne and OPSEU*, 75.

12 Albert O. Hirschman, *Exit, Voice, and Loyalty* (Cambridge, Mass.: Harvard University Press 1970); R.B. Freeman and J.L. Medhoff, "The Two Faces of Unionism," *Public Interest* 57 (1979): 69–93 and *What Do Unions Do?* (New York: Basic Books 1984).

13 It might be noted that systems of collective decision-making may not only be superior in a procedural and constitutional sense, but on efficiency grounds as well. See, e.g., Friedrich Hayek, *The Constitutional of Liberty* (Chicago: Regnery 1972), 276ff and Freeman and Medhoff, *What Do Unions Do*.

14 The Ontario Supreme Court has already come to this conclusion with respect to agency shop rules. See *Re Lavigne and OPSEU*.

15 Using the language of discrimination, the same point could be made by saying union security rules permit employment opportunities to be conditioned on an irrelevant criterion – a person's membership in a union. See Haggard, *Compulsory Unionism*, 278.

16 Since s.15 has come into force, the common exemption from union dues provided for religious objectors seems especially vulnerable. See, e.g., Ontario Labour Relations Act, s.47. Equal protection and benefit of the law would seem to rule out recognizing only those whose conscientious objection to membership in a union was based on religious principles. By comparison, the parallel exemption in English law includes those whose objection is based on "conscience or deeply-held personal conviction." See Employment Protection (Consolidation) Act 1978, c.44, ss.58 (3)–(13), 58A, as amended by Employment Act 1982, c.46, s.3. Our own statutory preference for individuals holding particular religious views about trade unions seems a clear violation of an atheist's or agnostic's freedom to remain outside of such organizations as well.

17 The reason compulsory membership laws do not violate a person's positive freedom to associate is that labour relations acts in Canada generally prohibit any attempt to limit a person's freedom to join other unions. Compulsory membership rules, in other words, do not entail a proscription against dual membership. In the absence of such statutory prohibitions, an argument that union security clauses violate a person's positive as well as negative freedom of association would be available. See, e.g., Arthur Lenhoff, "The Problem of Compulsory Unionism in Europe," *American Journal of Comparative Law* 5 (1956): 18–43, esp. 33.

18 The most influential essay arguing for this identity between positive and negative freedom was Gerald MacCallum's "Negative and Positive Freedom," *Philosophical Review* 76 (1967): 312–44. MacCallum's contribution and later essays which have considered this question are collected and discussed in Peter Westen, "'Freedom' and 'Coercion' – Virtue Words and Vice Words," *Duke Law Journal* 3 (1985): 541–93, esp. 549ff.

19 The leading exponent of this earlier view, on which the concepts of negative and positive freedom were sharply distinguished, was Isaiah Berlin. See his "Two Concepts of Liberty," in *Four Essays in Liberty* (Oxford: Oxford University Press 1969). See also Kahn-Freund, *Labour and the Law*, 196ff.

20 The other fundamental freedoms, such as speech and religion, manifest a similar Janus-like character. Constraints on the freedom of one person to shout fire in a theatre, spew defamatory and libellous remarks in public or do violence to others on film and in print all derive from the freedom of the listener to be free from behaviour which is invasive of her autonomy. Freedom of religion, as the American non-establishment clause makes explicit, is also derived from the same ideal of personal autonomy as the positive freedom to practice the religion of one's choice. See generally, David B. Gaebler, "First Amendment Protection Against Compelled Expression and Association," *Boston College Law Review* 23, no. 3 (1982): 995–1023; Frederick Schauer, *Free Speech: A Philosophical Inquiry* (Cambridge: Cambridge University Press 1982); and Kent Greenwalt, "Religion as a Concept in Constitutional Law," *California Law Review* 72, no. 5 (1984): 753–816. Canadian courts and commentators have already shown some recognition of this bilateral character of rights and freedoms: see *R. v. Big M Drug Mart* 354; *Re Lavigne and OPSEU*, 365–7; Lorraine E. Weinrib, "The Religion Clauses: Reading the Lessons," *Supreme Court Law Review* 8 (1986): 507–22.

21 Tribe, *American Constitutional Law*, 701. See also Renna Raggi, "An Independent Right to Freedom of Association," *Harvard Civil Rights-Civil Liberties Law Review* 12, no. 1 (1977); 1–30, where the basic value of freedom of association, permitting individuals to achieve through collective effort what they otherwise might not be able to achieve for themselves, is developed outside of the employment context. Cf. Kahn-Freund, *Labour and the Law*,

196ff, who regards the equation between the positive and negative as bad logic.

22 See Alexis de Tocqueville, *Democracy in America* (Garden City, NJ: Doubleday and Co. 1969), 193. See also *Re Lavigne and OPSEU*, 366–7.

23 See, e.g., R. Reich, "Why Democracy Makes Sense," *New Republic* (19 Dec. 1983); Tribe, "American Constitutional Law," 701.

24 The constitutional protections and the judicial interpretations of freedom of association in most of these countries is set out in the relevant monographs of the *International Encyclopedia of Labour Law*; Austria (p. 120); Italy (p. 106); Ireland (p. 130); West Germany. See also, M. Weiss, S. Smitis, and W. Rydzy, "The Settlement of Labour Disputes in the Federal Republic of Germany," *Industrial Conflict Resolution in Market Economies*, ed. T. Hanami and R. Blanpain (Deventer, Neth.: Klewer 1984), 81–106; Anne Staines, "Constitutional Protection and the European Convention on Human rights – An Irish Joke?" *Modern Law Review* 44 (1981): 149–65; J. Casey, "Some Implications of Freedom of Association in Labour Law: A Comparative Survey with Special Reference to Ireland," *International and Comparative Law Quarterly* 21 (1972): 699–717; and Kahn-Freund, *Labour and the Law*, 183, 195–6. And also see E. Cordova and M. Ozaki, "Union Security Arrangements: An International Overview," *International Labour Review* 119, no. 1 (1980): 19–38.

It should also be noted that in other countries where the commitment to freedom of association is made by statute rather than entrenched in the constitution, a similar interpretation has prevailed. Thus, in addition to those countries whose constitutions implicitly prohibit the union shop, there are others such as France, Belgium, and Switzerland which, by legislation, have recognized the right of each individual to be free to join only a union of his or her choice. (See *International Encyclopedia of Labour Law*.) Freedom in most of the democracies of western Europe includes the right to remain outside organizations to which one does not want to belong as much as to participate in those which one chooses to support.

25 *Education Co. of Ireland* v. *Fitzpatrick* [1961] I.R. 345, 362.

26 A majority of the court who heard the case declined to pass on whether the closed shop would violate the convention's guarantee of freedom of association. Of the ten judges who did consider it, seven were of the opinion that freedom of association necessarily implied freedom from association. See *Young, James and Webster* v. *The United Kingdom* (1981), 2 HRLJ 185 (Eur. Ct. HR), 195.

27 *Abood* v. *Detroit Board of Education*, 222, 234; and, generally, Haggard, *Compulsory Unionism*, 250–51. The Ontario Supreme Court came to the same conclusion in *Re Lavigne and OPSEU*.

28 Such an argument, obligating the state to enact such a law to protect the

workers' freedom of association, could be supported by reference to the ILO's Convention 98. See paragraph 23, *Freedom of Association*, Digest of Decisions of the Freedom of Association Committee, Geneva, 1974. See B.A. Hepple, *Hepple and O'Higgins' Employment Law*, 3rd ed. (London: Sweet and Maxwell 1979), para. 204ff.

29 See Kahn-Freund, *Labour and the Law*, 195.

30 Hayek, *Constitution of Liberty*, 278.

31 In Ontario, the legislative proscription is contained in the Labour Relations Act, RSO 1980, c.228 s.66(b).

32 This is the rationale that the American Supreme Court has turned to most consistently in justifying the agency shop variant of compulsory union association. See *Railway Employers' Department* v. *Hanson*, 238; *Abood* v. *Detroit Board of Education*, 215, 222. See also *NLRB* v. *General Motors*, 373 U.S. 734 (1963), 740; *Lanscott* v. *Millers Falls Co.*, 316 F. Supp. 1369, aff'd 440 F(2d) 14 cert. denied 404 U.S. 872.

33 See Haggard, *Compulsory Unionism*, 271 and 289ff. For an economic analysis of the free rider argument, see Alan G. Pulsipher, "The Union Shop: A Legitimate Form of Coercion in a Free Market Economy," *Industrial and Labor Relations Review* 19 (1965–6): 529–32.

34 See E. Cordova and M. Ozaki, "Union Security Arrangements: An International Overview," *International Labor Review* 11, no. 1 (1980): 19–38. See also Michael Dudra, "The Swiss System of Union Security," *Labour Law Journal* 10 (1959): 165–74; and ILO, Committee on Freedom of Association, 138th Report 1973, Case 631 (Turkey), holding that a solidarity fund levy set at two-thirds of union dues is consistent with freedom of association; and *NLRB* v. *General Motors*.

35 I offer this formulation as only one possible definition of the standard of review that courts might insist the other branches of government must meet. For a different formulation, see Cantor, "Forced Payments to Service Institutions."

36 This, in fact, was the line drawn by Mr Justice White in *Re Lavigne and OPSEU*. There is, however, no indication in his judgment that he appreciated the critical impact the legislative branch of government has on the definition and operation of our labour code and in particular on the processes and outcomes of collective bargaining when it promulgates rules related to everything from minimum standards of employment to monetary and fiscal policy to access to safe abortions. All of this legislation and more will directly affect the terms and conditions unions secure at the bargaining table and ought reasonably to be included within the purposes for which they have been recognized in law.

37 This basic division is the operative rule in American constitutional law. It has been accepted also in Great Britain since the enactment of the Trade Union Act in 1913 (2 and 3 George V, c.30). For an analysis of the operation

of this legislation, see E.D. Ewing, "Trade Union Political Funds: The 1913 Act Revised," *Industrial Law Journal* 13 (1984): 227–42.

38 See Haggard, *Compulsory Unionism*, for a summary of this jurisprudence. Many of these competing arguments are considered by Mr Justice White in *Re Lavigne and OPSEU*. For a pessimistic prognostication of the courts' ability to discharge this task, see Wellington, "The Constitution, the Labour Union and Governmental Action."

39 See, e.g., Alan Borovoy, "Charter of Rights Challenge Discriminates Against Unions," *Toronto Star*, 2 Dec. 1985.

40 For the purposes of our immediate inquiry, it is not relevant whether the payment given to an association (corporation or union) was effected by consent or by coercion. In either circumstance, the association would, for the reason reviewed in the text, have a legitimate claim to the money and could spend it on the purposes for which it was given/taken. Moreover, as the example of the consumer of a monopoly service or utility makes clear, in all these cases the difference in the consensual aspect of the payment is more a matter of degree than kind.

41 If it is felt that this principle allows corporations more effective opportunities to participate in the processes of politics (and ultimately in the formulation of our labour code), it would be entirely appropriate if not necessary for a legislature to meet this inequality directly by enacting spending and lobbying restrictions by corporations in the political processes. See, e.g., Canada Elections Act, Amendment (No. 3), SC 1980–81–82–83, s.8; Ontario Election Finances Reform Act, RSO. 1980, c.134, s.19. On this view, election expenses legislation would be an entirely legitimate response to address the differential opportunities of corporations and unions by limiting and thereby equalizing the influence financial resources can have in our legislative and executive branches of government. This view was recognized, but rejected without reasons, by Medhurst J. in *National Citizens Coalition et al.* v. *A-G for Canada* (1985), 11 DLR (4th), (Alta. QB). See also, to the same effect, *First National Bank of Boston* v. *Bellotti*, 435 U.S. 765 (1978). For one of many critiques of this judgment, see Charles R. O'Kelley Jr., "The Constitutional Rights of Corporations Resisted: Social and Political Expression and the Corporation after *First National Bank* v. *Bellotti*," *Georgetown Law Journal* 67, no. 6 (1979): 1347–83. For a pessimistic view of the effectiveness of legislation of this kind see E.D. Ewing "Campaign Financing: A Dilemma for Liberal Democracy," Osgoode Hall Law School, Public Law Workshops, 1982.

42 See L.C.B. Gower, *Gower's Principles of Modern Company Law*, (London 1979), and B.C. Welling, *Corporate Law in Canada: The Governing Principles* (Toronto: Butterworths 1984). For a particularly broad interpretation of the purposes of corporations, see Berger J. in *Teck Corp.* v. *Miller* [1973] 2, WWR 385 (BCSC).

43 *Central Mortgage and Housing Corp.* v. *Co-operative College Residences Inc.* (1977), 71 DLR (3d) 183 (Ont. CA); and see generally Gerald LaForest, *The Allocation of Taxing Power under the Canadian Constitution*, 2nd ed. (Toronto: Canadian Tax Foundation 1981), 46–7. See also Donald Smiley, *Conditional Grants and Canadian Federation* (Toronto: Canadian Tax Foundation 1963).

44 This was, in fact, precisely the basis on which Mr Justice White struck down the agency shop rule that was contained in the collective agreement governing the community college teachers in Ontario. See *Re Lavigne and OPSEU*, 386–7.

45 It should be recalled that in some sectors of the economy work-sharing may be another objective the legislature is pursuing in authorizing the closed shop.

46 Colleges Collective Bargaining Act, RSO 1980, c.74, s.59(2). In his judgment in *Re Lavigne and OPSEU*, Mr Justice White found that this section of the act did not violate the guarantees of expression, association, or equality set out in the Charter (389–392).

47 Labour Code of Quebec, SQ 1977, s97(a) as amended, SQ 1983, c.22, s.109(1).

THIRTEEN

1 The principle of exclusivity is included in our labour code by statute. See, e.g., Ontario Labour Relations Act, RSO 1980, c.228, s.67.

2 See Clyde Summers, "Freedom of Association and Compulsory Unionism in Sweden and the United States," *University of Pennsylvania Law Review* 112 (1964): 647–96.

3 The inconsistency comes about because of the way in which Labour Relations Boards define bargaining units. See, e.g., *Stratford General Hospital and OPSEU* [1977], OLRBR 70 (Ont. LRB). Whether such distinctions, drawn by agencies of the legislature, can withstand the scrutiny of judicial review is another question our courts may soon have to grapple with. For an introduction to how the definition of bargaining units would be evaluated under the Charter see the text at pp. 154–5.

4 *Young, James and Webster* v. *The United Kingdom* [1982], EHRR 38, 54.

5 The decision of The Ontario Divisional Court in *Service Employees International Union Local 204 and Broadway Manor Nursing Home* (1983), 44 OR (2d) 392; 4 DLR (4th) 231, was affirmed in the result, on other than constitutional grounds, by the Ontario Court of Appeal at 48 OR (2nd) 225. However, in an earlier decision the Ontario Court of Appeal explicitly rejected the conclusion that the Labour Relations Act offends the Charter of Rights. See *United Headgear, Optical and Allied Workers Union of Canada Local 3 and Biltmore Steteson (Canada) Inc.* (1983), 43 OR (2nd) 243. However, the court's opinion in this latter case was offered without

the support of any reasoning and specifically without consideration of the analysis we have been following. See also, *Re Prime et al. and Manitoba Labour Relations Board et al.* (1983), DLR (4th) 74; rev'd 8 DLR (4th) 641. The principle of exclusivity has since been challenged directly in the Supreme Court of Ontario in *Butters and Oberlein* v. *Attorney General of Ontario*.

In *Broadway Manor* the Divisional Court seemed to be alive to the limitation that the Labour Relations Act imposed on a person's freedom of association, but it suggested that the constraint was reasonable and justifiable within the meaning of s.1. However, this conclusion was clearly not essential to the issue before the court – which concerned the scope and meaning of the "positive" freedom of association, and so can be considered "obiter." The court also failed to consider the analysis we have been applying, and in a sense everything which follows in the rest of this part is an attempt to explain why, if it had, its conclusion on this point would have been different.

6 Statutory prohibitions against taking out membership in a union, other than chosen by the majority, at one time formed part of the labour code in Ireland. They were struck down in *National Union of Railwaymen* v. *Sullivan* [1947], IR 77. See also *Becton Ltd. and Company* v. *Lee* [1973], IR 1; and, generally, see *International Encyclopedia for Labour Law and Industrial Relations*, "Ireland."

7 The distinction between "positive" and "negative" freedom figures prominently in the literature of workers' freedom of association. See, e.g. *Freedom of Association and Industrial Relations*, Report VII, International Labour Conference, ILO, 30th Session, Geneva, 1947; ibid., 31st Session, Geneva, 1948; *Young, James and Webster* v. *The United Kingdom*, 4; P. Malles, *The Institutions of Industrial Relations in Continental Europe* (Ottawa: Labour Canada 1979); and Irwin Cotler, "Freedom of Assembly, Association, Conscience and Religion," in *The Canadian Charter of Rights and Freedoms; Commentary*, ed. Walter Tarnopolsky and Gérald Beaudoin (Toronto: Carswell 1982), 123–211.

8 The parallel between coercion which is effected by the denial of benefits and that which results from the imposition of punishments is recognized and justified in *R.* v. *Big M Drug Mart* (1985), 18 DLR (4th) 321, 354; *R.* v. *Video Flicks Ltd* (1984), 14 DLR (4th) 10, 38–41 (Ont. CA); and see, generally, Peter Westen, " 'Freedom' and 'Coercion': Virtue Words and Vice Words," *Duke Law Journal* (1985): 541–93. In *Re Lavigne and OPSEU* (1986), 29 DLR (4th) 321, Ont. SC, White J. also recognized that once they are certified unions cannot be characterized as voluntary associations.

9 Though the analogy is, I believe, close and informative, I do not intend to claim that it is exact. In the first place, unions obviously do not have the same sovereign authority in the rule-making processes of the workplace that a governing party does in the legislative processes of the state. However,

it is also true and widely recognized that a union which is granted the exclusive authority to represent the interests of all workers in an enterprise (or some segment thereof) is in fact and in law "clothed with a power not unlike that of a legislature ... [in] . .. its power to deny, restrict, destroy or discriminate against the rights of those for whom it legislates." *Steele* v. *Louisville and Nashville Railroad*, 323 U.S. 192 (1944). See also the concurring judgment of Mr Justice Powell in *Abood* v. *Detroit Board of Education*, 431 US 209 (1976) at 244ff., where the analogy between trade unions and political parties in a legislative, decision-making process is developed further. The same parallel is also discussed in R. Weland, "Majority Rule in Collective Bargaining," *Columbia Law Review* 45 (1945): 556; and G. Schatzki, "Majority Rule, Exclusive Representation and the Interests of Individual Workers: Should Exclusivity be Abolished," *University of Pennsylvania Law Review* 123 (1975–6): 897. For a similar analysis of the West German model, see R. Richardi, "Worker Participation in Decisions within Undertakings in the Federal Republic of Germany," *Comparative Labour Law* 5 (1982): 23.

A second difference between the position of an exclusive bargaining representative in our "private" system of industrial government and the ruling organization in a one party state is, of course, the provision in law in the former but not the latter of the governing association being replaced by a competing organization. However, when one contemplates the enduring security of major unions such as the Autoworkers, Steelworkers, Postal Workers, and Teamsters in the major units in which they hold bargaining rights, this difference is in practice only one of degree and one which could easily be exaggerated.

10 It is conventional wisdom of virtually all systems of collective labour relations that such terms of employment cannot fairly be regarded as the product of the employee's true consent. Even the most conservative interpretations of liberal political theory recognize that holders of private power, like employers, can act coercively against those they may hire. See Friedrich Hayek, *The Constitution of Liberty* (Chicago: Regnery 1972), 137.

11 The catalogue of conventional arguments in favour of union security are collected in Thomas R. Haggard, *Compulsory Unionism, the NLRB and the Courts* (Philadelphia: Industrial Research Unit, University of Pennsylvania 1977), 271ff. For an international perspective, see E. Cordova and M. Ozaki, "Union Security Arrangements: An International Overview," *International Labour Review* 119, no. 1 (1980): 19–38. The free rider and solidarity principles are the two most important and they are also the ones conventionally emphasized by those who defend the principle of exclusivity. See, e.g., Paul Weiler, *Reconcilable Differences* (Toronto: Carswell 1980), 142ff.

12 See Richard Freeman and Jim Medoff, "Two Faces of Unionism," *Public*

Interests 57 (1979): 69–93, where these ideas are initially introduced, and *What Do Unions Do?* (New York: Basic Books 1984), where they are developed more fully.

13 For summaries of the major principles embraced by these decisions, reference may be had to *Freedom of Association*; *Digest of Decisions of the Freedom of Association Committee* (Geneva: ILO 1974), esp. para. 30; and *Freedom of Association and Collective Bargaining*, General Survey by the Committee of Experts, ibid., 1983.

14 See *Abood* v. *Detroit Board of Education*.

15 To the extent that Canadian courts have already shown an inclination to adopt similar reasoning their conclusions would be similarly flawed. See, e.g., *Broadway Manor Nursing Home*.

16 For a discussion of the distinction between a concept and its various conceptions, see Ronald Dworkin, *Taking Rights Seriously* (Cambridge, Mass.: Harvard University Press 1977), chap. 5.

17 For an *a priori* argument that there is room, at least in theory, for a special industrial relations conception of this freedom, see Ferdinand von Prondzynski, "Freedom of Association in Modern Industrial Relations," *Industrial Relations Journal* 15, no. 1 (1984): 9–16.

18 *Minutes* of the Special Joint Committee of the Senate and of the House of Commons on the Constitution, vol. 43, (1981) pp. 67–77.

19 See *Freedom of Association and Industrial Relations*, Report VII.

20 Focusing on governmental interference with independent and autonomous associations is not unique to the ILO. For a similar preoccupation on the part of courts and commentators in Canada and the United States, see Cotler, "Freedom of Assembly, Association, Conscience and Religion," in Tarnopolsky and Beaudoin, *The Canadian Charter of Rights and Freedoms*.

21 Membership in the governing body of the ILO is divided between representatives drawn from employee, employer, and governmental constituencies in each country.

22 Most of these countries can point to a strong commitment in their constitutions to freedom of association as requiring a more liberal principle of representing employee interests than exclusivity. Austria, France, the Federal Republic of Germany, Ireland, Italy, the Netherlands, and Switzerland all have constitutional guarantees of freedom of association similar to that contained in the Canadian Charter. See generally, the national monographs for each of these countries in the *International Encyclopedia for Labour Law* (Netherlands: Kluwer); see also, Anne Staines, "Constitutional Protection and the European Convention on Human Rights – An Irish Joke," *Modern Law Review* 44 (1981): 149–65.

23 *NLRB* v. *Jones and Laughlin Steel*, 301 U.S. (1936).

24 The leading cases which signalled the court's retreat from its initial position in *Jones and Laughlin Steel* are: *Medo Photo Supply Co.* v. *NLRB*, 321

U.S. 678 (1944); *J.I. Case Co.* v. *NLRB*, 321 U.S. 332 (1943); *Order of Railroad Telegraphers* v. *Railway Express Agency* 321 U.S. 342 (1944).

For a discussion of these cases see Ruth Weyand, "Majority Rule in Collective Bargaining," *Columbia Law Review* 45 (1945): 446–599. It should be noted, however, that in none of these cases did the court even address the question of whether the designation of one union as the exclusive bargaining representative on the basis of its being chosen by one group of employees violated the freedom of those who voted against that selection. Even in the *J.I. Case* decision, where the court considered the position of the individual worker most directly, it pulled back from ruling out the possibility that collective agreements might be interpreted as establishing minimum standards on the basis of which individuals could negotiate more favourable terms for themselves directly with their employers.

25 *Steele* v. *Louisville and Nashville Railroad*, 323 U.S. 192 (1944).

26 See Haggard, *Compulsory Unionism*, 246ff., and J.E. Jones, "The Origins of the Concept of the Duty of Fair Representation," in *The Duty of Fair Representation*, ed. J.T. McKelvey (Ithaca: Cornell University Press 1977).

27 *Steele* v. *Louisville and Nashville Railroad*. The court's precise holding was that:

> If, as the state court has held, the Act confers this power on the bargaining representative of a craft or class of employees without any commensurate statutory duty toward its members, constitutional questions arise. For the representative is clothed with a power not unlike that of a legislature which is subject to constitutional limitations on its power to deny, restrict, destroy or discriminate against the rights of those for whom it legislates and which is also under an affirmative constitutional duty equally to protect those rights. If the Railway Labor Act purports to impose on petitioner and the other Negro members of the craft the legal duty to comply with the terms of the contract whereby the representative has discriminatorily restricted their employment for the benefit and advantage of the Brotherhood's own members, we must decide the constitutional questions which petitioner raises in his pleading.
>
> But we think that Congress, in enacting the Railway Labor Act and authorizing a labor union, chosen by a majority of a craft, to represent the craft, did not intend to confer plenary power upon the union to sacrifice, for the benefit of its members, rights of the minority of the craft, without imposing on it any duty to protect the minority (pp. 198–9).

28 See, e.g., *NLRB* v. *Allis-Chalmers Manufacturing Co.* 388 U.S. 175 (1967), and *Emporium Capwell Co.* v. *Western Addition Community Organization* 420 U.S. 50 (1975). For a critique of the American position, and discussion of the ways in which the same principle of exclusivity is thought to violate rights and freedoms of American workers, see George Schatzki, "Majority Rule, Exclusive Representation and the Interests of Individual Workers: Should Exclusivity be Abolished?" *University of Pennsylvania Law Review*

123, no. 4 (1975): 897–938. See also, Eileen Silverstein, "Union Decisions on Collective Bargaining Goals; A Proposal for Interest Group Participation," *Michigan Law Review* 77 (1979): 1485–1538; and Karl E. Klare, "The Quest for Industrial Democracy and the Struggle Against Racism: Perspectives from Labor Law and Civil Rights Law," *Oregon Law Review* 61 (1982): 157–200.

29 The case is discussed at length in Haggard, *Compulsory Unionism*, chap. 11. See also *Minnesota State Board for Community Colleges et al. v. Knight*, 104 S. Ct. 1058 (USSC 1984).

30 It should be noted that the U.S. Supreme Court's recent decisions on exclusivity seem defective even on their own terms. Certainly they seem inconsistent with its earlier holding, in *Shelton v. Tucker*, 364 U.S. 479 (1960) in which, as a derivative of the rights and freedoms set out in the First Amendment, the court had concluded that limitations on a person's freedom of association would attract the most rigorous standards of review. Part of the explanation of why the Court has not invoked the principle of reasonable alternative means in assessing whether exclusivity violates a person's freedom of association may lie in its derivative nature. Unlike other restrictions on freedom of association, exclusivity might not be seen to bear directly on a person's freedom of speech, dress, petition, and assembly, which are explicitly guaranteed by the First Amendment and therefore would not warrant the stricter scrutiny which is applied in the latter circumstances. Whether the Court should have seen exclusivity as violating fundamental freedoms set out in the American Bill of Rights is still a matter of some debate in the United States. See, e.g. Schatzki, "Majority Rule Exclusive Representation and the Interests of Individual Workers," and James E. Bond, "The National Labor Relations Act and The Forgotten First Amendment," *South Carolina Law Review* 28 (1977): 421–501. For a discussion of American jurisprudence on freedom of association as a derivative right, see Renna Raggi, "An Independent Right to Freedom of Association," *Harvard Civil Rights–Civil Liberties Law Review* 12, no. 1 (1977): 1–30.

It should be acknowledged again that what "authority" now exists in Canada on this question has not invoked this test of alternate means. See, e.g., *Broadway Manor Nursing Homes*; and *United Headgear, Optical and Allied Workers Union v. Biltmore Stetson (Canada)*. In neither of these decisions was any consideration given to this principle and to the analysis being followed here.

31 See Michael C. Harper and Ira C. Lupa, "Fair Representation as Equal Protection," *Harvard Law Review* 98, no. 6 (1985): 1211–85, for a description of how the rule of fair representation, interpreted to correspond with a "rationality" definition of equal protection, would be applied to a variety of distributional choices unions must characteristically make. See also Klare, "The Quest for Industrial Democracy and the Struggle Against Racism,"

pointing out that the courts' conception of the union's duty of fair representation did not even entail a requirement to admit all of those it represented to membership in the union. In addition to failing to meet a standard of proportionality between ends and means, it is notorious among labour law scholars in Canada how utterly ineffectual the duty of fair representation has been, especially in reviewing the decisions taken by unions in the negotiation context. See Bernard Adell, "Establishing a Collective Employee Voice in the Workplace: How Can the Obstacles be Lowered?" in *Essays in Canadian Labour Law*, ed. G. England (Don Mills, Ont.: CCH Canada Ltd 1986), 3–24, David M. Beatty, "Ideology Politics and Unionism," *Studies in Labour Law*, ed. Kenneth P. Swan and Katherine E. Swinton (Toronto: Butterworths 1983), 299–340, 335–7; Katherine E. Swinton, "Restraints in Government Effects to Promote Equality in Employment: Labour Relations and Constitutional Consideration," in *Report of the Commission on Equality in Employment*, Rosalie S. Abella, Commissioner (Ottawa: Canadian Government Publishing Centre 1985), 273–96 at 277.

32 See Francis G. Jacobs, *The European Convention on Human Rights* (Oxford: Clarendon Press 1975), 197. The importance of the legal practice of other free and democratic societies in providing benchmarks for the possibilities of our own constitutional order has been one of the few subjects on which almost all commentators are agreed. See, e.g., Peter W. Hogg, "Canada's New Charter of Rights," *American Journal of Comparative Law* 32 (1984): 283–305; John Claydon, "International Human Rights Law and the Interpretation of the Canadian Charter of Rights and Freedoms," (1982) 4 Supreme Court LR 287–302; Maxwell Cohen and Anne Bayevsky, "The Canadian Charter of Rights and Freedoms and Public International Law," *Canadian Bar Review* 61 (1983): 265–313; Errol P. Mendes, "Interpreting the Canadian Charter of Rights and Freedoms: Applying International and European Jurisprudence," *Alberta Law Review* 20 (1982): 383–433; and June M. Ross, "Limitations on Human Rights in International Law: Their Relevance to the Canadian Charter of Rights and Freedoms," *Human Rights Quarterly* 6, no. 2 (1984): 180–223.

33 It should be noted that in many of these countries there exists more than one process of decision-making at the level of the enterprise. In France, for example, there may be as many as five different institutions, some of which are cooperative bodies such as works councils and health and safety committees, while others replicate the more familiar (to North Americans) processes of local collective bargaining.

34 Being designated as a representative union in any of these systems invariably carries with it a range of benefits and opportunities to participate in various decision-making processes. Such a selective conferral of powers among different unions obviously interferes with the (positive) freedom of workers

to join the trade unions of their choice. Such designations can incline workers to join unions which can most effectively represent their interests in the different institutions and processes of decision-making. Notwithstanding the inherent limitation such rules impose on freedom of association, in at least two cases the European Court on Human Rights has confirmed their validity on the basis of the social benefits they secure. See *National Union of Belgian Police* (1975), 1 EHRR 578; *Swedish Engine Drivers' Union* (1976), 1 EHRR 617. More important for our purposes, because more than one union is designated, there is always some choice among the unions so classified. In Belgium, for example, where this system seems most highly developed, typically a worker would have a choice between five different trade union groups, while in Switzerland, where there is no governmental restriction on which unions are entitled to participate in these local decision-making processes, the choice would theoretically be unlimited. In systems like our own, where one union is made the exclusive representative of the workers' interests, even that freedom of choice is denied.

35 See supra, note 9.

36 The participatory rights of non-union workers may be marginally restricted by a rule that each candidate must be proposed by a minimum number of nominators. In the Netherlands this number is thirty. In West Germany there is a parallel though, more complex, requirement. See Works Constitution Act, 1972, s.14.

37 The term "bargain" is used intentionally, to underscore the fact that, even though they are part of what is characterized as a cooperative (rather than conflictual), system of labour relations, works councils do bargain and act very much as the German equivalent of local bargaining agents. In practice, all commentators seem agreed, there is less difference in the operation of these two models of collective labour relations than the theory and literature would sometimes suggest. See, e.g., *International Encyclopedia for Labour Law*, Germany, vol 5; Netherlands, vol 7; Austria, vol 2. See also Clyde Summers, "Worker Participation in the United States and West Germany: A Comparative Study from an American Perspective," *American Journal of Comparative Law* 28 (1980): 367–92; Adolf Sturmthal, *Workers Councils* (Cambridge, Mass.: Harvard University Press 1964); Roy Adams, "Two Policy Approaches to Labour Management Decision-making at the Level of the Enterprise," in *Labour Management Cooperation in Canada*, ed. W. Craig Riddell (Toronto: University of Toronto Press 1986), 87–109; *Collective Bargaining in Industrialized Market Economies* (Geneva: ILO 1974), 35; and *Workers' Participation in Decisions Within Undertakings* (Geneva: ILO 1983).

38 See Martin Pelzer, *The German Labour Management Relations Act* (London: MacDonald and Evans 1972), 43. See also Ivor L. Roberts, "The Works

Constitution Act and Industrial Relations in West Germany: Implications for the United Kingdom," *British Journal of Industrial Relations* 11 (1973): 338–67 at 340.

39 Brief descriptions of this system are set out in *International Encyclopedia for Labour Law*, Italy, vol. 6; Silvania Sciarra, "The Rise of the Italian Shop Steward," *Industrial Law Journal* 6 (1977): 35–44, and C. Guigni, "Recent Trends in Collective Bargaining in Italy," in *Collective Bargaining in Industrialized Economies*.

40 See *International Encyclopedia for Labour Law*, Germany, vol. 5, p. 187; Italy, vol. 6, pp. 118–19; Netherlands, vol. 7.

41 See *International Encyclopedia for Labour Law*, Germany, vol. 5, pp. 151, 166; Italy, vol. 6, pp. 104–7. The same rule appears to hold in Ireland as well: see vol. 6, pp. 161–2. See also Roy Adams, "Solidarity, Self-Interest and the Unionization Differential Between Europe and North America," *Relations Industrielles* 29, no. 3 (1974): 497–511, and F. Furstenberg, "Recent Trends in Collective Bargaining in the Federal Republic of Germany," *International Labour Review* 123 (1984): 615–33 at 620.

42 This must especially be true after the publication of Professor Otto Kahn-Freund's "On Uses and Misuses of Comparative Law," *Modern Law Review* 37 (1974): 1–27; *cf.* Clyde Summers, "American and European Labour Law: The Use and Usefulness of Foreign Experience," *Buffalo Law Review* 16 (1966–7): 210–28.

43 By contrast, distinction between and segregation of blue-collar and white-collar workers into separate decision-making processes, with separate representation, is one of our most durable and respected shibboleths. See Labour Law Casebook Group, *Labour Law: Cases, Materials and Commentary*, 4th ed. (Kingston, Ont.: Queen's University Industrial Relations Centre 1984), 198. For a discussion of the feasibility of incorporating interest group representation into the North American model of collective bargaining, see Silverstein, "Union Decisions on Collective Bargaining Goals."

44 In virtue of the fact some employees may be under the age of eighteen when they first begin to work, special provision for the representation of youth workers is included in the Works Constitution Act. See Pelzer, *The German Labour Management Relations Act*.

45 For a discussion of the circumstances in which the tenure of a member of a works council can be terminated, see ibid.

46 See Roy Adams, "Estimating the Extent of Collective Bargaining in Canada," *Relations Industrielles* 39, no. 4 (1984): 655–67.

47 It is a matter of some considerable controversy whether even the indirect effect of collective bargaining on the terms and conditions of employment in the unorganized sectors is a positive and beneficial one. For a review of the competing arguments, see Beatty, "Ideology, Politics and Unionism,"

in *Studies in Labour Law*, ed. Kenneth P. Swan and Katherine E. Swinton (Toronto: Butterworths 1983), 314–5.

48 See Summers, "Worker Participation in the u.s. and West Germany," 377.

49 *International Encyclopedia for Labour Law*, Germany, vol. 5. See also, Summers, "Worker Participation in the u.s. and West Germany," 378.

50 Academic commentators are unanimous that one of the most debilitating factors which has precipitated the enormous erosion in support unions now enjoy in the American workforce is the substantial increase in the unlawful practices employers use to frustrate and impede employee organization. See Paul Weiler, "Promises to Keep: Securing Workers' Rights to Self-organization under the N.L.R.A.," *Harvard Law Review* 96 (1983): 1769–827, and "Striking a New Balance: Freedom of Contract and the Prospects for Union Representation," *Harvard Law Review* 98, (1984): 351–420.

The federal government has made use of the West German model of "compulsory" collective relationships in responding to the problem of redundancies in the unorganized workforce. For a brief description of this experiment, see Roy Adams, "The Unorganized, a Rising Force," in *Jobs and Labour Peace and Agenda for Action*, ed. Lisa R. Cohen (Montreal: McGill University, Industrial Relations Centre 1983), 40–58.

51 See "Co-Determination in the Federal Republic of Germany," in *Workers' Control*, ed. Gerry Hunnius *et al.* (New York: Vintage Books 1973), 194–224 at 199–200.

52 Initially it might strike some as paradoxical that this model, by which a tiny fraction of the workforce can impose a system of collective labour relations on those who want no part of any formal association with their fellow workers, and who want to continue to bargain on their own as individuals, is being defended on the ground of enhancing freedom of association in the workplace. Whatever the comparative advantages and disadvantages of the two systems, it might be thought that to the extent the West German model effectively requires a system of collective labour relations to be utilized and, correspondingly, denies the possibility of bargaining by individual workers, it reduces rather than enhances freedom of choice. On this view, even if works councils could be defended as promoting the freedom of association of workers who presently bargain collectively through one exclusive agent, they would seriously interfere with the freedom of those in the unorganized sector who have no formal association with their fellow employees at all.

From our discussion of how the ethic of solidarity underlies all systems of collective labour relations in general and union security rules in particular, the error in perceiving the West German system in this way should be plain to see. Although it is true that all systems of collective labour relations will limit the freedom of those who want no formal association with their fellow employees in setting the rules which will govern their work, they do so to promote an equality of liberty of the workforce overall. By making the workers' involvement in fashioning the rules of the workplace with their employer more meaningful, as well as by equalizing the influence that each of them will have amongst themselves, the ethic of solidarity and the systems of collective labour relations to which it gives rise will enhance freedom overall. Solidarity is a constitutionally valid objective legislators are entitled to pursue notwithstanding the constraints it imposes on the freedom of those who do not want to associate legally with their fellow workers at all.

The critical comparison between the West German and Canadian systems is the reasonableness of the means they have devised to accomplish those ends. Moreover, because many of the individuals who work in the unorganized sector and bargain as individuals do so as a result of legal and practical limitations in their opportunity to organize collectively, rather than as a result of personal choice. European models like the West German works council can claim to directly promote and enhance the freedom of association of individual workers in this part of the labour market as well.

53 Allowing for the representation of different interest groups in a single decision-making institution might be justified as an attempt to get a qualitative as well as a quantitative measure of employee preferences. The latter is the only index a system of simple majority rule such as our system of labour relations can register.

54 Generally persons who wield powers which involve a special representation of the employers interest – e.g., the hiring and firing of staff – will be excluded. See Pelzer, *The German Labour Management Relations Act*.

55 The broad outlines of this area of our law are set out in Labour Law Casebook Group, *Labour Law: Cases, Materials and Commentary*, chap. 3, 199–200. See also George W. Adams, *Canadian Labour Law* (Aurora: Canada Law Book, 1985), chap. 7.

FOURTEEN

1 Labour Law Casebook Group, *Labour Law: Case, Material and Commentary*, 3rd ed. (Kingston, Ont.: Queen's University, Industrial Relations Centre, 1981), 37.

2 See, especially, Kahn-Freund, "Uses and Misuses of Comparative Law"; Summers, "American and European Labour Law"; and Derek Bok, "Reflections on the Distinctive Character of American Labor Law," *Harvard Law Review* 84 (1971): 1394–463.

Of the three commentators, certainly Summers is the most optimistic about the practical value of comparative labour law scholarship. Although he concedes the danger of trying to borrow directly the legal rules of another country, he does recognize such research can "open doors to constructive changes in the system. Awareness of gaps and weaknesses points towards places where changes are most needed; recognition that certain elements in the existing system are not immutable broadens the range of possibilities; and knowledge of the variety of arrangements in other systems provides suggested solutions. This does not mean we can borrow from another system; legal rules transplanted from one society to another are likely to be rejected. But comparisons in labor law do open our minds to the need for change, the possibility for change and the range of potential solutions" ("Worker Participation in the u.s. and West Germany," *American Journal of Comparative Law* 28 (1980), 368).

3 "Co-Determination in the Federal Republic of Germany," in *Workers' Control*, ed. Gerry Hunnius *et al.* (New York: Vintage Books 1973), 195.

4 Cf. Paul Weiler, who argues the strike is an essential component of any revitalized system of collective bargaining. See "Striking a New Balance: Freedom of Contract and the Prospects for Union Representation," *Harvard Law Review* 98 (1984), 351–420.

5 In an important sense the ultimate differences in the strike and arbitration as methods of dispute resolution are the criteria each invokes in fashioning solutions to the conflict. The strike, obviously, relies on market criteria. It counts all the resources one can invoke in asserting one's bargaining power in the market place. Arbitration, by contrast, commonly makes reference to some distributive criteria as well. See Morley Gunderson, *Economic Aspects of Interest Arbitration* (Toronto: Ontario Economic Council 1983); Joseph Weiler, *Interest Arbitration: Measuring Justice in Employment* (Toronto: Carswell 1981).

6 Brief descriptions of the Italian model are contained in the *International Encyclopedia for Labour Law*, Italy, vol 6 and in C. Guigni, "Recent Trends in Collective Bargaining in Italy," in *Collective Bargaining in Industrialized Market Economies* (Geneva: ILO 1974), 273–94.

7 Gerhard Leminsky, "Worker Participation: The German Experience," in *Labour Relations in Advanced Industrial Societies*, ed. Benjamin Martin and Everett M. Kassalow (Washington, D.C.: Carnegie Endowment for International Peace 1980), 139–60 at 155. See also *International Encyclopedia for Labour Law*, Netherlands, vol. 7 and *Workers Participation in Decisions Within Undertakings*, 22, 142.

8 The description of works councils functioning very much as local bargaining agents features prominently in the literature on works councils. See note 37 in section 13 above.

9 If there were any doubt on this point, the appropriate Canadian compromise might be a rule which gave the workers the freedom to choose which technique of dispute resolution – cooperative or conflictual – they wanted to use to resolve impasses in the decision-making process. Such a solution would

certainly comport with the ethic of autonomy and self-government which infuses the constitution as a whole and is one which Canadian public servants, in the federal sector at least, have long enjoyed.

10 For a description of this development in Canadian industrial relations policy, see Roy Adams, "Two Policy Approaches to Labour Management Decision-making at the Level of the Enterprise," in *Labour Management Cooperation in Canada*, ed. W. Craig Riddell (Toronto: University of Toronto Press 1986): 87–109. See also, Bernard Adell, "Establishing a Collective Employee Voice in the Workplace: How Can the Obstacles Be Lowered," in *Essays in Canadian Labour Law*, ed. G. England (Don Mills, Ont.: CCH Canadian Ltd. 1986), 3–24.

11 A recent study commissioned by the AFL-CIO in the United States is reported to have recommended the more widespread use of arbitration in place of the strike as a means of reviving the attractiveness of collective bargaining to American workers as a whole. See *Herald Tribune*, 25 Feb. 1985, p. 3.

12 For a description of the operation of the West German industrial relations system over the recent past, see Otto Jacobs, "World Economic Changes and Industrial Relations in the Federal Republic of Germany," in *A Decade of Economic Change in Industrial Relations*, ed. Hervey, Jutis *et al.* (Madison, Wis.: IRRA 1985), 211–46.

13 For a description of the relationship between the industry-wide and local processes of decision-making, see "The Federal Republic of Germany," in *Industrial Conflict Resolutions in Market Economies*, ed. T. Hanami and R. Blanpain (Deventer, Neth.: Kluwer 1984), 81–133.

14 *Collective Bargaining in Industrialized Market Economies*, 111; Clyde Summers, "The Usefulness of Unions in Major Industrial Society – A Comparative Approach," *Tulane Law Review* 58 (1984): 1409–40 at 1412; Roy Adams, "Solidarity, Self-Interest and the Unionization Differential Between Europe and North America," *Relations Industrielles* 29, no. 3 (1974): 497–511; Silvania Sciarra, "The Rise of the Italian Shop Steward," *Industrial Law Journal* 6 (1977): 35–44.

15 Adams, "Solidarity, Self-Interest"; Summers, "The Usefulness of Unions in Major Industrial Society," 1413–16.

16 See *Collective Bargaining in Industrialized Market Economies*, 126–7, 262; *International Encyclopedia for Labour Law*, Italy, vol. 6; R. Blanpain, "Recent Trends in Collective Bargaining in Belgium," *International Labour Review* 123, (1984): 319–22. This trend seems to have been particularly pronounced in Italy where, it will be recalled, collective bargaining is predicated on a principle of voluntary representation. See T. Treu, "Conflict Resolution in Industrial Relations," *Industrial Conflict Resolutions in Market Economies*, 137–58.

17 For descriptions of this division in decision-making responsibility, see *International Encyclopedia for Labour Law*, Germany, vol. 5; *Workers*

Participation in Decisions Within Undertakings, Collective Bargaining in Industrialized Market Economies; Summers, "Worker Participation in U.S. and West Germany"; and Martin Pelzer, *The German Labour Management Relations Act* (London: MacDonald and Evans 1972).

18 *Collective Bargaining in Industrialized Market Economies*, 262; *Worker Participation in Decisions Within Undertakings*, 142; and Summers, *Worker Participation in the U.S. and West Germany*; 374, 376. This seems especially true in Italy where bargaining on any subject can, in theory, take place at any level. See Treu, "Conflict Resolution in Industrial Relations."

19 Summers, "The Usefulness of Unions," 1413.

20 These wage differentials are reported in most of the European countries we have identified. See *International Encyclopedia for Labour Law*, Germany, Austria, Netherlands. See also Sturmthal, *Workers Councils*; Roberts, "The Works Constitution Act," 352; Summers, "American and European Labour Law"; and Bok, "Reflections on American Labour Law." For a description of the relationship between these different decision making levels in one representative establishment, see W. Rydzy, "Settlement of Labour Disputes in Private Industry: The Example of Adam Opel Ag," in Hanami and Blainpain, *Industrial Conflict Resolutions in Market Economies*, 113–33.

21 T. Treu and M. Roccella, "The Settlement of Disputes in a Large Enterprise: The Case of Alfa Romeo at Arese," in *Industrial Conflict Resolutions in Market Economies*, 179–95; C. Guigni, "Recent Trends in Collective Bargaining in Italy," in *Collective Bargaining in Industrialized Market Economies*, 273–94.

22 See, e.g., John C. Anderson, "The Structure of Collective Bargaining," in *Union Management Relations in Canada*, ed. John Anderson and Morley Gunderson (Toronto: Addison-Wesley 1982), 173–95.

23 In some sectors they were. From the earliest beginnings of collective bargaining some industries, like the garment trades, moved quite quickly to a system of industry-wide bargaining.

24 See Anderson, "The Structure of Collective Bargaining," 176.

25 Pattern bargaining to establish industry-wide standards is perhaps most developed in the auto sector, but it is used in many others as well, including steel and municipal services. Indeed, even arbitration awards for particular institutions, in sectors like health care, are consciously arranged by the parties to have an industry-wide effect.

26 See Milton Derber, *The American Idea of Industrial Democracy: 1865–1965* (Urbana: University of Illinois Press 1970); see also Summers, "Worker Participation in the U.S. and West Germany," 384; and Bok, "Reflections on American Labor Law."

27 See Leminsky, "Worker Participation – the German Experience," 159–60; and Roberts, "The Works Constitution Act," 351.

28 See Morley Gunderson and Katherine Swinton, *Collective Bargaining and Asbestos Dangers at the Workplace*, Study No. 1 (Toronto: Royal Commission on Matters of Health and Safety Arising from the Use of Abestos 1981).

29 For a discussion of recent developments in multi-party bargaining structures in Canada, see Anderson, "The Structure of Collective Bargaining"; Kenneth Strand, "Altering Union Bargaining Structures By Labour Board Decision," in *The Labour Code of B.C. in the 1980's*, ed. Joseph Weiler and Peter Gall (Calgary: Carswell 1984), 99–129; Joseph B. Rose, "Mandatory Bargaining Structures: What are the Consequences," in *Essays in Labour Relations Law*, ed. Geoffrey England (Don Mills, Ont.: CCH Canadian Ltd. 1986), 25–56.

30 For a brief description of the bargaining structures in the construction sector, see Labour Law Casebook Group, *Labour Law: Cases, Material, and Commentary*, 4th ed. (Kingston, Ont.: Queen's University Industrial Relations Centre 1984), chap. 3, 214ff.

31 Strand, "Altering Union Bargaining Structures."

32 Kahn-Freund, "Uses and Misuses of Comparative Law."

33 A convenient summary of the legal authorities bearing on the question of the burden of proof under s.1 can be found in Peter Hogg, *Constitutional Law of Canada*, 2nd ed. (Toronto: Carswell 1985), 681, "Canada's New Charter of Rights," *American Journal of Comparative Law* 32 (1984): 295. As Hogg points out, from the outset Canadian courts have put the burden of proof on those who, like the defenders of the principle of exclusivity, invoke s.1 of the Charter to justify some limitation or restriction of some fundamental right or freedom. In the context of the present stage of the conversation, defenders of exclusivity would be trying to establish that proposition by demonstrating that the European systems we have been considering are not reasonable alternate means because of the results they would be unable to achieve. What the authorities referred to by Hogg state is that they will bear the burden of establishing that fact.

34 See Summers, "Worker Participation in the U.S. and West Germany," 380–4.

35 Writings on the theoretical correlation between productivity and participation is extensive. Useful expositions include; Carole Pateman, *Participation and Democratic Theory* (Cambridge: Cambridge University Press 1970); and Richard Freeman and Jim Medoff, *What Do Unions Do* (New York: Basic Books 1984).

36 The comparative statistics on industrial conflict show the relative strength of the Western European systems on this criterion; see also *Yearbook of Labour Statistics, 1985* (Geneva: ILO 1985), chap. 9.

37 See Roberts, "The Works Constitution Act," 300; M. Weiss, S. Simitis,

W. Rydzy, "The Settlement of Labour Disputes in the Federal Republic of Germany," in *Industrial Conflict Resolutions in Market Economies*, ed. Hanami and Blanpain, 81–106.

38 Roy Adams, "Solidarity, Self-Interest and the Unionization Differential Between Europe and North America," *Relations Industrielles* 29, (1974): 497–511, 497. See also, Derek Bok, "Reflections on the Distinctive Character of American Labor Law," *Harvard Law Review* 84: (1971) 1394 and 1411ff; Paul Weiler "Promises to Keep: Securing Workers' Rights to Self-organization under the N.L.R.A." *Harvard Law Review*, 96, no. 8 (1983): 1769–1827.

39 It will be recalled that not only are trade unions in some European countries precluded from entering into union and closed shop arrangements, they are not even able to restrict the benefits they are able to secure to those who join the union and pay their dues.

40 Summers, "The Usefulness of Unions," 1438.

41 For a descriptin of the scope of bargaining that typically takes place in larger industrial enterprises in Italy, see T. Treu and M. Rocella, "The Settlement of Disputes in a Large Enterprise: The Alfa Romeo at Arese."

42 It bears repeating that in theory, industry-wide negotiations and not the works councils themselves set the levels of wages, hours, and other fringe benefits such as vacations, leaves, etc.

43 For a more detailed description of the powers of co-decision-making that works councils enjoy in these matters, reference may be had to *International Encyclopedia for Labour Law*, Germany; Pelzer, *The German Labour Management Relations Act*; and Summers, "Worker Participation in the U.S. and West Germany," 111.

44 For a discussion of the authority of the works councils on dismissals in particular and staffing (including the appointment of supervisors) generally, see Roberts, "The Works Constitution Act," 348 and Leminsky, "Worker Participation: The German Experience."

45 See, e.g., Ontario Employment Standards Act, RSO 1980, c.137, s.40; see also RRO 1980, reg. 286.

46 See *International Encyclopedia for Labour Law*, Germany; and Pelzer, *German Labour Management Relations Act*.

47 See Roberts, "The Works Constitution Act."

48 For a discussion of the Canadian and American authorities on the rights of workers to be informed about and be involved in such matters as corporate reorganizations, plant closings, and contracting out of work, see Brian Langille, "Equal Partnership in Canadian Labour Law," *Osgoode Hall Law Journal* 21, no. 3 (1983): 496–536.

49 See Summers, "Worker Participation in the U.S. and West Germany," 382; Roberts, "The Works Constitution Act," 344.

50 Our earlier observation of organized labour's resistance to minimum wage and just-cause standards legislation makes their hostility to changes of this kind a real possibility as well.

51 To ensure that judicial review does offer realistic means by which individuals can have a more effective and more equal role in the development of social policy, courts have a special obligation to make its procedures and results available and intelligible to those who will be governed by it. See Michael Walzer, "Philosophy and Democracy," *Political Theory* 9, no. 3 (1981): 379–99. For a polemic which argues that the popularization of law is highly problematic, see Zenon Bankowski and Geoff Mungham, *Images of Law* (London: Routledge and Kegan Paul 1976). Pragmatically, to ensure judicial review realizes its potential of democratizing the law-making processes in our community requires attention to a wide range of procedural issues, including rules of access and standing funding of interest group advocacy centres, as well as the appointment and tenure of judges. For a discussion of some of these issues, see W.A. Bogart, "Standing and the Charter: Rights and Identity," and Kenneth Swan, "Intervention and Amicus Curiae Status in Charter Litigation," in *Charter Litigation Symposium* (Faculty of Law, University of Toronto, 28 Feb. 1986); H.N. Janisch, "Administrative Tribunals in the 80's: Rights of Access by Groups and Individuals," in *Windsor Yearb. Access Justice* 1 (1981): 303–28; C. Baar, "Judicial Appointments and the Quality of Adjudication: The American Experience in a Canadian Perspective," *La Revue Juridique Thèmis* 20 (1986): 1–26; Jacob S. Ziegal, "Federal Judicial Appointments in Canada: The Time Is Ripe for Change," 37 *University of Toronto Law Journal* (1987): 1–24.

52 For one account of the potential of activist lawyering and how it conforms to our theory of government and social ordering, see Bruce Ackerman, *Reconstructing American Law* (Cambridge, Mass.: Harvard University Press 1984). For a less sanguine view, see Marc Gold, "The Constitutional Dimensions of Promoting Equality in Employment," in *Research Studies of the Report of the Commission on Equality in Employment*, Rosalie S. Abella, Commissioner (Ottawa: Canadian Government Publishing Centre 1985), 249–72, esp. 262–4.

53 *Reference Re Language Rights under the Manitoba Act, 1870* (1985), 19 DLR (4th) 1 (SCC).

54 A not incidental by-product of such cooperative action between legislatures and courts would be that s.33 would be invoked in a way that enhanced rather than derogated from the force of the Charter as an instrument of social justice.

POSTSCRIPT

1 In addition to formulating complementary standards of judicial review to

assess the proportionality between the social benefits and constitutional costs of any legal rule, the most urgent questions the courts must address relate to the judicial process itself. The processes by which and criteria on which judges are appointed, as well as the question of standing and access, are among the more critical issues determining the extent to which judicial review can realize the objectives which, on the interpretation we have been following, it is meant to achieve.

2 The best-known work arguing for this position is C. Pateman, *Participation and Democratic Theory* (Cambridge: Cambridge University Press 1970); see also R. Reich, "Why Democracy Makes Economic Sense," *New Republic*, 19 Dec. 1983.

3 The relationship between liberal legal theory and community is discussed in Ronald Dworkin, *Law's Empire* (Cambridge, Mass.: Harvard University Press 1986), 206. See also Amy Gutmann, "Communitarian Critics of Liberalism," *Philosophy and Public Affairs* 14, no. 3 (1985): 308-22.

Index